The Battles of Texas

The Battles of Texas

Adjuncts, Composition, and Culture Wars at UT Austin

Nate Kreuter and
Mark Garrett Longaker

The Pennsylvania State University Press
University Park, Pennsylvania

Library of Congress Cataloging-in-Publication Data

Names: Kreuter, Nate, author. | Longaker, Mark Garrett, 1974- author.
Title: The battles of Texas : adjuncts, composition, and culture wars at UT Austin / Nate Kreuter and Mark Garrett Longaker.
Description: University Park, Pennsylvania : The Pennsylvania State University Press, [2025] | Includes bibliographical references and index.
Summary: "Explores how the pressures of austerity, diversity, and university politics shaped the writing program and curricula at the University of Texas at Austin in the 1980s, with relevant parallels for writing programs today"—Provided by publisher.
Identifiers: LCCN 2024039374 | ISBN 9780271099194 (hardback) | ISBN 9780271099200 (paperback)
Subjects: LCSH: University of Texas at Austin. Department of English—History—20th century. | English language—Rhetoric—Study and teaching (Higher)—Texas—Austin—History—20th century. | Multicultural education—Texas—Austin—History—20th century. | Education, Higher—Economic aspects—Texas—Austin—History—20th century. | Education, Higher—Political aspects—Texas—Austin—History—20th century.
Classification: LCC PE1405.U6 K74 2025 | DDC 808.0071/176431—dc23/eng/20241028
LC record available at https://lccn.loc.gov/2024039374

Copyright © 2025 Nate Kreuter and Mark Garrett Longaker
All rights reserved
Printed in the United States of America
Published by
The Pennsylvania State University Press,
University Park, PA 16802-1003

The Pennsylvania State University Press is a member of the Association of University Presses.

It is the policy of The Pennsylvania State University Press to use acid-free paper. Publications on uncoated stock satisfy the minimum requirements of American National Standard for Information Sciences—Permanence of Paper for Printed Library Material, ANSI Z39.48–1992.

For Lester and JR
Multa novit vulpes

Contents

Acknowledgments   ix

Introduction: History, Narrative, Pedagogy
1

1 The Composition Revolution
24

2 The Saturday Night Massacre
48

3 The Battle of Texas
77

4 Revision and Division
112

Conclusion: Memory, Responsibility, History
143

Notes   159

Bibliography   183

Index   199

Acknowledgments

At the University of Texas at Austin we would first like to thank the Digital Writing and Research Lab—particularly, Casey Boyle, Jessica Solace, and Laura Excudero—for hosting and maintaining RhetCompUTX. The Office of the Vice President for Research, Scholarship and Creative Endeavors of the University of Texas at Austin also deserves thanks for providing a generous subvention in support of this book's production. Additionally, we are grateful to the graduate students who initially helped us conceptualize and create the digital archival exhibit: Jane Aman, Hannah Foltz, Tristan Hanson, Cindy Lou Holland, Tristin Hooker, Martha Sue Karnes, KJ Schaeffner, Sarah Schuster, and Kiara Walker. We are finally thankful for the primary source materials gifted to us by John Ruszkiewicz, Lester Faigley, and Susan Wells.

At the University of Georgia we wish to thank the First-Year Writing program's administrative team, Joshua King, Sara Steger, and Clare Reid Baeckeroot, who demonstrate their phronetic wisdom daily. Also in Park Hall, we thank Laurie Norris, Kensie Poor, Roland Végső, Richard Menke, Cynthia Camp, Casie LeGette, Lindsey Harding, Elizabeth Davis, and Isiah Lavender. In Peabody Hall we thank Aaron Meskin. We would also like to acknowledge the contributions of Nicholas Allen and Winnie Smith, as well as the University of Georgia's Willson Center for the Humanities, which generously provided research support for this project.

To Archna Patel at Penn State University Press we extend our gratitude and appreciation for her editorial direction and, in particular, her confidence in our narratological approach to disciplinary history. For putting us in touch with her, we thank Eric Detweiler at Middle Tennessee State University. For their sharpening of our text and generous engagement with our work, we thank the external reviewers.

For their time, their candor, and their willingness to revisit a sometimes uncomfortable past, we express our deepest thanks to the twenty-seven former undergraduates, graduate students, lecturers, professors, and administrators at the University of Texas at Austin who agreed to be interviewed for this project. Their generosity and their perspectives were both humbling. These interviewees are Michael Adams, Valerie Balester, Lance Bertelson, Jerome Bump, Hugh Burns, Joyce Locke Carter, Larry Carver, Evan Carton, Rod Davis, Geoff Henley, Scott Henson, Susan Jarratt, David Jolliffe, Fred Kemp, Michael King, Robert King, Carol MacKay, James McDonald, David McMurrey, Paul Meyer, Thomas Miller, Wayne Rebhorn, James Skaggs, Mary Trachsel, John Trimble, Susan Wells, and Robert Wren.

Within our homes, we thank Michelle, Rozi, and Lidia, and Lindsay and Will.

Introduction
History, Narrative, Pedagogy

Ours is a seismic era. So much can be said for all humanity in every corner of the globe, and for the duration of the twenty-first century, but it's especially true for higher education because of what the last two and a half decades have witnessed: the erosion of tenure track employment and the eruption of nontenure track faculty; the explosion of digitized, remote instruction, along with its requisite worries about equity, access, and intellectual property; the expanding enrollment of increasingly diverse students and the invention of initiatives intended to welcome the marginalized; the growing demand for professional credentials and the related diminishment of the liberal arts. As if all this weren't enough, in 2020, a global pandemic accelerated trends toward distance education and away from staples like the credit hour and the fifteen-week semester, while adding psychological trauma, political unrest, and unimaginable uncertainty to an already volatile mix.

Though no single book can account for all the factors contributing to our contemporary convulsions, attention to two complicated, long-standing, and interacting trends—which we refer to hereafter as "austerity" and "diversity"—can go a long way. To better understand these two dynamics, we should look not at the present century but at the long history of American higher education, going back to the late 1800s. Since the emergence of what contemporary scholar Michael Smith calls the industrial era "education factory," US colleges and universities have been shaped by the need to open their doors and accommodate new students. Dedicated to the principle of access and dedicating the requisite attention to diversity, state legislators, university administrators, and college professors have endeavored "to figure out how to deliver higher education at a scale far greater than had ever been tried before."[1] This mission, like all operations of scale, required significant financial investment. Through the middle of the twentieth century, between the attack on Pearl Harbor and the fall of Saigon, US higher education relied on generous state support. But when that flood of federal and state dollars dwindled to a modest trickle, colleges and universities looked for ways to earn revenue and cut costs, seeking innovation and imposing austerity, while continuing to attract students. This incentive to expand access and its corollary effort to reduce costs have been the economic motor of American higher education since the industrial revolution, an eight-cylinder, fuel-injected engine revving high in the latter decades of the twentieth century and driving the precipitous growth in college enrollment that Smith admiringly reports: "In 1870, the total number of students enrolled in college represented just 1 percent of the number of eighteen- to twenty-four-year-olds in the United States. In 2020, the ratio was 65 percent."[2]

Focused on this economic model and this historic outcome, one might assume that the history of American colleges and universities is an even and easy process of growth and improvement. An advanced economy creates the demand for skilled workers. Colleges and universities open their doors, inviting consumers hungry for skills and diplomas. Initially, state support incentivizes growth and innovation, but later privatized innovation and lean budgets fund the enterprise. As competition increases, institutions cut costs to deliver a better product at a lower rate, muscle out pricey alternatives and lure new clients. Diversity and austerity work together in a salubrious symbiosis. Unfortunately, this market model, like many economic ideals, is troubled by the specifics of history. Smith is an economist, so he sees things with the elegance and clarity that only his discipline can bring. David Labaree, on the other hand, is a historian, noticing contingencies and peculiarities. According to Labaree, US higher education is not a well-timed engine but a complicated, layered, contradictory Rube Goldberg machine, the result of historical accidents that fell in an auspicious way, leaving us with a "system of higher education that is enormously productive and useful" but that also "makes no sense to outsiders." While Smith wants to reform the contemporary university so that it better resembles the elegant simplicity of a competitive market, saying, "It's time . . . for us to look to the business world for new ideas," Labaree suggests that the system, inelegant and inefficient thought it may be, is nonetheless "enormously effective," so we should resist those who, like Smith, urge us "to remake it in a more rationalized form."[3]

We open with this distinction between the conservative historian who wants to preserve the "perfect mess" of higher education and the radical libertarian who wants to "remake higher education" in the image of market-driven corporations not because we want to champion one vision over the other but instead because we want to maintain both arguments in productive tension. Yes, higher education is driven by the symbiosis of diversity and austerity, and yes, it is also a contradictory mess of historical contingencies. Both an efficient market for instruction and accreditation as well as a complex and variegated historical sedimentation, higher education is prone to moments of crisis and transition, brief periods when the calcified layers of tradition crack and reform under the pressures exerted by the drive toward diversity and the imposition of austerity. The 1980s is one such moment. Ours is another. We begin, therefore, with a brief history of the interaction between diversity and austerity, asking you to shift your attention away from present pains and toward previous paroxysms. For if you can understand the 1980s, you might better understand the 2020s.

Our analogical argument begins by recounting the long history of the modern university with a specific focus on three dynamic and interacting elements: the industrial incentive to increase access to higher education, the political demand to accommodate diversity (of many types) on college campuses, and the national commitment to civic edification. These are the historian's contingencies that constitute the economist's incentive, the moving parts in the diversity machine. Since the industrial revolution, students have sought credentials and skills that promise advancement into the professional-managerial class. Colleges and universities proliferated and grew in a country increasingly dependent on knowledge production. College graduation rates for males increased nearly threefold between 1870 and 1950 and more than threefold among women between 1870 and 1980. College attendance rates grew nearly sixfold in the same century. Factors allowing for such growth are many—including a laissez-faire system, public support for higher education, and open enrollments—but the main force pushing students into postsecondary education is personal advancement.[4] As more people seek higher economic status through college accreditation, more students enroll. As more students enroll, the student body becomes more diverse—first in terms of economic class, then in terms of gender, and then, finally, by race.

Colleges and universities have responded, sometimes slowly, by broadening access. In the first half of the twentieth century, states created two-tiered systems. California exemplifies the trend, and the logic driving it.[5] The California Master Plan (1960) coordinated efforts among state colleges, which serve underrepresented students, and research universities, which employ star intellectuals. According to the master plan, the University of California system provides the intellectual innovation to fuel an increasingly technological society, while the California State University system trains professional workers who can thrive in a (post)industrial economy. The University of California, Berkeley, would pursue research excellence, while Cal State, Fresno, would strive toward accessibility. Alongside these economic and institutional development frameworks, population growth and legislative assistance contributed to early twentieth-century enrollment. An unprecedented swell in population (the postwar "baby boom" of 1947–60) and a new source of college funding (the G.I. Bill of Rights, 1944–56) pushed universities and colleges to proliferate and expand even more. Further legislative efforts to expand access, such as the Basic Education Opportunity Grant (also known as the Pell Grant, 1972), tried to ensure that every capable student could afford college tuition.

Since the late nineteenth century, because students matriculated largely for professional advantage, historians such as John Guillory trace higher education's evolution over the last century or better to the rise of a professional society and the emergence of the professional-managerial class.[6] Nonetheless, our long history would be incomplete without attention to the political pressure coming not from US industry but from students themselves. In the latter decades of the twentieth century, those excluded from college classrooms began to demand a seat: working-class students, women, people of color, and the LGBTQ+ community. These demands became especially loud during the 1960s and 1970s when students proclaimed and the wider electorate agreed that everyone has a right to higher education.[7] Frequently understood in terms of "access," this political pressure is far more complicated than the word implies, for students don't simply demand admission. They also want to be represented in governance, reflected in curricula, acknowledged by the faculty, and accommodated by the institutions. This garland of demands has recently inspired one historian of higher education to rightfully remark that the struggle for access cannot end with "proportional representation." Even if a university's faculty and students include people of every race, gender, and ethnicity, proportional to the larger population, this same university may still be "ignoring other factors that contribute to racial equity."[8] Cultural centers, curricular reforms, and pedagogical accommodations are also requisite.

The economic push is thus assisted by a political pull. In the twentieth century, US higher education witnessed a protracted legal and cultural war over programs designed to diversify college campuses by admitting and assisting women and people of color. This ongoing fight is documented by a series of landmark Supreme Court cases: *Sweatt v. Painter* (1950), *Regents of the University of California v. Bakke* (1978), *Grutter v. Bollinger* (2003), *Fisher v. University of Texas* (2016), and most recently *Students for Fair Admissions v. President and Fellows of Harvard College* (2023). Outside the courtroom, students and administrators wrestled over how best to accommodate, welcome, and assist diversifying populations.[9] In the 1960s and '70s, college and university administrators (allied with like-minded citizens and politicians) responded with meager provisions or reactionary measures. It was never enough for industry to incentivize access. Students had to demand it. Tense and tumultuous, the rights revolution and the conservative backlash are both integral moments in the century-long march toward greater access in American higher education, a journey significantly advanced but far from over.

The last element in our long history of American higher education, alongside the economic incentive toward accommodation and the political struggle over access, is the historic US commitment to civic edification. Since the colonial era and extending through the antebellum period, American colleges and universities have been committed to civic training, preparing republican leaders for their roles in government and society. Thomas Miller, in a sweeping history of American language arts education, affirms this judgment when he comments that "republican values were fundamental to . . . colleges" prior to the industrial revolution.[10] Higher education's civic mission expanded considerably in the twentieth century, as the federal government boosted efforts that were previously local and otherwise piecemeal. Beginning in the interwar years and extending through the Cold War decades, the US federal government acknowledged and supported higher education's civic mission by funding and often creating a wide range of "parastate" institutions, establishing a pattern that historian Christopher Loss calls "mediated governance."[11] During the Depression era, the Works Progress Administration (1935–43) funded construction projects on college campuses, giving students jobs, improving physical plants, and asking people to invest their professional and civic identities in their local colleges.[12] Toward the end of World War II, the G.I. Bill (1944) helped more than half of America's veterans readjust to civilian life by providing college tuition—a notable break from previous veterans' benefits programs, which emphasized financial support but not emotional well-being or educational growth.[13] And during the Cold War era, the National Defense Education Act (1958) supported research at colleges and universities, directly funding student enrollment by introducing federal loans.[14] But students committed to access and accommodation eventually rejected the midcentury civic mission in higher education.

Emerging from the skirmish between uniform civic education and multiform campus residents was a new politics of diversity. The rights revolution (raging through the 1960s and '70s) clashed with higher education's civic mission (pursued in the 1940s and '50s). Colleges and universities realized that they couldn't accommodate a racially diverse student body while also preserving a uniform civic identity. Women and students of color demanded "liberation from the white middle-class adjustment regime."[15] All this came to a head in the 1970s when "a new understanding of higher education emerged, one that prized the rights-bearing educated citizen and embodied her identity through a new variant of pluralist politics known as diversity."[16] Access and inclusion could only advance when Cold War civic education retreated. A new civic education, gathered under the banner of "multiculturalism," began to take hold in the 1980s. Close attention to the late twentieth century reveals that its last two decades were such a revolutionary moment because the century-long drive toward expanding higher education combined with a new incentive to cut costs. So, to our long history of diversity in higher education we append a short history of austerity in the 1980s.

In the middle of the twentieth century, block federal grants and guaranteed state support contributed to record growth and glorious stability among institutions of American higher education. Clark Kerr, one-time president of the University of California system and the mastermind of the California Master Plan, began pontificating about higher education in the 1960s, at the modern university's zenith. By the early 1990s, Kerr was lamenting its nadir: "The twentieth century was a grand century for the cities of intellect. The century, that golden century, is now past, never to be replicated."[17] He marked 1990 as the limen between an era of publicly funded "rapid expansion and extension" and an age of privately endowed, "constrained resources."[18] Investigating the last two decades of the twentieth century, Sheila Slaughter and Larry Leslie identify the primary reason for this change: "academic capitalism." In the United States, they explain, the "corporate quest for new products converged with faculty and institutional searches for increased funding."[19] Slaughter and Leslie investigate research partnerships, while Derek Bok, former president of Harvard University, notices another area where late twentieth-century entrepreneurial incentives rapidly altered college curricula. Research labs chased patents and grants, while administrators hunted tuition dollars. Dangling inexpensive distance education and valuable professional accreditation, colleges and universities have enticed students seeking a high return for a low investment.[20]

Students and their families have most acutely felt the effects of this late century shift to marketized resources and market-like behaviors. In 1960, tuition accounted for 20 percent of most universities' budgets. In 1987, tuition only contributed 24 percent of the typical college's or university's revenue. By the end of the century, however, tuition rarely accounted for less than 35 percent and often accounted for 50 percent of total income.[21] In the twenty-first century, tuition rates have only continued to rise. Within a single generation, higher education costs primarily borne by the state were shifted onto the backs of individual families. When the price of college essentially doubled, people began to see postsecondary education less as a public good and more as private capital. Students began to seek job skills, a return on their investment, rather than personal growth, a luxury in lean times. Summarizing these marketized developments while glancing back at the golden age of public support for higher education, David Labaree describes 1940–70 as a brief stretch when Americans viewed college as a "public good." We are now, Labaree contends, "back to the place where we have always been, where the university's primary role is to provide individual consumers a chance to gain social access and social advantage."[22] Since the late nineteenth century, students have expected professional status when paying for college credits, but beginning in the 1980s, their expectation became an insistence, and their attention to marketable skills an obsession.

Among university administrators and faculty, a combination of the constant demand for professional skills and the new push toward private revenue inspired corporate practices and entrepreneurial thinking. That shift in perspective led institutions to reduce labor costs and imitate corporate management. Derek Bok, while admitting that entrepreneurial thinking inspired these trends, concedes that hiring nontenure track instructors might be "exploitative," but he defends the practice with typically laissez-faire panache: "If the pay seems low, the root problem is probably that too many students have attempted to earn a PhD."[23] Frank Donoghue, critical of the managerial turn in higher education, remarks that after a brief hiatus in the mid-twentieth century, the pressure to run universities like for-profit corporations returned.[24] Presaging Donoghue's concerns, another critic of privatized higher education, Marc Bousquet, finds that corporate culture invaded university norms in the 1980s, as administrators embraced a "competitive, market-based, high-performance" mindset typically associated with capitalist enterprise.[25] All these commentators would agree with the assessment of Charles Smith, who also served in academic administration during the last two decades of the twentieth century: "Faculty innovations, often claimed to be market oriented, [were] introduced to cut costs and increase income."[26] Market pressures led to market values and then to market-like behaviors.

The 1980s not only witnessed an intensification of financial austerity in higher education; this decade also experienced a revitalization of the civic mission that higher education pursued before the industrial revolution and the federal government supported through the first half of the twentieth century. The politics of diversity, born in the 1960s Civil Rights Movement and flourishing in the 1970s rights revolution, pitted itself against the civic mission that higher education had assumed for centuries. This conflict between a midcentury commitment to uniform civic education and a late century respect for a diverse citizenry flared up in the 1980s. Andrew Hartman, a historian of these culture wars, explains that "debates about higher education have long acted as a proxy for arguments about whose values will shape the nation's future."[27] This could be seen nowhere better than in the conflict between civic-minded conservatives and diversity-concerned liberals. Multiculturalism was championed as a curricular ideal on the left, while intellectuals as diverse as the revanchist Allan Bloom and the progressive Todd Gitlin resuscitated "an Enlightenment appeal to common humanity."[28] The culture war over civic education might seem a far cry from the financial austerity inspiring a reduction in public money and a turn toward casualized labor, but that is not the case. In fact, the culture wars provided cover for many of the financial reforms in late twentieth-century higher education. This revolutionary symbiosis between diversity and austerity was not lost on those living through the trauma. Paul Lauter, a literature professor writing at the end of the 1980s, remarked that the "real crisis of higher education has to do with the sharp decline of its authority," a decline brought on by the culture wars and permitting further cuts to public funds.[29] Carol Stabile, a communications studies professor writing at the same time as Lauter, put the matter more bluntly, saying that the culture wars "succeeded in diverting attention from a number of urgent economic issues."[30]

The long saga of the modern university combined with the short history of the 1980s reveals that diversity and austerity shaped one hundred years of higher education, especially reforming the second to last decade of the previous century. Turning our attention to the present, we can see that these same forces continue to interact, resulting in undeniably revolutionary, though arguably different, results. Entrepreneurial thinking and market-like behaviors increased in the spring of 2020 when growing digitization met a global pandemic. Even prior to COVID-19, students were demanding—and universities were providing—digitally assisted remote instruction, already drifting away from the standard semester and the typical credit hour. Early in 2019, only 104 institutions offered primarily online degree programs, and 5 percent of these 104 programs served nearly half of all the students pursuing online degrees. By 2021, every institution had substantial experience with remote instruction in a variety of formats: synchronous, asynchronous, hybrid, hyflex, just-in-time, competency-based, and so forth. In the intervening years, enrollments skyrocketed among peripheral players. The University of the People, a nonprofit offering online degree programs for free, grew by 75 percent during the pandemic. Modern States Education Alliance, another nonprofit offering online courses that fulfill core requirements, doubled its enrollment in 2020.[31] The pandemic encouraged university administrators to expedite their efforts, lest they lose "customers" to new outfits.

Meanwhile, as economic pressures roiled higher education, political turmoil rocked the country. A rightward lurch in electoral politics and two social movements (now known as Me Too and Black Lives Matter) brought entrenched sexism and racism to the forefront of national consciousness. A new culture war was brewing, catalyzing with economic pressures in a bubbling stew. Over the course of the twentieth century, the accommodation of increasingly diverse students inspired changes to curricula and campuses, including new majors (such as "area" studies in Asian and African diaspora, Latino/a, and disability studies, to name a few) and new institutions (such as diversity offices and accessibility institutes). The most famous, perhaps, are the Black studies program at the University of Illinois Urbana–Champaign (1968) and the ethnic studies program at the University of California, Berkeley (1969), both created in response to student protests. Such efforts only increased during the pandemic as colleges and universities responded to progressive demands for greater accommodation (now gathered under the umbrella of "diversity, equity, and inclusion," also known as "DEI"). All the while, as DEI expanded, administrators struggled to maintain enrollments by offering accessible online education.

All these efforts were admirable and necessary. However, just as diversity politics inspired a recrudescence of Cold War civic education in the 1980s, so did anti-racist pedagogy and DEI policy trigger conservative backlash in the 2020s. Legislatures in states like Texas and Georgia have outlawed funding for diversity, equity, and inclusion initiatives at publicly funded colleges. Other laws aim to restrict the discussion of controversial subjects such as critical race theory and human sexuality. According to a PEN America study, twelve such laws were passed in 2021. One hundred and thirty-seven more bills were proposed in 2022, 39 percent of them targeting higher education, and seven becoming law.[32] As public arguments about the politics of higher education boil over, they inadvertently lend steam to efforts that increase managerial control by redefining tenure, thus making university faculty into contract employees without the job security or academic freedom they won in the 1920s when the American Association of University Professionals fought against the proletarianization of the academic profession, preserving academics' "status as independent guildmasters."[33] As of this writing, tenure has been legislatively reconnoitered in Wisconsin, Georgia, and Texas. Popular support for these efforts stems from public distrust of academics and their heresies. So it was in the 1980s, and so it remains today, as pundits cry about critical race theory, while legislators conspire to casualize academic labor and constrain university budgets. In the 2023 legislative session, for instance, Wisconsin lawmakers, ostensibly incensed about DEI programs, cut $32 million of public funding from the state university system, despite a surplus of $7 billion in the state coffers, promising to restore the money if colleges and universities demonstrated that they would better serve the market for professional skills rather than invest in the diversity of their student body.[34] To be fair, no one advocating critical race theory in higher education intends to advance managerial control over precarious college faculty. And no effort at advocating for social justice in the classroom should be blamed for reductions in public funds. The privatization of higher education long predates the legal theories of Richard Delgado and Kimberlé Crenshaw, and the erosion of tenure will easily outlast Ibram X. Kendi's anti-racist activism. The reappearance of diversity politics has clearly been exploited as a cover for neoliberal reform, allowing opportunistic politicians to justify their efforts at privatizing higher education with promises to protect American citizens from "dangerous" ideas.

    The analogy is undeniable, but so are the exceptions. The 2020s are like, but not exactly like, the 1980s. College enrollments are no longer increasing. In 2008, the US economy entered a tailspin now known as the Great Recession. Since then, birth rates have plummeted, as have college applications, leaving us on the edge of an "enrollment cliff."[35] Nonetheless, those students who remain are increasingly nonwhite and nontraditional. But this time, not public institutions but private initiatives serve the new demographics. When Michael Smith writes glowingly about the educational institutions expanding access, he turns to private outfits, like Southern New Hampshire University, which increased its enrollment from 3,000 in 2003 to 175,000 in 2023.[36] These marketized solutions come with their own problems, such as low graduation rates and record defaults on the loans needed to afford pricey private colleges. Heavy marketing campaigns and paltry post-enrollment advising have lured many students to colleges and universities where they receive insufficient support, take on burdensome debt, yet earn no diplomas.[37] Public control over higher education slips away as private firms flood the industry with classes and content, bringing a host of additional new concerns: the digital, just-in-time delivery of content to suit consumer demands; the intensifying drive toward outcome-based learning; the proliferation of new accreditation instruments, such as certificates, microcredentials, and badges.[38] Moreover, our present-day culture wars are different from those experienced forty years ago. James Davison Hunter, the sociologist who coined the term "culture wars" in 1990, recently told the left-leaning magazine *Politico* that what we are seeing today is better described as a "class-culture conflict."[39] Ben Domenech, writing for the conservative *Spectator*, contends that the issues themselves have changed—we're no longer wrestling over curricular diversity or civic ideals. Instead, today conservatives fight over "a radical trans agenda and a race-focused education regime."[40] Despite all these differences, the present moment shares a common composition with the 1980s: Then as now, diversity politics meets economic austerity, creating opportunity for radical change. So, if you're invested in higher education today, then you should also be interested in the 1980s.

We've relied on an elaborate analogy to justify the temporal scope of our study, but we haven't justified the institutional emphasis. Our study is among numerous others that focus on particular institutions. We focus on the University of Texas at Austin (UT Austin) rather than an array or cross-section of institutions, raising the question: Even if you agree that the 1980s are interesting because they're similar to the 2020s, why should you care about the writing program at the University of Texas at Austin? To justify the object of our study, we point first to the unique place that all writing programs occupy in modern higher education. Since the industrial revolution, the core curriculum at most colleges and universities has boasted one constant—the universal writing requirement. At the beginning of chapter 1, we explain in much greater detail why writing requirements became such a fixture. For now, suffice it to say that because every college student in the United States for the last century or better has had to take a first-year writing class or fulfill some other type of writing requirement, the history of higher education can be traced through the development of this class, the curricula of its teachers, and the experience of its administrators. Historians of rhetoric and composition know how central the writing curriculum is to higher education, so they have told rich stories by situating a given program in a wider context. So have Lisa Mastrangelo, Suzanne Bordelon, and Barbara L'Eplattenier when situating composition pedagogy and writing program administration at the Seven Sisters colleges in the wider context of democratic progressivism and Deweyan pragmatism.[41] Likewise do the contributors to *In The Archives of Composition* (2015) as they chronicle writing instruction at normal schools during efforts in the late nineteenth and early twentieth centuries to accommodate women and students of color.[42] So also have David Gold and Catherine Hobbs when placing the writing pedagogy at southern public women's colleges in the circumstances of postbellum industrialism, regional patriarchy, and women's suffrage.[43] And finally so do we when placing the writing program at the University of Texas at Austin in the wider political and economic context of higher education toward the end of the twentieth century.

While any history of twentieth-century higher education could be told through the microcosm of a specific university's writing program, the impact of diversity and austerity on colleges and universities is especially relevant to writing program administration. As recent scholars have argued, the politics of diversity requires that we rethink easily overlooked topics, such as the assessment of student work and the teaching of grammar.[44] Moreover, writing programs are typically scrutinized in moments of financial austerity because writing classes are costly. As a result, writing programs were among the first to experiment with marketized solutions, a tendency leading two experts on writing program administration and higher education employment, Eileen Schell and Patricia Lambert Stock, to conclude, "Composition studies is a particularly fitting vantage point from which to study the academy's turn toward contingent labor."[45] Additionally, two crises involving the writing program at the University of Texas at Austin speak directly to the effects of austerity and diversity on higher education. The Saturday Night Massacre (1985), chronicled in chapter 2, is an academic tragedy resulting from fiscal austerity, and the Battle of Texas (1989), covered in chapter 3, is a quarrel fought over a "multicultural" writing curriculum. Finally, the combined ability of austerity and diversity to enable dramatic change in higher education is recounted in chapter 4, as we explain how these two crises inspired an administrative overhaul of the core curriculum and the writing program at UT Austin. Therefore, a close study of one writing program in the 1980s will not only contribute to our knowledge of writing program administration but also expand our understanding of higher education's evolving trends. We conclude this segment of our introduction, the justification of our temporal scope and institutional focus, with an encapsulation of our core *historical* argument: Austerity and diversity in the 1980s, just as today, have dramatically reshaped higher education, and this revolution can be glimpsed by focusing on the writing program at UT Austin. But that is not our primary purpose. While exploring an era of diversity and austerity in microcosm through the deep study of one academic unit at one university, we will primarily advance an *ethical* argument—a disposition we think most suitable to the writing program administrator living in transitional times, regardless of where they find themselves institutionally or geographically.

The chapters that follow primarily offer a narrative history with an ethical upshot. To better explain this effort, we contrast our narrative/ethical approach with the more common analytical/polemical argumentation among scholars in the discipline of critical university studies. Analytical histories of higher education attempt a universal perspective through causal analysis—a distant, clear-eyed, critical gaze at a broad ocean, seeking patterns on a distant horizon or penetrating beneath the choppy surface to identify a tidal flow. For example, Matthew Johnson, when detailing the history of affirmative action policies at the University of Michigan, focuses on one cause, "co-optation . . . the process of selectively incorporating activism, while preserving long-standing values and priorities."[46] Once Johnson has shown that upper-level administrators consistently co-opted activists' demands, neutering their potential through bureaucratic procedure, he can conclude, "If we agree that inequality is a choice, then we can hold universities accountable. We can demand choices that lead to equality."[47] Sharon Lee similarly identifies three causes that frustrated efforts to make the University of Illinois an inviting place for Asian students in the 1960s, '70s, and '80s: the belief that Asians are a model minority, the assumption that proportional representation is the end of diversity policy, and the focus on Black-white race relations in the United States.[48] As her analysis unfolds, Lee zeroes in on one cause above the other two: "ultimately . . . [rejecting] higher education's narrow goal of statistical parity as the sole measure of assessing minority student experience."[49] Johnson's and Lee's detailed case studies draw policy-oriented conclusions applicable to other institutions.

But we aren't writing to high-level administrators capable of realizing grand policy designs. Instead, we primarily address an audience of rhetoric and composition specialists, workaday instructors and midlevel personnel (in our case, writing program directors and departmental administrators), academics who, like us, will spend their lives teaching undergraduates, designing curricula, and chairing committees. While we value policy recommendations and scholarly polemics, we also believe that teachers and administrators laboring at a lower institutional tier will benefit more from circumspection. As Susan McLeod explains, writing program administrators work in a "variety of exigencies and contexts," meaning that for the writing program administrator, "context is all."[50] Since the 2020s have been so different from the 1980s, and every writing program, like every college or university, is institutionally unique, our study of the writing program at the University of Texas at Austin can teach us about the 1980s, but it cannot promulgate principles or programs suitable to the present day or our audience's professional lives. Nonetheless, a study promoting a circumspect disposition, rather than a five-point plan or a generalizable principle, can reflect McLeod's contextualism. In every era, but especially in our moment, the writing program administrator needs to see things as Leonidas saw Thermopylae, barking orders on the front line, not as Xerxes witnessed the battle, perched atop a high bluff, far above the fray. Rather than telling you how to fight your battles, we will suggest a suitable vantage and an advisable posture, leaving the tactics to those who know the terrain. Since we are making assertions about how to be, rather than what to do, we characterize our argument as *ethical* rather than *polemical*, and we distinguish our narrative from others' analyses.

Following the example of cultural rhetorics scholars, who likewise see potential in narrative as a mode of scholarly inquiry, we have chosen to tell a story with an emotional effect rather than write an analytical account with a polemical conclusion. In this introduction and our conclusion, we offer a metacommentary on the encapsulated narrative. The story told in our four body chapters is vital because, as the members of the Cultural Rhetorics Theory Lab at Michigan State University explain, "If you're not practicing story, you're doing it wrong."[51] The metacommentary is also necessary because, as critical race theorists in the discipline of composition studies explain, narratives blend theory and method.[52] In the body chapters, we traverse this blurry terrain. In the framing chapters, we draw analytical lines on a rhetorical map, distinguishing the theory from the method, explicitly tracing an argument that we elsewhere advance sub rosa. V. Jo Hsu points out that "many academic fields remain suspicious of narrative, experience-based, and affective methodologies."[53] But these suspicions are unwarranted; for narrative, when incorporated into scholarly inquiry, can arrive at conclusions and exert influences not available in other academic genres. Aja Martinez, for example, has developed her method of "counterstory," quasi-fictionalized narratives, so that people and especially women of color can locate themselves in "rhetoric and writing studies pedagogy and curriculum development."[54] Similarly Hsu analyzes the narratives of those who experience LGBTQ+ diaspora, "a constellation of stories that determine with whom, where, and how we belong."[55] Such narratives commit an "act of defiance" against exclusion and bigotry, "continually reinterpret[ing] events."[56] For Martinez and Hsu, narrative's myriad potential lies in its radical particularity, its deferral of analysis, and its demand for experience. Our story leverages the same rhetorical potential to a new effect. Narrative allows us to explore character portraits and re-create events. We can reveal personality types responding in their typical ways to their turbulent times. Because of narrative's affective potential, we agree with Lynée Lewis Gaillet, who states, "I believe storytelling—with a purpose, based on painstaking research, tied to a particular cultural moment, making clear the teller's prejudices—is the real task of the historian."[57]

The suasive possibility offered by characters and dramas is fundamentally an emotional appeal, a rhetorical quality that Debra Hawhee, following Aristotle, calls *alogos*. *Alogos*, Hawhee explains, must be approached "in positive terms" as something that happens not in the absence of logic but alongside and likely prior to the logical appeals of a given artifact.[58] The *alogical* dimension of our persuasive effort—"surges of highly complex feelings, snap judgments, changes of heart, *transformation*"—matters more than the historical-logical argument presented in this introduction. The characters themselves count more than the combined economic and political forces chronicled in our history; the Saturday Night Massacre and the Battle of Texas teach more than the analogy between the 1980s and the 2020s because these stories invite you (our reader) to connect with and emulate certain types of academic professionals. This search for professional identity in scholarly narrative is common among rhetoric and composition specialists, as evidenced when the coauthors of *GenAdmin* (2011), all seasoned writing program administrators (WPAs), remark that "the narratives we have inherited may help us to realize ... aspects of WPA work and identity."[59] They furthermore notice that historical narratives shape future professional identities by teaching young academics "to act and think as WPAs."[60] Two pioneers in narrative analysis, Wayne Booth and Walter Fisher, explain how narratives can elicit such a response. Booth and Fisher explain that narratives ask readers to build a common world and identify with protagonists in that world.[61] This is a sensuous response. The principle of narrative appeal is, as Fisher explains, "*identification* rather than deliberation."[62] Following Fisher's insight, throughout this book's body chapters we present three types of protagonists—the tragic, the romantic, and the phronetic—placing all three in the wider setting of a transitional decade, hoping that while witnessing

Introduction

each character's response to austerity and diversity, the reader will identify most with the phronetic protagonist.

We borrow two of these terms, "romantic" and "tragic," from Hayden White, who studied the use of narrative among nineteenth-century historians. These Victorian antiquarians adopted an "organicist explanatory strategy," imagining that people are "awash in a historical sea" but nonetheless able to direct their course through this "Chaos of Being."[63] Nineteenth-century romantic historians found in the "'Chaos of Being' notion of history" a "historical consciousness" released "from the kind of determinism which had driven the historical thought of Enlightenment rationalism."[64] If history is an organic tangle, not a mechanistic process, then individuals may influence its growth. While we don't want to extenuate a comparison between nineteenth-century historians of Western politics and contemporary historians of writing pedagogy, we nonetheless believe that a rough parallel exists. Like historians in the middle of the 1800s, many contemporary historians of rhetoric and composition adopt an organic view of history. Thomas Masters, for example, objects to sweeping intellectual histories of writing pedagogy, with their inevitable ideological trends and overbearing grand narratives. According to Masters, such intellectual histories fail to engage with "practice-based history . . . a detailed examination of the particulars of writing and its instruction at a given moment in history."[65] In practice-based history Masters finds individual agency. The turn among historians of writing pedagogy toward what David Gold has called "microhistories" further allows romantic protagonists to shine. Gold complains, "Too often, progressive-minded scholars do a disservice to the agency of their subjects by presuming them to be helpless victims of social forces beyond their control."[66] Gold's "microhistorical approach" allows the historian to "see teachers and students as potential agents and active shapers of their educational experiences."[67] Other historians follow suit, using archival sources to tell local stories about romantic protagonists. Kelly Ritter, for example, tells the tale of midcentury writing instruction at the Women's College in North Carolina, where "the general education movement rolled through the Women's College like a passing freight train, but the department held firm and resisted."[68] In Ritter's and Gold's scholarly works, we see the characteristic romantic defiance of history's movement toward mechanistic progress and diminished modernity.

Gold's and Ritter's romantic celebrations contrast with another trend in scholarly works about the history of writing program administration: a tendency toward what we, again echoing White, will call a "tragic" narrative. White contends that nineteenth-century organicism allowed the historian to emphasize the individual's agency or their ultimate "resignation to a condition from which" each person "perceived little prospect of liberation." The tragic historian acknowledges the complexity of history, the "Chaos of Being," but finds that any attempt to swim against the current will only result in movement with the tide. The tragic character is stuck, inconsolably, between historical forces and individual agency, ultimately unable to exercise individuality and finally unwilling to succumb to causality. The characteristic tragic action, therefore, is struggle.[69] Two recent institutional histories tell such narratives. David Fleming's *From Form to Meaning* (2011) spins two tragic narratives: the first about left-leaning teaching assistants who tried to realize "an emergent, self-directed, and meaning-driven curriculum run by genuinely empowered and collaborative staff"; the second about a faculty-led effort to abolish the required first-year writing course in favor of a writing-in-the-disciplines program.[70] Fleming's protagonists could neither overcome nor endure because the first-year writing requirement is marked by contradictions: "precariously 'empty' and dangerously full, relatively untethered to disciplinary content and authority, on the one hand, but replete with all our social concerns and anxieties about language, reason, identity, and community, on the other."[71] A similarly tragic story is told by Ryan Skinnell, who chronicles curricular changes to the first-year writing program at Arizona State University, each made at an important moment, each trying to achieve a university-level goal. When Skinnell assumes "the narrow scope of micro-history alongside the comprehensive scope of macro-history," he finds a vain struggle to slip historical shackles. His conclusion captures this frustration: "Composition's value as an institutional concession helps explain why the [first-year writing] course endured in American higher education and why it thrived, despite a steady procession of complaints from all quarters that composition did not (and does not) meet its ostensible purposes of remediating underdeveloped matriculants, preparing students for subsequent college writing tasks, or helping students to write better more generally."[72] Fleming's protagonists fight for curricular innovation and pedagogical autonomy but fail. Skinnell's protagonists angle to improve education, always frustrated by the institutional drive toward national status.

These quick glances of ours at several recent microhistories of rhetoric and composition overlook a heap of complex arguments and careful documentation by their authors. But we focus on the characterological features and the narrative contours so that we can describe the romantic and the tragic characters and explain why these character types are suitable to writing program administration in the contemporary university. We are all struggling to exert some agency in fraught economic and political circumstances, often despite Byzantine administrative environments. By asking us to identify with their protagonists, the tragic and romantic microhistories caution against hubristic assumption and fatalistic resignation. Those of us who find ourselves running programs and chairing departments should endeavor for agency while acknowledging limitations. To these two common characterological types we add a third, the phronetic protagonist, whose persuasive potential can be analyzed using Walter Fisher's criteria for good narrative reasons. The phronetic protagonist appeals to an ethical fact (prudence), suits a contemporary relevance (our transitional circumstances), behaves in a measured way that achieves desired consequences (departmental gains, functional governance, pedagogical improvement), is consistent with the midlevel administrator's experience, and points to a transcendent valuation of the actual good over the potential ideal.[73] Needless to say, this dry taxonomy of characterological types and their rhetorical-ethical potential is unappealing. In order to identify with the phronetic protagonist, the reader must encounter the character as you will, dramatized in tense situations.

Our narrative favors the phronetic protagonist because this character type is suitable to writing program administration and appropriate to transitional times. Such a phronetic disposition is regularly praised among scholars of rhetoric and composition. Joseph Harris, for instance, has argued that program administrators should pay close attention to the "here and now" because this *"programmatic"* approach is capable of "changing local, material conditions."[74] Donna Strickland has similarly recommended that rhetoric and composition specialists "put our considerable intellectual abilities to work on the pragmatic, transformative tasks of tweaking," which she defines as "working together to pose unpredictable futurities."[75] Most recently, Kathryn Gindlesparger challenges middle managers in higher education to "change . . . systems from the inside" by leveraging their "rhetorical investment in shared governance through participation that 'exceeds expectations.'"[76] All three scholars, each of them a writing program administrator, champion the phronetic disposition that our story favors. They make their arguments explicitly and logically. In the chapters that follow, we will make a similar claim implicitly and emotionally. We choose this narrative mode of argumentation because, as Linda Adler-Kassner, another writing program administrator/scholar, points out, the logical work of scholarly theory can lead to pragmatic administrative strategies, but this logical work itself is fundamentally supported by a deeper identification "rooted in other stories, ones that we tell about *why* we do the work that we do."[77] Adler-Kassner recalls the opening line to Aristotle's treatise on rhetoric: "Rhetoric is an *antistrophos* to dialectic."[78] Recognizing that others before us have made a dialectical case for a phronetic disposition in contemporary writing program administration, we offer a rhetorical counterpart, a story about phronetic writing program administrators.

In addition to suiting the enterprise of writing program administration, the phronetic disposition also speaks to our present transitional moment. Clark Kerr has called our era "a century for foxes."[79] Metaphorically, we face famine and predation. Among such pointed terms for scarce resources and political minefields, Kerr wants university administrators "looking around every bush, avoiding every trap, eating everything that happens to come along."[80] Since the twenty-first century is a transitional era like the 1980s, but only more so, we need new narratives with new protagonists. Surviving tragedy requires some acquiescence to the fates. Achieving agency requires scrappy determination. For all these reasons, we tell a story here that favors the phronetic protagonist, encouraging versatility, advocating opportunism, and forgiving compromise. Though it doesn't showcase resistance, our history of the writing program at the University of Texas at Austin is radical in the sense that Hayden White predicted, emphasizing the underlying dynamics of diversity and austerity, grasping higher education by its political and economic root.[81] Additionally, our story is pragmatic—in Joseph Harris's words, "more concerned with the here and now."[82] While chapters 2 and 3 tell of administrators who tragically failed to overcome austerity and romantically fought to preserve civic education, chapters 1 and 4 spin another yarn about phronetic actors who achieved an imperfect and tenuous advantage—for themselves, their programs, and their students. The body chapters prove that the rhetoric and composition faculty at UT Austin were most successful when they put aside ideological rigidity, accepted their limited agency, paid less attention to their disciplinary legacy, and closely regarded their administrative purview. In our first and last narrative chapters, we chronicle their always imperfect, typically short-sighted, consistently cautious, yet regularly effective solutions. In the ancient fables of both Eastern and Western traditions it is the opportunistic, clever fox who usually survives and often thrives. Altogether, our story positions the vulpine writing program administrator as the accidental exemplar of our academic age.

We have so far presented this book's principal contributions: the first, a *historical* argument made analogically; and the second, an *ethical* appeal presented narratively. We append to this introduction a discussion of a third contribution, one simultaneously archival and pedagogical. For the same reason that scholars in critical university studies find themselves rummaging through crumbling boxes of sepia papers, the microhistorical turn among historians of rhetoric and composition has directed many toward primary source research. Together composition and critical university studies have generated a litany of institutional histories derived from such archival evidence. Rhetoric and composition scholars have also produced a series of reflections on how researchers go about their craft—where they look, what they examine, which sources are revelatory, and which repositories are helpful. Barbara L'Eplattenier calls this a conversation about "methods," which she distinguishes from the more common chatter about "methodology."[83] In this introduction we've offered an extensive discussion of our narrative methodology. Following L'Eplattenier's suggestion, we here append some commentary on our archival methods with reflections on their pedagogical potential in the graduate classroom.

We have chosen to complement this scholarly narrative with a digital archive, RhetCompUTX (https://rhetcomputx.dwrl.utexas.edu), featuring all the primary sources and many of the secondary sources (newspaper and magazine articles) that we cite, along with many others that we do not reference but are nonetheless relevant to the history of writing program administration at UT Austin. We present this digital archive as a resource and a guide. Barbara L'Eplattenier and Lisa Mastrangelo comment that histories of writing programs are difficult to write because "administrative work is not always easy to find in archival documents."[84] Our digital archive speaks directly to their concern by making the source material about one influential writing program easily accessible and therefore a resource for future research. This public presentation of our primary source research can also serve as a guide for future researchers. The digital exhibition of our archival evidence responds to a call made more than twenty years ago by Linda Ferreira-Buckley for more "archival training" in rhetoric and composition graduate study.[85] Instead of describing the collection, our digital archive shows the collecting. James Purdy explains that digital archivism promises "accessibility" because digital archives "eliminate many temporal and spatial obstacles" to primary source research.[86] Our exhibit does more than offer access to our archival research; it also publicly reveals our research process.

In a separate article composed with others who helped us construct RhetCompUTX, we more fully explain the rationale behind our digital archive.[87] And in the conclusion to this book, we offer additional reflections on its potential. For the purposes of this introduction, we briefly mention that RhetCompUTX includes four types of items, which are related to classroom instruction, departmental governance, university administration, and local and national context, each imagined as a layer of information. These items were culled from a variety of sources, including personal papers housed in repositories, official records of university administration (e.g., meeting minutes and committee reports), digitized archives of newspaper and magazine articles, and syllabi and other such materials found in personal files. We encourage the would-be researcher to peruse these sources directly, noticing how we rely on them in the narrative chapters that follow. We believe that direct digital access to such materials can teach the novice researcher so much more than any dry recounting of our research process ever could. The digital space that we created is itself an artifact of our research and our writing because we built the site as an aid to this book's composition, organizing and chronologizing nearly thirteen hundred items. The public presentation came as an afterthought, a way for us to show our work. Therefore, when paired with this book, RhetCompUTX allows the novice researcher to see how "writing and research . . . occur together in the same virtual space, which frames these activities as integrated parts of knowledge production, rather than as separate and separable steps."[88] The complementary digital archive realizes the potential that Alexis Ramsey-Tobienne sees in digital archives, creating a "partner space" that can "help us elucidate our own research endeavors in traditional archives."[89]

While the digital archive complementing this scholarly book is both a resource for future research and a guide to would-be researchers, we suggest that it can do something more for graduate education in the discipline. Reflecting on their efforts at teaching archival research methods to graduate students in the field of rhetoric and composition, Jonathan Buehl, Tamar Chute, and Anne Fields remark, "Now that the field has a substantial body of scholarship on ways of *doing* in the archives, scholars of rhetoric and composition should further discuss ways of *teaching* and *learning* in the archives."[90] It is time for graduate classes to engage the archive, as Charles Morris once encouraged, as a "dynamic site of rhetorical power."[91] Doing so allows graduate students to "intervene in current conversations" about writing program administration, as Patty Wilde, Molly Tetreault, and Sarah Fraco attest, based on their experiences in the graduate classroom.[92] Writing program administrators have long recognized the potential of archival research for reflections on and reformations of their professional identity. Susan Wells commented more than twenty years ago that archives give rhetoric and composition specialists "the possibility of reconfiguring our discipline."[93] James Purdy adds that digitization extends this possibility by making archives, such as

RhetCompUTX, "a (or even the) site of disciplinary formation."[94] To realize the potential that Purdy has identified, researchers must get beyond the referential/evidential function of archival data. As exhibited in this book, our references do what Jenny Rice says many bodies of primary source research must. The notes documenting our archival sources boost "the feel of legitimacy for [our] epistemic claims."[95] Readers are often invited to regard but not to explore sources. But with the digitization of our evidentiary body and the addition of material, we offer something more than an exhibition of our data or an exposition of our process. With the digital archive we also create what Barbara Biesecker calls a "scene of invention," a place where the user can make something new while interacting with something old.[96] This gets us to the pedagogical potential of digital archival exhibits.

By constructing RhetCompUTX, we tap the potential that Wendy Hayden sees in digital archivism, expanding the scope of scholarly work beyond the published essay or book while inviting students to engage in the "critical imagination" that Gesa Kirsch and Jacqueline Jones Royster advocate among historians of rhetoric and composition.[97] According to Kirsch and Royster, critical imagination requires "listening respectfully" to past actors, "hypothesizing" about their motives and actions, and "tacking out" to take a wider and longer view, so we can "learn to look more systematically beyond our own contemporary values and assumptions."[98] Like Kirsch and Royster, we argue that direct engagement with our primary source data facilitates such critical imagination. Enabling students to interrogate a robust digital archive about writing program administration, RhetCompUTX asks graduate students to "consider *why* and *how* they might engage the archives on their own."[99] The digital exhibit enables students to vicariously experience the administrator's quotidian life by allowing them to peruse the documentary traces of a writing program plagued by the imposition of economic austerity and blighted by conflicts over political diversity. Graduate students can, in short, step into a historical moment not unlike their own. Such an encounter, fueled by the sources that we provide and ignited by the students' critical imagination, empowers the user to think like a university administrator—strategically yet hopefully, with circumspection and compassion, seeking opportunity while acknowledging restriction. Approached pedagogically in a graduate class filled with students interested in writing program administration, the digital archive and its scene of invention matter just as much as (or perhaps more than) the scholarly narrative.

We return to this digital archive and its pedagogical potential when reflecting on the ethics of historical scholarship in this book's conclusion.

The framing paragraphs to each of the four substantive chapters explicitly propound the contemporary relevance and scholarly purpose left otherwise implicit in the stories we tell. Beyond the framing segments to each narrative chapter and outside the introductory and concluding chapters of this book, everything hereafter is a chronological narrative told with careful attention to characters and events. We conclude this introduction by confessing that our initial interest in this project did not stem from the historical analogy, ethical narrative, or pedagogical potential presented in this chapter. You should care about the 1980s because this period was similar to our own. You should be interested in the narrative chapters because they present a phronetic disposition appropriate to writing program administration in times of economic austerity and political diversity. And you should consider perusing the digital archive because of the pedagogical potential that it lends to your critical imagination. All these justifications occurred to us as we organized the evidence, digitized items, ordered events, sketched characters, and recounted episodes. But at first blush, we were attracted to this study because of the narrative, a decade-long tale of faculty infighting, institutional evolution, disciplinary revolution, and programmatic adaptation. Likewise, we encourage you to enjoy the story that unfolds in the next four chapters. We promise it's a good one.

1
The Composition Revolution

Stories about late twentieth-century developments in higher education tend to privilege economic causes and slight individual agency. Recounting his experiences in the 1980s, Clark Kerr makes it seem like history simply shifted, its actors swept up in the tide: "Higher education became even more of an adjunct to the immense and changing labor market.... The economic return to a college degree dropped precipitously.... Many students came to college looking for job training, not a philosophy of life.... Enrollments in engineering, business administration, and computer science went up drastically, and departments involved became among the most dominant on campus. College became less a professional and class-oriented institution for an elite and more a market-oriented instrumentality for the masses. It was a fundamental restructuring."[1] More recent scholars note that this broad narrative about how the publicly supported midcentury university transformed into a commercial, market-oriented enterprise suffers from two related problems: (1) "Like all quasi-determinist theories of history, this story is in a tangle about agency," and furthermore (2) this narrative "assumes that changes in society will simply be reproduced in the same form in universities."[2]

But individual conditions at each institution and the complexity of each institutional setting give the lie to any such determinacy, calling into question the "quasi-determinist" character of economically inflected histories. Program administrators are well aware of each institution's peculiarity and each actor's agency. Such an awareness led two professors of writing and rhetoric at the University of California, Davis to describe their institutional environment—including many of the factors that we found at UT Austin, such as disciplinary status, labor issues, and writing-across-the-curriculum initiatives—as a "complex ecology."[3] Such an awareness also inspired professors at the University of Minnesota Duluth to describe the forced merger of their independent writing program with the Department of English as "an exercise of power" by administrators demanding that they "realign budgets with enrollment." While acknowledging the restraints, these same writing program administrators also detail their successes, documenting, for example, those instances when they believe that they "succeeded in resisting the exercise of power."[4]

To slice through the Gordian knot about agency and recognize the ineluctable variation among institutions, in this chapter we tell a story about how specific actors exercised some, albeit limited, influence during a transitional decade. In the 1970s a long-standing approach to teaching writing, which served the conservative politics of Cold War America and the professional aspirations of incoming students, was challenged when the political winds shifted and pedagogical efficacy was called into question. Upper administration at the University of Texas at Austin mandated or incentivized several reforms to the writing program. But change didn't just happen, nor was it entirely aimed at professional training and marketable skills. As we explain, writing program directors, departmental administrators, and regular faculty were able to tack into these shifting political winds and adjust to the changing economic currents while also advancing a uniquely effective curriculum and an interestingly civic pedagogy. The composition revolution of the 1970s at the University of Texas at Austin, therefore, gives the lie to Kerr's static verb. Higher education did not simply *become* "an adjunct to the immense and changing labor market."[5] Middle managers accommodated their curricula to economic pressures while leveraging local possibilities, thus realizing their own agendas.

At the beginning of the 1970s, UT Austin English department chair Neill Megaw and writing program director James Sledd contributed complementary articles to the university's alumni magazine, the *Alcalde*, both deploring literacy instruction. They blamed financial pressures and ballooning enrollments, the most salient economic forces shaping higher education in the late twentieth century.[6] In the spring of 1975, no longer administrators, they nonetheless teamed up again, submitting a proposal at a faculty meeting: "That every member of the regular faculty of the [UT Austin] Department of English will teach at least one section of composition . . . every three semesters."[7] At the time, all students had to take nine hours, equaling three classes, dedicated strictly to writing. Everyone had to take E 306, a first-year writing class, in their first year. Thereafter, during the first and the second years of enrollment, students fulfilled the remainder of their three-course requirement by selecting from a bevy of electives. In order to explain the magnitude of the writing program at UT Austin, allow us a quick digression on course numbering and a brief note on enrollments. The first number in each class signifies the number of credit hours, the second number indicates the level of instruction, and the third number (along with the added letter) indicates the special topic or theme in the course. Thus, E 306 (Rhetoric and Composition) is a three-hour course (3), taught as a requirement in or before the first semester of formal enrollment (0), and designated by the number 6. E 307 (Literature and Composition) is similarly a required first-year course, distinguished from E 306 by the final digit (7). E 317 (Technical Writing) and E 314 (Survey of Literature) are intended for second-year students (hence the 1), and 325 (Advanced Writing) is intended for upper-division students (hence the 2).

The upshot of all these numbers is that the English department taught a lot of writing to students at various points in their academic careers. Students typically took E 306 in the first semester of their first year and either E 307 or E 317 in the second semester. In the first semester of their sophomore year, they often took E 314. Another number demonstrates the writing program's magnitude. In the fall of 1975, roughly 4,500 students took the required writing class (E 306). Assuming that all 4,500 of these students marched through the typical curriculum, we can speculate that an equal number of first-year students was split between E 307 and E 317 in the subsequent spring, and another 4,500 sophomores had to take E 314 in the 1975–76 academic year. Therefore, four separate required writing classes had to serve 13,500 students each academic year. With so many classes to offer and so many students to serve, the English department resorted to graduate instructors and nontenure track faculty. According to Sledd and Megaw, staffing so many classes with such "unqualified" personnel had cheapened the quality of instruction. Their solution was to require that seasoned, tenure track professors staff required writing classes. Responding to Sledd and Megaw's proposal, the English department formed a committee and produced a tedious report with a scandalous revelation: Only 2.5 percent of the tenured faculty taught first-year writing classes![8] The faculty entertained several administrative solutions to such an appalling statistic—drop the first-year writing requirement or maybe hire "specialists" to handle the course load. Nevertheless, asking tenured faculty to step into the lower-division writing classroom was simply a nonstarter. Even the students objected, with one saying, "I . . . would not want to . . . feel the wrath of a bored professor for a whole semester."⁹ The tenured faculty's reason for rejecting Sledd and Megaw's proposal is best summarized by Wayne Rebhorn, who called the first-year writing course "drudgery."¹⁰

Like many other professors, Rebhorn never liked to teach E 306. But his objections were understandable. The class was not intellectually challenging. It was typically assigned to graduate instructors and nontenure track faculty. Worst of all, it was boring to teach. Rebhorn's story explains his sentiment. He migrated south from New Haven in the late 1960s, shortly before Megaw arrived to chair the English department. Though arriving at UT Austin around the same time, the two men could not have been more different. Megaw was hired in 1968 by Dean John Silber not for his scholarly profile but for his pedagogical commitments. Megaw and Sledd saw eye to eye, so in 1968, Sledd accepted Megaw's invitation to direct the first-year writing program. He resigned just two years later. Not long after, Megaw was replaced by a new department chair.¹¹ Rebhorn later described Megaw as "really not much of a researcher." In the early 1970s, Rebhorn himself was already on the fast track to a high-profile academic career. A Yale alumnus, he published several articles before leaving graduate school. As a professor, he penned numerous academic books and scholarly translations, earning a "lucrative" endowed professorship and retiring as one of the department's most decorated members. Rebhorn knew the university was making a big "push" toward becoming a "research institution." His tall stack of scholarly titles magnified the university's grand achievement and secured his good fortune.¹² So in 1975 when Sledd said the English faculty was building a "research machine" at the expense of undergraduate education, he was looking at Rebhorn and the like, those careerists who had become "the real enemy of education in the American state university."¹³

Sledd's critique was nothing new. Since the rise of the German research university, humanist teachers have criticized professional scholars for their poor performance in the classroom, their refusal to invest in the collegiate community, and their selfish personal advancement.¹⁴ The Sledds and the Rebhorns of the academic world have been at odds for more than two centuries. And it would be hard to blame an upwardly mobile academic for disdaining the first-year-writing chore. While early nineteenth-century humanists found substantive intellectual engagement in the introductory writing classroom, late twentieth-century English professors found nothing of the sort. Additionally, even if E 306 allowed a sure path to academic publication, its status would dissuade tenure track faculty. By midcentury, the typical American university had become a series of missions, institutions, and populations

The Composition Revolution

living alongside one another in mutual support, if not purposeful cooperation. Graduates and professors stand at the upper tier, building a German-style research university where they can advance knowledge. The public occupies the commons, benefiting from an American-style college that serves their professional needs.[15] Students come to enjoy a liberal, community-oriented undergraduate education. The undergraduate college funds the research mission, and the research mission burnishes the graduate university, providing fresh PhDs to continue the educational enterprise. One historian of education calls this dynamic "cross-subsidy," a central organizing principle of the modern university.[16] Responding to Sledd and Megaw's proposal to upset this long-standing cross-subsidy by putting tenured faculty in the first-year writing class, a UT Austin literature professor snorted that first-year writing is "an elementary course . . . taught by teaching 'interns.'"[17] The rest of the English department decided to form an ad hoc committee, which dismissed Sledd and Megaw's proposal as well intentioned but flawed, offering instead a series of alternate proposals aimed at improving writing instruction.[18] Sledd dismissed the report and its recommendations, saying the document was "weak because of its specious arguments and obvious contempt for lower-division teaching."[19]

Sledd's slander notwithstanding, the faculty's concerns about the intellectual rigor and institutional status of first-year writing instruction were completely sensible. So were their complaints about the experience of teaching E 306. The class *was* "drudgery." In 1975, the first-year writing curriculum was dominated by what scholars have since termed "current-traditional rhetoric," an approach to writing instruction that promises basic writing skills. The pedagogy is as uninspiring as the name. Its features will be familiar to most who have taught or taken a first-year composition course in the last fifty years: abstract topics, formal argumentation, and strict grammar. Students write about subjects they can readily learn (the research paper, the literary analysis); they imitate "modes" or strict genres (the expository essay, the descriptive paper, the narrative account, the argumentative editorial); they obsess about grammatical correctness (comma splices, pronoun disagreement, proper source citation). One of current-traditional rhetoric's most enduring aspects is its emphasis on prescriptive grammar, which is enforced by tests of grammatical proficiency intended to measure student achievement.[20] Rebhorn confirmed this perennial commitment to formal instruction and grammatical correction, saying it was "a time-consuming, boring, uninspiring chore primarily because so much of one's effort is spent correcting merely mechanical errors."[21]

Recent scholarship complicates this view in important ways. To begin with, the monolith of "current-traditional rhetoric" appears much less integral when the historian's lens focuses on particular sites. In practice, current-traditional pedagogies have challenged dominant ideological norms and enabled underrepresented students.[22] Nonetheless, in the mid-1970s at the University of Texas at Austin, first-year writing instruction was in the doldrums. Dedicated teachers like Sledd and Megaw championed literacy, wanting to deliver it to the masses. But most of the faculty understood how tedious and ineffective the dominant pedagogical approach could be. Gazing upon this dysfunctional mess, the rhetoric and composition faculty told themselves a story now common in their disciplinary field—a story not unlike the one we've told so far. The intellectual rigor, low status, and pedagogical drudgery of teaching writing had plagued their enterprise for too long. But pedagogical solutions and administrative innovations could save them yet.[23] By revitalizing the study of first-year writing instruction and tying the required writing curriculum to democratic ideals and professional credentials, the rhetoric and composition faculty hoped to improve their status, restructure their discipline, and revolutionize higher education. Rebhorn himself marched in the vanguard, authoring an extensive report in 1979 that compares the teaching of writing in his own classes with the teaching of writing outside the English department. He found that those teaching writing in the English department did much more than focus on grammatical correctness and generic form. He personally gave feedback on students' "clarity of exposition" and "rhetorical strategy." He often required revisions based on instructor feedback.[24]

A more sustained indication of how much things were changing can be found in the career of John Trimble. Educated at Princeton, Trimble decided to forego a career in law so he could study English literature at the University of California, Berkeley. The first to admit that he was no bookish scholar, Trimble came to UT Austin in the early 1970s. Despite the senior faculty's admonition to write an academic book about Alexander Pope, Trimble gambled on a textbook. *Writing with Style* differed from the impersonal handbooks that dominated the market. It was not a grammar guide but a personalized "conversation" about composition. And it paid off. Along with two major teaching awards, *Writing with Style* earned Trimble tenure with promotion to associate professor. The book was adopted broadly in writing programs across the country. Next, Trimble pioneered a new course: E 325 (Advanced Writing). At a spring 1973 meeting where the faculty narrowly voted to approve E 325, Trimble recalled a senior literary specialist describing writing instruction as "mere technician's work." He remembered another faculty member harrumphing, "We are not in the remediation business." Both comments "stung."[25] Nonetheless, committed to making the writing classroom something more than a gray space for tedious formalism, Trimble revamped E 325, developing strategies that he would employ every semester until his retirement in 2004: working through students' writing in class, having students peer-review one another's papers, emphasizing audience rather than form and rhetorical impact rather than grammatical rule. Sledd and Megaw's proposal, Rebhorn's complaints, and Trimble's innovations all evidence the rapid and needed change in writing pedagogy that was happening at UT Austin and across the country. To better understand how the teaching of writing had become so widely mandated yet so curiously ineffective nationwide, we should look beyond local, institutional concerns, surveying instead a century of writing pedagogy.

The first-year writing requirement so common at US colleges and universities was fired in the crucible of economic pressures brought by the industrial revolution and political demands specific to postwar America. As one historian comments, the late nineteenth century was a "new era" for the American college.[26] Another corroborates this judgment, adding that "the American university of 1900 was all but unrecognizable in comparison with the college of 1860."[27] Through the eighteenth and the early nineteenth centuries, colleges and even a few universities decorated the American landscape, but these were traditional and regional institutions teaching the same curriculum to every undergraduate while offering a few graduate degrees, usually in theology or law. They provided cultural polish and mental discipline through a common course of study. They catered to a small, privileged, almost exclusively male population. Writing instruction was a mainstay. From the colonial period to the Civil War, students at American colleges studied rhetoric and writing every year. In the first year, they typically learned grammar and basic prose composition by translating Latin and Greek. In their second and third years, they debated one another in written prose and public speech in both Latin and English. Often they declaimed—in either strict syllogisms or loose "forensic" debates—before the entire student body or in front of townspeople, family, and faculty. In their last undergraduate years, they attended a series of lectures on rhetoric, where they learned about the fine points of literary style, aesthetic taste, sound argumentation, and persuasive logic.

After the Civil War, American higher education changed its stripes. This transition from a "classical" curriculum to various "professional" curricula has been recounted by many historians, especially those invested in the history of language arts education. Perhaps most recently, John Guillory describes an "epochal break" between "the arduous system of embodying knowledge as *technē*" and the modern efforts "in which access to knowledge was 'methodized.'"[28] At Harvard and elsewhere, student demand for professional instruction inspired the elective system famously introduced by Harvard president Charles Eliot in 1885.[29] In the US Congress, this pragmatic ethos elicited the Morrill Land-Grant Acts (1862 and 1890), which provided federal support for professional education in the applied fields of engineering and agriculture, satiating the era's hunger for "practical public service."[30] Adding to this professional ethos was an egalitarian, albeit meritocratic, undercurrent, which included the supposed "equality of all fields of learning," the "equality . . . among all the students," and the "ease of admission to the university."[31]

However, despite their career aspirations, these students were not prepared for a college-level education. So, one universal curricular requirement remained. At Harvard, as elsewhere, every student had to take English A, an early and paradigmatic version of what is now the first-year writing class.[32] Such are the demographic and economic forces that created the need for a universal writing requirement. What was the curricular response? Antebellum rhetoric and writing instruction had a rich foundation drawing on Greek philosophy, Enlightenment psychology, and Romantic transcendentalism.[33] Back then, rhetoric was a liberal study that empowered leaders and enabled citizens. After the Civil War, now pared down to a first-year course, instruction in rhetoric and composition chased a single practical goal: competency. Like most historians of rhetoric, Guillory focuses on the "universal requirement" as a telling moment in the history of language arts education. He notes one unintended consequence of the first-year writing course: "The vernacular curriculum was prevented from achieving anything like the dominant position formerly held by classical languages."[34] Harvard's admission requirements in the 1870s reflect the universal writing course's diminished standing and curtailed reach. At the turn of the century, Harvard asked applicants to "write a short English Composition, correct in spelling, punctuation, grammar, and expression."[35]

Textbooks from the era similarly demonstrate that the universal requirement guaranteed a place, but not a grand seat, for writing instruction in the modern university. In 1896–97, students in Harvard's required first-year writing course studied Adams Sherman Hill's *Principles of Rhetoric*, a tedious volume that reduces the language arts to three stylistic abstractions: clearness, force, and elegance. Instead of a rich liberal arts education, students in the typical first-year writing class read little beyond the required textbook, wrote regular (if not daily) themes, suffered through a few substantive writing assignments, and paid close attention to form, especially grammatical correctness (e.g., subject-verb disagreement errors) and generic features (e.g., the five-paragraph essay).[36] Because the required writing class was so central to American higher education's pragmatic turn, in the mid-1970s Richard Ohmann, former editor of the flagship journal *College English*, and Wallace Douglass, one-time director of Harvard's English A, labeled its curriculum a "rhetoric for the meritocracy," a booster course for technocrats and engineers.[37] Ohmann and Douglass's critique presaged Guillory's recent argument that the "postrhetorical" curriculum serves "the new class of knowers," the professional-managerial class of the modern world.[38]

The current-traditional rhetoricians of the late nineteenth and early twentieth centuries, the people who taught writing and wrote textbooks, were not building their professionalized curriculum on a robust intellectual or scholarly tradition. They were accumulating practices with an eye toward what works or might work in the classroom. Rather than choosing the best, they collected the most. One scholar of composition studies famously called these people "practitioners," a weathered lot who gathered tricks, ignored theories, and trusted their gut rather than researchers' reports.[39] The expert practitioner was not a scholar versed in liberal culture but a calloused hand at the composition plow, the teacher "who stay[ed] in the field long enough . . . to keep making practice their inquiry."[40] When such a "rare" practitioner-expert appeared, however, they didn't write a magnum opus of rhetorical theory. They wrote a compendium of their accumulated classroom activities. As rhetorical pedagogy developed by industrial era practitioners, such compendia are the monuments of current-traditional rhetoric, which Wayne Rebhorn discovered and disdained at UT Austin in the late 1970s.

To the lifelong teacher, a practitioner is a master of the craft. To the scholar, however, the practitioner is unreflective and naive. In addition to seeming vacuous, the practitioner's pedagogy was also ineffective. Scholars of composition have repeatedly critiqued current-traditional rhetoric's most glaring flaw, the damning sin at the heart of UT Austin's obsession with formal grammar. It may have offered a "schema of discourse that could be easily taught and learned," thus assuring students and teachers that higher education could be open to all. But current-traditional rhetoric "did not help students learn to write better."[41] In fact, the focus on formal genres and the harping on grammatical errors may have interrupted students' ability to learn effective prose composition. In the early twentieth century, this unreflective approach to writing instruction was challenged by Progressive era researchers who offered philosophical vision and empirical assessment. They wanted to recenter the uniform writing curriculum around the view that human experience structures knowledge, a pragmatic epistemological framework borrowed from John Dewey and others. Furthermore, they wanted to apply the new tools of statistical inquiry to educational institutions. Under the twin standards of "exploration" and "science," a cadre of educational reformers marched on traditional writing instruction.[42] And they won many battles. The Progressive era testing regime systematically evaluated students before and after their classroom experience, codifying capacity and achievement and determining what worked and what didn't. These early studies had "serious flaws" in their "experiment design."[43] Nevertheless, armed with the philosophical ideal of "experience" and fiercely brandishing Gestalt psychology and the project method of teaching, young researchers broke the current-traditional line. The Progressive era's intellectually robust and (pseudo)scientific revolution demanded the "abandonment of formal grammar in favor of functional instruction."[44] In the 1930s, the current-traditional writing curriculum beat a rapid retreat.

Given such progress in the 1930s, one has to wonder why Wayne Rebhorn was complaining about the widespread application of current-traditional writing pedagogy in the late 1970s. No single answer suffices, but two trends certainly assisted the resurgence of formalistic writing instruction. On the one hand, a trend in politics and higher education, which Lisa Mastrangelo calls "administrative progressivism," favored top-down management and measurable outcomes. Deweyan pragmatism focused on the individual student and encouraged the instructor to nurture their unique flourishing. Current-traditional rhetoric sated the manager's thirst for standardization and fed the administrator's hunger for efficiency.[45] On the other hand, mid-century American politics favored a conservative turn toward curricular uniformity in service of Cold War civic ideals. The years 1930–50 witnessed what one historian of higher education calls a return to the "traditional educational emphasis on intellectual training and cultural heritage," good grammar and great literature.[46] Practitioner lore came back for cultural reasons. The old ways appealed to traditional American values resuscitated in the postwar era: "democratic ideals . . . individuality and egalitarianism."[47] Cold War values furthermore inspired the implementation of general education requirements at US colleges and universities. A robust suite of required classes would provide basic skills and teach core values in line with economic industry and conservative culture. Recent historians of liberal arts education explain that such general education requirements born in the 1950s, such as the nine-hour writing requirement at UT Austin, "institutionalized these promises" to teach practical skills and humanistic ideals.[48]

But disciplinary advances would challenge and eventually topple current-traditional rhetoric just thirty years after its renaissance. While the Cold War instigated the resurgence of traditional writing instruction, it also sabotaged the revanche. The postwar enrollment boom made possible by the G.I. Bill (1944) created a demand for remedial instruction, unintentionally giving writing teachers a stable place within the developing university. Writing teachers created their own professional societies—most famously, the Conference on College Composition and Communication (1949). Between 1950 and 1965, new journals were founded, such as *CCC* and *College English*. More important, the scholars publishing in these journals were competent in the conventional research modes of textual and qualitative analysis. By the late 1950s, a discipline dedicated to a "more scholarly trajectory for the field" of writing instruction was taking shape.[49] Then Cold War defense spending lent a hand. An extension of the National Defense Act in 1964 provided funds to support some of the most robust empirical research in writing instruction to this day.[50] During the 1960s, study after study criticized current-traditional rhetoric for being ineffective and outdated. Researchers experimented with a range of new psychological theories, empirical methods, and philosophical perspectives. Some turned to British theorists who relied on the psychology of Lev Vygotsky and Jean Piaget. Others brought back the Progressive era emphasis on experience.[51] Unable to justify itself, tedious to teach, dumb, and boring, the uniform curriculum of current-traditional rhetoric was finally expiring after a century of dominance. And from its ashes arose the modern discipline of rhetoric and composition.

Aware that current-traditional rhetoric was ineffective and outdated, yet still committed to offering practical skills and humanistic education, dedicated to the midcentury resurgence of civic education, and constantly pressured to serve a growing and diversifying body of students who sought professional accreditation, the UT Austin English department decided to fully revamp its curriculum in the late 1970s. John Trimble was the perfect man to spearhead this initiative. In January 1980, he produced an eight-page report chronicling one department's plan to escape current-traditional "drudgery." His report glows with the faculty's hope for what could be and rots with their despair for all that was.[52] Other English departments, like the one at The Pennsylvania State University, were similarly bulldozing their writing curricula for similar reasons.[53] While Trimble focused on E 325, two other writing specialists, James Kinneavy and Maxine Hairston, aimed at broader reforms. They were supported by fresh blood, a cohort of young, talented professors: Greg Myers, Ted Smith, John Ruszkiewicz, Steven Witte, and Lester Faigley. Kinneavy's and Hairston's stories give the lie to the deterministic tale often told by those who focus on economic causes, for their initiatives did not simply kowtow to students' professional demands or cater to administrative dictates. Instead, Hairston and Kinneavy recognized the shifting institutional winds while acknowledging the persistent demographic and economic tides; this circumspection allowed them to develop programs and pedagogies that were both responsive to the moment and pursuant to their agenda. Change didn't simply happen to them; Hairston and Kinneavy played a vital role by exerting their influence without bucking the trends.

An orphan who first sought refuge in the Congregation of Christian Brothers, Kinneavy had taught secondary education in the American West. He eventually earned an EdD from the Catholic University of America before leaving the order and teaching high school in New Orleans. In 1958, he joined the faculty at Western State College in Colorado. While at Western, he began work on a hefty book. Along with others, such as Edward Corbett's *Classical Rhetoric for the Modern Student* (1965), Kinneavy's *Theory of Discourse* (1971) rehabilitated classical rhetoric for the postwar era. He lamented the status of rhetoric and composition within English departments, saying, "Composition is so clearly the stepchild of the English department that it is not a legitimate area of concern in graduate studies, is not even recognized as a subdivision in the discipline of English . . . and is generally the teaching province of graduate assistants or fringe members of the department."[54] Stretching across an unimaginably wide intellectual terrain, Kinneavy rustled up ancient Greek rhetoricians with mid-twentieth-century Continental philosophers and branded all their ideas as "discourse," a capacious term that encompassed all communication. He ranged wildly, in one chapter analyzing a scientific paper on vitamins, in another dissecting the literary works of Albert Camus, and in another still exploring the poetry of Gerard Manley Hopkins. Kinneavy subsumed all English studies—literature, technical communication, classical rhetoric, philology, and critical theory—under a dizzying theoretical edifice built primarily of triangles, the most foundational being his famous triad of encoder, decoder, and reality (with "signal" floating eerily in the center space).[55] He loved to hang glide on ideas. Toward the end of his life, he described his academic career as an odyssey of theory.[56]

For all this high-flown philosophy, Kinneavy's great intellectual adventure began with practical intent. While at Western State College hunting a contract for his textbook, he realized that no publisher would consider anything by a professor from a regional institution. So, in 1963, he got another job. At UT Austin, he realized that his ideas were not suitable for a textbook, and he should pursue instead "scholarly monographs." But he never lost his interest in pedagogy, for he believed that theory requires practice, and composition instruction cannot be reduced to the "mechanical pedagogical procedure passed on in a teaching tradition."[57] Kinneavy's commitment to the interplay of rhetorical theory and pedagogical practice anticipated similar conclusions reached by later scholars, a commitment best demonstrated not by Kinneavy's *Theory of Discourse* but by the syllabus he designed for E 306.[58]

The "Kinneavy syllabus" was the new uniform curriculum in all E 306 classes from the mid-70s until the spring of 1985. Like his *Theory*, Kinneavy's syllabus connects rhetorical aims to discursive modes, teaching students to write in certain genres (modes), so that they might speak to particular audiences in specific ways at appointed times (aims). While Kinneavy's *Theory* covers five aims of discourse (informative, explorative, persuasive, literary, and expressive), his syllabus attempts a pared-down list: self-expression, argumentation, and explanation. Each unit addresses a specific aim, which is often dissected into argumentative strategies. For instance, "explanation" is divided into description, causal analysis, classification, and purposive explanation. Kinneavy offers advice about each strategy. Classificatory explanation is discussed in the first unit of the course and subdivided into genus-species differentiation, exemplification, description, and operational division. "Argumentation" is treated in two units, induction and deduction, with each unit exhaustively covering one rhetorical strategy.[59] In 1978 Susan Rodi, a non-tenure track lecturer, revised Kinneavy's syllabus, emphasizing inductive and deductive reasoning as well as classification.[60] Rodi's was the first in a series of revisions that expanded the initial fifty-plus pages of course material into a final (1983) multiauthored oeuvre, completed by John Ruszkiewicz, newly appointed director of composition, and his assistant director, Mary Trachsel, a graduate student.[61]

The English department faculty, Rebhorn included, held Kinneavy in high esteem.[62] He was a slight, "unprepossessing" professor who physically resembled the stereotypical scholar. One graduate of the rhetoric PhD program recalls: "He was sort of like Mr. Everyman coming out of a 1940s movie."[63] By many accounts, he was a masterful and riveting public speaker.[64] Kinneavy gave extracurricular lectures on rhetoric in the basement of Parlin Hall, where the English department was housed. Many graduate students attended voluntarily.[65] Some faculty lingered outside the classroom door or wandered in to listen. Referring to Kinneavy's *Theory* and honoring its author, graduate students had T-shirts made up that read "I got lost in Kinneavy's Triangle."[66] He leveraged his standing as a scholar and the growing disciplinary stature of his field (rhetoric and composition) into a series of reforms that promised the professional skills that students wanted while also emphasizing the rhetorical pedagogy that he believed in. The Kinneavy syllabus was no rhetoric for the technocracy; it was a thoughtful, sophisticated, and philosophical attempt to teach a wide range of humanistic skills, made possible in a specific moment of economic pressure and disciplinary advancement.

Kinneavy's coleader of the composition revolution was Maxine Hairston. One graduate student recalls that she dismissed pretension. Once, after returning from a northeastern university where she'd given a guest lecture, she remarked that she'd been "some place where the pricks all dress in three-piece suits and call each other 'doctor.'"[67] Another graduate student recalls Hairston saying something to the effect of "I never considered myself to have a first-rate mind, but I've done pretty good with what I've got."[68] She was confident and often brash, essential survival tools for a female tenure track faculty member—one of very few in the English department—when many, both male and female, thought the departmental culture alarmingly sexist, even by the standards of its time.[69] She earned her PhD from UT Austin at the age of forty-six. When Sledd unexpectedly stepped down just three years after Hairston joined the faculty, she found herself installed as the English department's director of composition. She quickly gained a national reputation primarily by publishing a number of highly regarded and widely adopted writing textbooks. She didn't downplay her success, nor did she apologize for her pedagogical commitments. Like Kinneavy, she was quite visible in her outreach to high school teachers throughout the state of Texas.[70]

Most important, Hairston was "student centered."[71] Her enduring contribution to the first-year writing curriculum was an emphasis on writing as a process. Rather than obsessing about a sentence's correctness or a paragraph's coherence, those interested in teaching the writing process told students to do what good writers do: brainstorm with some prewriting exercises, try throwing together a draft just to get some ideas on the page, show your work to someone else, revise based on your reader's comments, then repeat the process. Though this approach to the writing classroom borrowed teaching methods from creative writers—as did John Trimble's writing workshops—process pedagogy justified itself by referencing scientific studies. Empirical research reveals that real writers think recursively, not linearly, engaging and reengaging specific cognitive activities, not aiming toward an ordained outcome.[72] Hairston calls it a "paradigm shift in the teaching of writing."[73]

Process pedagogy didn't interest Kinneavy in the least. But Hairston's enthusiasm overcame his obstinance. The 1976 version of Kinneavy's syllabus features pages upon pages of advice about how to teach the "aims" and "modes" of discourse, applying Kinneavy's argot to first-year writing assignments like the research paper. But there is no mention of revision or peer review.[74] The 1978 syllabus is even more elaborate in its adoption of Kinneavy's rhetorical theory, featuring his famous "triangle of discourse." In 1978, instructors might have conceded that "journal writing" could be used as an important step in the development of a writer's ideas, but these same instructors were encouraged to present journaling as another of Kinneavy's modes (expressive writing) with its own particular aim (revelation of the self).[75] In 1982 and 1983, students were still writing eight or nine papers, all graded on a rubric, with no expectation of revision.[76] But in 1984, Hairston's "winds of change" finally blew across E 306. Instructors were told that "revision should be a regular, fully-integrated component in every E 306 course. Students need to be encouraged to revise and to be taught how to do it."[77] By 1985 this brief paragraph on revision had evolved into an entire unit dealing with "writing as process."[78]

Just as Kinneavy had strategically approached this moment in his institution's history, recognizing a chance to insert rhetorical theory into writing pedagogy, Hairston similarly surveyed the landscape, noting an opportunity for a student-centered, female faculty member to climb the professorial ranks with her pedagogical achievements. Her success stems in part from her savvy awareness that process pedagogy would serve the students' professional interests and accommodate their increasing diversity. Process pedagogy allows instructors to grade students based on their investment in learning, not their mastery of white, upper-middle-class English. To a curmudgeon like Sledd, Kinneavy's classicism and Hairston's process pedagogy were needless because the real solution was simply hard work in the undergraduate classroom. The innovators were just throwing their dung on the already sky-high pile of "research and publication." Sledd chuckled, "They cannot give us answers, [but they] will provide an endless series of always changing fads."[79] He scoffed at initiatives now common among US universities: empirical research in writing studies, graduate programs in rhetoric and composition, writing centers, digital writing labs, and writing-across-the-curriculum programs. Sledd's easy dismissal overlooks their achievement. Kinneavy's rhetorical approach and Hairston's process pedagogy still satisfied the mid-century interest in professional training and civic education, but they did so without the burden of current-traditional drudgery. Other initiatives in the UT Austin writing program similarly suited the political and economic circumstances of the time while improving the quality of instruction.

In the late 1970s, the UT Austin rhetoric faculty became part of a research project bankrolled by the Fund for the Improvement of Postsecondary Education (FIPSE). Created in 1972 by the Department of Health, Education, and Welfare, the FIPSE grant was another in a rash of federal programs, including Project English (1964), passed as an extension of the National Defense Education Act. Like Project English, FIPSE encouraged educational experimentation and innovation in the service of practical skills. These were Cold War efforts aimed at training a professional-managerial class for an industrial economy capable of competing with and ultimately defeating communism. In 1978, the rhetoric faculty at UT Austin joined researchers at the University of Michigan under the auspices of the Formative Evaluation Research Associates (FERA) to "conduct a nationally comprehensive and systematically controlled evaluation of writing programs. The project would assess the effectiveness of writing programs by analyzing their impacts on students, faculty members, and the colleges and universities that sponsor them."[80] UT Austin's writing program was one of the first to be courted. FERA initially proposed to undertake a study in Kinneavy's and Susan Wittig's E 306 courses. Members of the Freshman English Policy Committee at UT Austin narrowly voted to participate.[81] Shortly after their arrival on campus, Lester Faigley and Stephen Witte won another FIPSE grant for their qualitative and comprehensive study of writing instruction. Faigley and Witte collected reams of survey data, along with many close analyses of particular programs. They maintained a separate office, paid graduate assistants out of an independent budget, authored several federal reports, published numerous articles, and eventually coauthored an empirical study on writing assessment.[82]

Simultaneous with the launch of the FIPSE project, Kinneavy, Witte, and graduate student Thomas Cameron proposed another qualitative study of writing instruction, looking at the Kinneavy syllabus and an alternate model developed by Cameron and based on Francis Christensen's popular "sentence-combining" pedagogy.[83] Inspired by the potential of such empirical research, in 1983 Witte wrote to associate dean John Weinstock to request $9,500 and a permanent office where he could manage a new journal.[84] *Written Communication* published its first issue in 1984. One of the first in the field to use double-blind peer review, *Written Communication* soon became a clearinghouse for empirical research in writing studies.[85] Even Hairston got into the grant-finding game. In June 1985, she attended a meeting hosted by the Ford Foundation, which was seeking to fund further improvements in writing pedagogy.[86] She soon had the ear of the university's vice president, who talked with her for nearly an hour about the importance of writing in a university education.[87] Student demographics, professional demands, and private funding allowed the rhetoric and composition faculty to expand their programs and increase their stature. Kinneavy, Hairston, Faigley, and Witte seized the opportunity with both hands.

This same institutional investment in writing's professional potential allowed program administrators on the UT Austin faculty to achieve other successes within their departments. In 1979, for example, the English department created a graduate concentration in the then-emerging field of rhetoric and composition. Thomas Miller, a graduate student who would establish himself as a leading scholar in the field, later bragged that the graduate concentration managed to "professionalize and raise the standard of composition teaching by making it a philosophically sound enterprise, and also give it professional credibility."[88] Hairston and Kinneavy hounded the department to hire more writing specialists.[89] Their department chair acquiesced, though he worried about recruitment, saying, "True specialists in composition and rhetoric—the only area where student demand regularly exceeds faculty capability—are scarce and in high demand."[90] With the promise of additional faculty and on behalf of the English department's Rhetoric/Composition Interest Group, Kinneavy initially pitched the idea for a rhetoric graduate concentration to the department's Graduate Programs Committee.[91] After considering an independent graduate degree, they agreed to a new concentration within the English department's established PhD program.[92] Hairston and Kinneavy barnstormed nationally, pitching their new concentration at speaking engagements. Kinneavy was particularly successful at attracting promising scholars.[93] He preferred older graduate students who already held MAs, most with extensive teaching experience.[94]

The initial success of the graduate program in rhetoric and composition can be partly attributed to Hairston's and Kinneavy's recruitment efforts, but proper due must be paid to the collegial environment created by junior faculty. In 1978 when Trimble—then associate director of the first-year writing program—welcomed new graduate students, he boasted that "UT's English Department . . . has perhaps the largest number of nationally known rhet/comp specialists of any department in the country."[95] Graduates of the program recall young professors socializing with graduate students who resembled junior faculty in not only age but also their family lives. Mary Trachsel, for example, vacationed in Mexico with rising star Lester Faigley and his wife and sons. She played tennis regularly with Steve Witte and his family. Social events where faculty and graduate students mixed were frequent, with Hairston and Kinneavy often hosting at their homes. Faculty collaborated with graduate students on scholarly projects and invited them to participate in departmental governance.[96]

Another initiative highlights how faculty made the most of an institutional interest in professional skills and credentials. In the 1970s, the Writing Lab (which years later evolved into the Undergraduate Writing Center) wasn't a space at all but rather a sequence of exercises designed to help underprepared students succeed in their college English classes.[97] The dean of the College of the Humanities praised the lab, suggesting that university funding be dedicated to its expansion, so that "students who are having difficulty in English writing can be referred for assistance by their faculty members."[98] Like many such institutions, the Writing Lab began as a remediation center.[99] Following the dean's suggestion, in 1977 the Freshman English Policy Committee considered hiring a director. They settled on a nontenure track faculty member (a graduate of the UT Austin English program), and the Writing Lab was given a small space on campus.[100] The Writing Lab hosted self-paced courses, tutored individual students, and developed placement tests.[101]

The idea for a separate computer lab, which would evolve into what is now known as the Digital Writing and Research Lab, was hatched while graduate students and professors carpooled to a conference in Galveston.[102] The director of the Writing Lab had applied for and received a private grant of IBM personal computers. When the director of first-year writing, John Ruszkiewicz, received the computers in January 1985, he planned to have them all installed in the Writing Lab by September, but he had no idea what to do with them. He found himself fishing for suggestions at faculty meetings.[103] While unintentionally eavesdropping on a bathroom conversation, Fred Kemp, a graduate student who would later pioneer the use of networked writing environments, overheard Ruszkiewicz complain that no one there knew how to use the computers. Kemp recalls: "So I came out of the stall, and I said to John, 'Hey, I'm a computer guy.' I really wasn't. I'd been on a computer for about four months, a TRS80 model four.... He said, 'Do you know anything about IBM PCs?' I said, 'Oh yeah, sure, no problem!' I had never seen one."[104] Kemp soon found himself in charge. In October, not long after taking over, Kemp severed the brief union between the Writing Lab and the computer lab. He realized that Writing Lab tutors were using their last remaining PC for mundane chores like word processing. So he confiscated their machine.[105] Jerome Bump, originally a scholar of Victorian poetics, took an early interest in digital composition and soon became the PC lab's director. Like Ruszkiewicz, he placed great trust in the graduate students. Kemp, along with a number of other graduate students such as Joyce Locke Carter, developed an early program that facilitated collaborative writing on a closed network of personal computers. Daedalus, as they'd named it, proved commercially viable. The graduate students formed their own company, signing its articles of incorporation in Hairston's living room. They sold stock to faculty (and others), and they maintained a healthy business for several years to come. By the fall of 1996, Carter was writing Kinneavy on Daedalus Group letterhead, telling him how to install their software and assuring him that they would soon sell their wares through a large distributor.[106] All these initiatives—grant-seeking, the writing lab, and the computer lab—were possible because of a long-standing investment in professional accreditation, an interest that peaked during the Cold War and tied directly into instrumental writing instruction. By promising to teach practical literacy, the rhetoric and composition faculty ameliorated their pedagogy and improved their status.

In the early 1980s, rhetoric and composition was riding high at UT Austin, cresting on the demographic and economic waves that buoyed postsecondary writing instruction throughout the mid-twentieth century. The undergraduate writing curriculum was sophisticated and well established. The faculty were publishing rafts of exciting new research. The graduate concentration was in full swing. Kinneavy sought one more achievement, a new writing-across-the-curriculum program that imitated a program developed at Beaver College in Pennsylvania. Kinneavy corresponded with the writing program director, learning of her efforts. He also built on Hairston's suggestion at a 1977 meeting of the University Faculty Council. Hairston argued that "if the faculty would like to require an upper-division writing course or would like to change the second-semester composition to an upper-division level," such a change would require more time and consideration.[107] The exigency for curricular overhaul built up over time as faculty expressed increasing concerns about student writing. A 1975 campus-wide study conducted by James Sledd and Susan Hereford concluded that student writing was "quite important," yet students' writing was quite inadequate.[108] Hairston noted the "conscious . . . widespread concern by faculty, parents, and the general public about dropping scores on college entrance examinations."[109] Kinneavy participated in a study of fifty-nine teaching assistants, concluding that students "fail[ed] to face up to a fundamental holistic discourse situation."[110] The 1975 report indicates a faculty preference for "specialized upper division composition courses" and intensive writing instruction spread across every year of undergraduate instruction.[111]

In 1980, as the university geared up for a major overhaul of its core curriculum, Kinneavy saw a clear line of attack. The English department formed several committees. After a flurry of memos, a rush of meetings, and an efflorescence of possibilities, Kinneavy's vision prevailed. He wanted a curriculum that stretched across three courses and as many years. The new writing requirement would consist of the required first-year writing course (E 306), a new sophomore-level literature course (E 316), and a new junior-level writing-across-the-curriculum course (E 346K). A draft proposal was circulated for the entire English faculty's consideration in April 1980.[112] After much deliberation, the new plan was approved by the faculty, with sixty-one in favor, fifteen against, and two abstentions.[113] Nearly a year later, Kinneavy's proposal had worked its way up the ladder of committees and procedures, finally winning University Faculty Council approval.[114]

Kinneavy's vision for E 346K resembled the writing-across-the-curriculum programs at other universities.[115] But one key difference captures his ability to conciliate institutional demands, harness economic pressures, and account for midcentury investments, while advancing his own intellectual and pedagogical agenda. The main difference between Kinneavy's vision and the curricular innovations pursued elsewhere can be grasped at their intellectual root. Most writing-across-the-curriculum programs at the time were informed by research in educational psychology. Scholars like James Britton (borrowing liberally from the psychological theories of Jean Piaget and Lev Vygotsky) contend that people first learn expressive communication, which focuses on the self; only later do we come to transactional communication, which involves a community of others. These same researchers argue that transactional communication is always peculiar to a community, so it must be studied within that community. Based on this educational-psychological foundation, writing specialists determined that literacy is plural, and literacies are situated in specific communities, so students in upper-division college classes should learn to write within their disciplines.[116] Though the psychology justifying many writing-across-the-curriculum programs was admirable, Kinneavy built on the intellectual foundation of classical rhetoric, which allowed him to insert a civic dimension into an otherwise practical course.

He would offer professional skills and civic education, a clear sop to the midcentury investment in educating industrial workers and democratic citizens. E 346K would feature four variants—Writing in the Humanities, Writing for the Social Sciences, Writing for Business, and Writing for the Natural Sciences and Technology—each taught by a nonspecialist (an English faculty member), thus requiring that students learn to communicate the core ideas of their chosen disciplines to an educated outsider. Kinneavy saw this as a boon: "It is not enough to teach the practitioners of a craft to communicate with one another in the jargon of their department. They must also be taught the common language of humanity in its full rhetorical scales."[117] E 346K would require sophisticated rhetorical accommodation by the student and equally sophisticated rhetorical instruction from the teacher.

Since the industrial revolution, US higher education has promised a "practical public service" that relies on democratic access to higher education while providing pragmatic preparation for professional careers. The pursuit of this ideal intensified during the Cold War. In the early twentieth century, the ideal of liberal culture, the "militant insistence of the humanists" who struggle against the modern university's pragmatic drive, opposed professional skills and democratic access. Alongside pragmatic skills, democratic access, and liberal culture sits a fourth ideal motivating the modern university—the undying hope to advance knowledge in all its forms.[118] All four of these interests came together in the midcentury as universities tailored humanistic education toward liberal democratic citizenship, allowing humanists to conduct research that advanced the national ethos, teach classes that taught practical literacy, and design curricula that promised civic edification. Historians of rhetoric and composition have already noted how these ideals animated writing pedagogy through the first half of the twentieth century.[119]

Recent commentators have lamented that the professional turn at US colleges and universities has extruded the civic training once baked into American higher education. Wendy Brown, for example, criticizes late twentieth-century higher education for abandoning its civic mission, arguing that "the saturation of higher education by market rationality has converted higher education from a social and public good to a personal investment in individual futures."[120] While Brown's assessment is broadly accurate, it does not apply to every institution or academic program. The example of James Kinneavy's E 346K curriculum proves that a circumspect administrator can pander to the interest in marketable skills while preserving the democratic ethos once driving higher education. Kinneavy promised that E 346K would uphold liberal culture and provide civic education by promoting the central mission of humanities education since the ancient Greeks: "compassion for one's neighbors." Delivered to an audience of scholars at Ball State University in 1984, Kinneavy's defense of E 346K blistered with Greek etymologies, scholarly references, and historical gravitas. He promised that "the English teacher can unify the university conceptually and linguistically." E 346K would braid the "dialectical and scientific strands of the liberal arts tradition." Set atop a heap of scholarship and rescuing liberal education, E 346K also promised practical skills by teaching students technical writing. This was not current-traditional rhetoric or practitioner's knowledge, and it certainly was not a grab bag of classroom exercises. It was, according to Kinneavy, the "basis of all culture and civilization."[121]

In pilot sections, undergraduates adored the class, with one student commenting that they "never enjoyed (English) writing until now," yet these classes "made me learn to like it." Students in Kinneavy's fall 1984 section of E 346K expressed similar appreciation. Eighty-four percent said the course was either excellent or very good. And a comprehensive review of student evaluations in the fall of 1984 found that most students liked the class regardless of their instructor (see table 1).[122] An accounting senior called E 346K "beneficial."[123] A communications student said it was the "most worthwhile" writing course he had ever taken.[124] Another undergraduate majoring in communications said the class rightly emphasized professional writing skills, a sentiment echoed by a journalism undergraduate and an electrical engineering student.[125] A lecturer on the English department faculty who had taught all four variations of E 346K said, "Professors and students report glowing success with the course."[126] Punning on a recent blockbuster film based on Tom Wolfe's depiction of the Apollo program, a *Houston Post* columnist called E 346K "the write stuff."[127]

In 1984, President Reagan ran a now famous political ad that touted the country's blossoming economic recovery. He said it was "morning again in America." In November of that year, not long after Kinneavy told an audience at Ball State University about the professional and civic potential of his writing-across-the-curriculum program, a bright optimism, a rejuvenated promise, and an overwhelming vote carried Reagan to reelection. That same promise, shining with faith in the free market and hope for the entrepreneurial spirit, suffused the UT Austin writing program. New initiatives, bold programs, and curricular innovations promised to train a large and diverse population of students for a range of technically sophisticated professions and their place in a vibrant liberal democracy. A new day for America, a new chapter for writing program administration, was dawning.

Table 1 UT Austin Undergraduate Students' Opinions of E 346K

	E 346K Writing in the Humanities	E 346K Writing in the Natural Sciences	E 346K Writing in the Behavioral Sciences
Percentage of students who rated the course above average or excellent	68	74	85
Percentage of students who thought the class was average	24	22	13
Percentage of students who thought the class was below average or poor	8	4	2

Historian of writing program administration David Fleming contends that the writing requirement, which is nearly universal in modern American higher education, has been shaped by both economic and civic motives. On the one hand, the required writing course is part and parcel of capitalist society, another instrument in the preparation of the professional-managerial class. On the other hand, the universal requirement and the civic component lingering in much composition pedagogy and many composition classes makes postsecondary writing instruction into something more than professional education. Like many writing teachers before him, Kinneavy wanted to see "students not as future engineers, nurses, or managers, but as *citizens*." Because every writing program is caught between these two places (the economic and the political, our professional and our civic roles), Fleming argues that the college writing requirement occupies a "liminal" space, a "middle place in social life that contains profoundly transformative possibilities."[128] We don't take issue with Fleming's analysis. In fact, our discussion of the composition revolution at the University of Texas at Austin proves that writing pedagogy and writing programs owe their potential to this liminal space, ripe with possibility, as was Kinneavy's E 346K class. We do suggest one amendment to Fleming's argument, however. The potential in the writing program's liminal space is just that—potential. Its realization requires action by individuals, often the program directors left out of histories of higher education. This chapter has shown that with the right circumspection, a middling program director—a Hairston or a Kinneavy—can harness and redirect the economic and political forces shaping their career, their discipline, their program, and their institution.

Contemporary writing program administrators often assume that in order to achieve the institutional agency revealed in this chapter, they must learn the circumspection modeled by its protagonists. For that reason, when introducing institutional efforts similar to the reforms central to the composition revolution at UT Austin, many writing program administrators insist that institutions themselves "do contain spaces for reflection, resistance, revision, and productive action," and they furthermore argue that program administrators can "rewrite institutions through rhetorical action."[129] Another scholar-administrator also looking for opportunity in seemingly inopportune places promotes an "operative approach" to writing program administration, "a kind of *intuiting* into what might work differently."[130] In similar fashion but different form, yet another proposes "a focus on the here and now" and places "a high premium on self-awareness and situated action."[131] Finally, the authors of *GenAdmin*, like everyone mentioned so far, agree that the writing program administrator must exhibit "a flexible context-dependent way for people to intervene in the world."[132] All of these scholar/administrators advocate scrupulous administrative activism. In this chapter, we offer a narrative argument, emotionally exalting the same prudence.

The composition revolution at UT Austin allowed faculty (such as Faigley and Witte) to raise their disciplinary standing and advance their careers, marginalized people (such as Hairston) to claim a place in an otherwise exclusionary institution, and program administrators (such as Kinneavy) to promote a civic agenda in an otherwise professional writing course. These victories did not come without compromise or through complaisance. While they rejected current-traditional rhetoric, they maintained a midcentury dedication to civic education and professional training. This chapter and its story present Kinneavy and Hairston as phronetic actors, aware of their institutional environment and attuned to their historical moment. But they did not always embody such prudence. The next chapter reveals what happened when their attachment to full tenure track employment and democratic self-governance ran aground of the university's turn toward precarious employment and managerial administration. The times were changing. Kinneavy, Hairston, and Sledd committed themselves to outdated ideals and expiring institutions, ensuring that the institutional progress achieved during their composition revolution would not survive the coming transitional decade.

2
The Saturday Night Massacre

The history of higher education since the industrial revolution is often told as a story of struggle between academics who demand job security, intellectual autonomy, and institutional influence and managerial administrators who take their cues from private industry, searching for low-cost labor, asserting ham-fisted control, and reducing faculty to a precarious and impecunious status. This century-long struggle has been characterized as a "fluctuation between absolute [faculty] autonomy and totalitarian [administrative] control."[1] There is substantial truth to this narrative. A commonly told spinoff is about middle managers, the writing program administrators, complicit with the deans and the presidents, happily doing their managerial bidding in exchange for professional status. James Sledd was among the first to paint his fellow writing program administrators as toadies to their corporate university masters. Sledd, always good for an epithet, coined the term "boss compositionist." He directly accused many of his colleagues, including Maxine Hairston, of building an intellectual edifice to justify academic programs that exploited nontenure track instructors. Calling Hairston out by name, he said that she and others had waged a "non-intellectual, non-pedagogical campaign for limited academic power [. . . duplicating], on a small scale, the encompassing society's division into haves and have-nots."[2] Sledd's criticisms of his colleagues have recently been echoed by academic labor activist and media studies scholar Marc Bousquet, who alleges that many of the achievements mentioned in the previous chapter—writing labs, research budgets, tenured status, graduate programs—have been afforded to writing program administrators solely because they oversee "a large, cheap labor force" of adjunct instructors who lack tenure, academic freedom, or any say in faculty governance.[3]

Indeed, no one can deny that writing programs have historically relied on exploited instructors. The industrial era universal writing requirement demanded a large, costly workforce, lending itself to capitalist managerial practices, which now infiltrate other disciplines, departments, and programs. These managerial practices date back to the late nineteenth century.[4] Bousquet argues that academic capitalism came early to composition programs. Writing program administrators were among the first middle managers told to respond to "exterior forces" such as student demand and financial austerity, so they were also among the first to adopt "marketlike behaviors" such as the employment of precarious workers.[5] While we don't disagree with Bousquet's analysis, we do contend that he might be wrong in his assessment of writing program administrators, their motives, and their actions. Calling into question the existence of craven "boss compositionists" and their sinister assistance to an exploitative regime, this chapter chronicles the decline and fall of James Kinneavy's writing-across-the-curriculum program, an initiative doomed from the beginning by an English department split between tenured "haves" and nontenure track "have nots." The outcome of this story is exactly what Bousquet might predict: Faculty infighting incited by unbearable exploitation was finally resolved with cruel fiat. This episode's drama was so cinematic, its staging so theatrical, and its resolution so bathetic that national news outlets and professional magazines ran with the story, printing headlines about a mass firing often referred to as the "Saturday Night Massacre" of the UT Austin lecturers.

This chapter reveals that most of the rhetoric faculty—far from enacting a "management theory of agency," appealing to a rhetoric of "pleasing the prince," or pursuing limited concessions from dictatorial university higher-ups—demanded that the lecturers be given tenured rank and full privileges.[6] In fact, when the lecturers themselves organized, as Bousquet argues they should, they demanded far less than the rhetoric faculty tried to achieve for them. Lecturers collectively asked for multiyear contracts, a living wage, and some limited say in departmental governance. Additionally, this chapter reveals that the forces leading to the final, managerial, solution were beyond both the lecturers' and the faculty's command. Managerial authority, exercised by the upper administration, ended the turmoil within the English department, in part because the English faculty failed to develop a workable governance system that would include nontenure track faculty without causing resentment among the tenured professors and without handing total departmental control over to the swelling majority of nontenure track instructors.

Corporate managerialism and faulty governance, not boss compositionists or their management theory of agency, doomed Kinneavy's writing program. This chapter, therefore, is not about complicit middle managers but about stumbling program administrators. It's about people who tried to oppose marketized precarity but failed to overcome external economic forces (such as students' demand for professional skills), internal market-like behaviors (such as managerial action by upper administration), and departmental dysfunction (including an unworkable governance of a faculty split between tenure track professors and nontenure track lecturers). This chapter's story is much more complicated than any tale about fat-cat presidents who demand assent, the boss compositionists who do their bidding, and the victimized academics who suffer from fiscal austerity. The complications, we suggest, are what really matter to the middle manager searching for workable solutions or substantive improvements.

In the early 1970s an enrollment boom and a literacy crisis confronted the writing program at UT Austin. In 1971, 39,503 students stampeded onto campus. A decade later, in 1981, the herd was 48,145 large. Throughout the 1980s, enrollments occasionally crested above 50,000, but never dipped below 47,000.[7] Additionally, low standardized test scores funneled students into E 306. In 1971, nearly half the entering class tested out, but in 1975, barely 25 percent were exempted.[8] The local media reported the problem. A 1979 *Alcalde* article lamented that the "writing skills of today's students have deteriorated to near non-existence."[9] A 1983 *Texas Monthly* article said UT Austin fiddled with the "Rhetoric of Popular Culture" while statewide literacy rates burned.[10] A 1984 letter to the editor of the UT Austin student newspaper, the *Daily Texan*, reported that the university's graduates couldn't write.[11] The university's provisional admissions program compounded the problem. Begun in 1978 as an effort to increase accessibility to disadvantaged students of color, the program allowed students who had not qualified for regular admission to take an intensive summer session in order to prove themselves in several core classes such as E 306.[12] As is common with such efforts, the provisional program pitted the university's desire for inclusion against its aspiration toward excellence.[13] One English professor dismissively sneered that the "provisional program is a method by which students can enter the university, even if they're dopes," suggesting that the university mission to achieve national stature would be harmed by their simultaneous effort to serve the underprivileged.[14] In addition to this exacerbating and already felt conflict among institutional values, the provisional program also placed a significant financial strain on the English department. Most provisionally accepted students succeeded and had to take the second-semester writing course (E 307). In September 1977, Hairston told Kinneavy to start preparing for another "staffing crunch."[15] In 1978, only 13 percent of enrolling students tested out of E 306, while the provisional program continued to grow.[16]

In 1980, the situation had gotten so bad that the English department seriously considered lowering the bar for E 306 exemption, while the general faculty considered canceling the provisional program altogether.[17] James Sledd could not abide by this near brush with low standards. He called the department's pedagogical "irresponsibility . . . typical." According to Sledd, the situation was hopeless: "Barring a miraculous procession of sinners to the mourning bench, the only reasonable decision is to abolish the requirement."[18] Though they did not accept Sledd's recommended penance, the English faculty did mourn at the bench. At a February 1981 faculty meeting, one literature professor wailed about their inability to meet student demand, despite offering a record-high 452 individual composition sections.[19] In 1982, the English faculty gnashed their collective teeth over an even larger number: 559 writing classes.[20]

While the English department drowned in the flood of underprepared students, one person glimpsed a rainbow. James Kinneavy listened closely to the crisis rhetoric, meticulously clipping articles from local newspapers, popular magazines, and trade publications.[21] He heeded the campus conversation. He participated in a study of fifty-nine teaching assistants, concluding that students didn't get to write for a variety of audiences, so they "fail[ed] to face up to a fundamental holistic discourse situation."[22] He gleefully noted that faculty preferred "specialized upper division composition courses" and intensive writing instruction spread across every year of undergraduate instruction.[23] Kinneavy knew that other universities were revising their core curricula in response to nationally declining test scores. In 1978, The Pennsylvania State University witnessed a twenty-one-point drop in overall SAT scores among incoming students. Beaver College and the University of Michigan saw similar declines.[24] Kinneavy had contacts at all these schools. He had also heard Hairston recommend a curricular overhaul in her 1977 report to the General Faculty Council.[25] He felt the time was ripe.

The core university curriculum was thirty-five years old and sorely outdated. Soon James Vick—a UT Austin professor of mathematics—found himself chair of the ad hoc University Council Committee on Basic Education

Requirements. They completed their work in December 1980, delivering what would thereafter be called the "Vick report."[26] Among other things, they concluded that E 306 was a remedial course whose role should diminish as the university's stature rose. They further concluded that all students should take four writing-intensive classes beyond E 306, two at the lower division and two at the upper division. And, finally, they decided that the two upper-division courses should be taken in each student's chosen major. Among the faculty on the Vick committee was a young English department faculty member by the name of Alan Friedman, a New Yorker, a University of Rochester graduate (1966), and a believer in shared faculty governance. Friedman slyly reported the committee's activities to the English department administration. Eleven months before the Vick report appeared, Friedman told his fellow English professors that they should start working on a complementary proposal of their own. Kinneavy agreed, partly because he opposed any effort to abolish E 306.[27] By late February, thanks to Friedman's dutiful reporting, the English faculty marshaled a quiet insurrection. In multiple subcommittees, each ginning up their own proposals, they devised a set of reforms.[28] From the outset, the faculty saw this as a two-pronged effort. On the one hand, they would improve writing pedagogy to address the literacy crisis. On the other hand, they would streamline the curriculum to manage student enrollment and address the staffing crunch. These were their "pedagogical" and "logistical" motives.

The faculty were still thinking about their dilemma in the previous decade's terms. They thought they faced a pedagogical problem that they could solve with teacherly know-how. But they didn't realize that the country at large was turning toward fiscal conservatism with uneven consequences. Describing the federal economic policies under President Reagan, one historian explains that despite the common belief that "Reagan changed American conservatism by bringing to it a sunny, optimistic visage," his "economic conservatism . . . was in truth deeply traditional and administered harsh medicine—but not to all."[29] This evaluation of federal policy applies equally to the departmental response to the labor crisis at UT Austin. It initially looked sunny and hopeful, a new day for the core curriculum. But the benefits of this curricular overhaul only came to tenure track faculty, while austerity punished precariously employed lecturers. As the faculty focused on the pedagogical promise of their new curriculum, they initially ignored the logistical problem of rising enrollments and dwindling revenue.

In response to the enrollment crisis, the UT Austin English department chair convened the "Task Force on Composition" with multiple "teams" of faculty, each studying a specific issue. He wanted a "package of coordinated proposals."[30] They looked at everything—admissions, degree requirements, exemption options, course sequencing, and course content.[31] The department chair told the task force to focus on the logistical problem: rising enrollments.[32] The subcommittees generated a flurry of mimeographed paper. One report prevailed. Professor Lester Faigley wrote the committee report, but his recipes came right out of Kinneavy's cookbook.[33] While the department chair had requested a logistical solution with pedagogical garnish, Faigley and Kinneavy plated a pedagogical solution with logistical flavor. They suggested three required classes to satisfy the university's standing nine-hour requirement: E 306, E 316 (a new sophomore-level literature survey with a substantial writing requirement), and E 346K.[34] Bucking the logistical emphasis, Kinneavy claimed a "faculty mandate" to reform the curriculum.[35] When he pitched this proposal to the general faculty, Kinneavy didn't mention the logistical value added until the end.[36] Kinneavy believed that by distributing the nine hours of required courses across a student's first three years (rather than across their first three semesters), the new curriculum would prevent student demand from piling up.[37] Furthermore, Kinneavy wanted the English department to determine which classes could substitute for E 346K. If student demand for this junior-level course rose too high in a given year, the English faculty could open the spillway, approving more petitions for substitution or transfer credit. Finally, Kinneavy wanted to give E 346K credit for any second-semester college composition course taken at another university.

While Kinneavy's proposal sailed ahead, the Vick report trudged through the university bureaucracy. The general faculty questioned the Vick report's proposals.[38] A government professor declared, "If things are not being done well at the lower level . . . what we ought to do is maintain and strengthen the lower-division." Others confessed their ignorance of composition pedagogy. A physics professor stated that faculty in his department were trained to teach science, not syntax: "Very few of my colleagues are qualified or willing to teach a course with a substantial writing component." Faculty opposed to the recommendations of the Vick report mounted an onslaught of counterproposals, such as a new, required second-semester writing class.[39] The Vick report recommendations were never formally approved for the entire university. Instead, the colleges were told to develop their own plans for curricular reform in the "spirit of" the report's recommendations.

Kinneavy's proposal was approved in October 1980 by the College of Liberal Arts.[40] Along the way, however, this shiny pedagogical solution lost some of its logistical luster. The general faculty decided that the English department would not be able to determine which courses would count for E 346K credit.[41] All the same, both the Vick report and the English proposals were approved by June 1981. The faculty had essentially agreed to a four-course writing requirement, two at the lower division and two at the upper division.[42] The individual colleges could decide how to wed the Vick report and the English proposals. Vick conceded that E 346K could satisfy one of the two required upper-division writing courses proposed by his committee.[43] So, all the colleges saddled the English professors with most of the newly required writing courses. Students would have to take three courses in the English department (E 306, E 316, and E 346K) and one additional upper-division writing course in their home departments.[44] None of this deterred Kinneavy. The English faculty were so confident in his program that they started developing syllabi for E 346K in November 1980, not long after the college approved it, but several months before the University Council would begin to deliberate, seven months before the general faculty would endorse, and two years before the president of the university would finally approve their plan.[45] In September 1982, UT Austin president Peter Flawn finally assented to the entire four-course requirement. Then he inserted a disastrous provision. Flawn declared that second-semester courses taken at other universities would not transfer for E 346K credit.[46] Flawn's decision, in effect, guaranteed that every student had to take three classes taught by the English department, no exceptions. The trouble with asking the English department to teach so many classes was that they would have to hire so many more teachers.

Kinneavy stood firm. Others retreated. Sledd immediately petitioned the University Council to reinstate their second-semester course (E 307) and allow E 317 (an existing sophomore-level technical writing course) to substitute for E 346K. In response, Kinneavy defended his proposal's pedagogical promise: "We will have a freshman composition course, E 306; it is not a remedial course. We will have a sophomore literature course with a substantial component of composition. . . . We will then have E 346K at the junior level. It will ask the student, at a time when he has a fairly mature grasp of this content, to write prose on the subject matter, addressed to the general reader."[47] When it became evident that the University Council would vote down his proposed reinstatement of E 317, Sledd predicted the fall of Kinneavy's program: "I am sorry that my motion will now be defeated. . . . I have let a little light shine in—maybe nothing much to be proud of."[48]

Robert King always viewed himself as a problem solver. As the founding dean of UT Austin's College of Arts and Sciences, he had many problems with the Department of English: "the usual composition/literature thing" and the "pain-in-the-ass egos that are so frequently overrepresented in English departments."[49] But Dean King had bigger problems still. He was caught between the university's competing values. He wanted to build a research university, yet he needed to staff composition classes that would increase accessibility. Through the latter half of the 1970s, tenured and tenure track faculty had regularly taught first-year composition, and they took on extra courses when enrollments surged. They taught three courses (nine credit hours) per semester, including at least one section of first-year writing. In the fall of 1979, for example, tenure track faculty committed to sixty-three sections of first-year writing. They took on an extra seventy-one sections when enrollments ballooned later that year.[50] They expected the same of new faculty, stipulating in job ads that successful candidates must be willing to teach required writing courses.[51] However, King's quest for national prestige worked against the faculty's commitment to instructional access. In August 1979 when the chair of the English department reminded the faculty of their mandated nine credit-hour teaching load, he also explained that there were ways to reduce the burden, like teaching a graduate course (which counted for 4.5 credit hours), giving individual instruction to an undergraduate (which counted for 0.3 credit hour), mentoring a graduate student (which counted for 0.6 credit hour), supervising a master's thesis (which counted for 0.5 credit hour), or serving on a doctoral thesis committee (which counted for one credit hour).[52]

A few years later, Dean King quick-marched the English department chair's initiative to reduce faculty teaching hours. As he pushed the college toward research prestige, he wanted English professors teaching only two courses (six credit hours) per semester, like other departments in his college. The English faculty appointed a Teaching-Load Credit Committee, which recommended further ways to avoid the classroom.[53] Their proposal was approved by a departmental vote of 13–0, a rare moment of consensus among those pain-in-the-ass egos.[54] Not long after, with King's blessing, the next chair of the English department formally reduced the teaching load of tenured and tenure track faculty to six credit hours per semester. King was soon caught in his own trap. He needed teachers, but he had reduced teaching loads. At one point, he forced the literature faculty to teach at least one composition course per year, over howls of protest. That gambit had earned him the moniker "King Dean." In the late 1970s president Lorene Rogers pressured him to admit more graduate students, who could serve as teaching assistants, the most economical solution.[55] But overreliance on graduate instructors had embarrassed the university already. In 1976, the Texas state legislature had investigated complaints initiated by constituents. As it turns out, members of the Texas House of Representatives didn't care about teaching assistants whose poor training hindered first-year composition. They cared about teaching assistants whose foreign accents impeded calculus instruction.[56] But that didn't stop James Sledd from making a fuss. Testifying before the Texas House in August 1979, Sledd alleged that the English department failed to train the graduate instructors who taught the overwhelming majority of their required first-year class (E 306). He called the teaching practicum intended to train new graduate instructors a "phony course."[57]

Despite President Rogers's assurances that English graduate instructors were well trained, the issue dragged on for years, resulting in a massive university report and a failed legislative proposal.[58] Sledd told the local press that he had been given relief from teaching to serve on dissertation committees that he never belonged to.[59] Rejoicing in his newfound status as the "most hated man on campus," Sledd sanctimoniously promised to teach his three courses per semester.[60] Sledd and King didn't have much in common, but they shared a clear-eyed view of their predicament. Enrollments were climbing steeply, tenure track faculty took on fewer classes, and graduate instructors could not make up for the shortfall. Sledd and King also noticed another important factor, something Sledd viewed as a travesty and King saw as an opportunity. They both spied a precipitous downturn in employment prospects for tenure track professors. The midcentury bloom of professorial opportunity was miraculous. Thanks to rising national enrollments, tenure track jobs outnumbered qualified personnel. Between 1958 and 1972, the production of PhDs in the humanities rose from a valley of 300 to a peak of 1,200 per year.[61] The system worked well for a time. Graduate students climbed the ranks to tenure track employment, tenure track professors dripped knowledge in their research publications, and research publications festooned the reputations of flagship universities.

But in the 1970s, the once-reliable crop of stable jobs withered. In 1975, Sledd declared that it was "criminal that the professors are still recruiting more assistants while the old ones can't get jobs with their new PhDs." In an antebellum analogy, he called the literature professors "white folks," applying an ineffable epithet to the graduate instructors.[62] Once again, Sledd was treading on worn ground. Since the early nineteenth century, research universities have depended on precarious lecturers and other such adjuncts, so that their resident scholars could focus on research and publication.[63] But there was something new about this situation. Private docents assisting instruction at the University of Berlin in the mid-nineteenth century were likely not graduates of the institution. But US lecturers had received their PhDs from the universities now employing (and underpaying) them. Like many roads to hell, this new exploitative labor practice was paved with the best intentions. King knew that UT Austin PhDs weren't moving on to stable academic careers. He settled on what seemed to be a humane, practical solution. The English department would hire its own recently graduated doctoral candidates to serve as lecturers. The graduates would have jobs, and the university would cover its staffing shortfall. In 1978, the English department offered nontenure track positions to several of their own graduates at a rate of $6,000 per year (approximately $28,700 in 2023 dollars).[64]

UT Austin had been down this road before. At the university's very beginning, courses in English were taught by two people: a tenured professor of rhetoric and English literature, and an assistant professor of history. The tenured professor taught the senior course in literature, while the assistant professor taught the first-year course in writing. In 1889, to alleviate the first-year writing professor's obligation to read and correct more than one hundred essays per week, the university hired an undergraduate senior to teach one section of first-year writing per term. Then in 1894, they hired another nontenured (adjunct) professor to teach first-year writing and speech.[65] In the late 1930s the exploitation of nontenure track faculty had become so deplorable at UT Austin that faculty decried their "academic proletariat."[66] Likely unaware of this calamitous past, Dean King expanded the number of lecturers from five to twelve, then twenty, and then forty.[67] At the beginning of the fall 1979 semester, the English department chair reported that they would have to hire forty new assistant professors, each teaching three classes per semester, to staff their first-year composition classes.[68] In that same year, Kinneavy moved to hire six tenure track faculty who could teach first-year writing and staff the new graduate concentration in rhetoric and composition.[69] His motion never got past committee. In February 1982, the English Department Senate voted unanimously to hire eight more lecturers, bringing the total up to fifty-eight contingent faculty teaching 230 individual courses (compared to the seventy-eight visiting and tenure track professors who were slated to teach 190 sections).[70]

Such numbers fail to capture the human variables in King's economic equation. David McMurrey, a UT Austin PhD candidate, best represents the sort of lecturer that King imagined. In 1980, McMurrey was teaching in Kansas while completing his literature dissertation. He was also revising his scholarly profile, becoming an expert in technical communication.[71] Kinneavy invited him into a nontenure track position not long after McMurrey defended his dissertation. As a lecturer, McMurrey kept his head down and developed a niche, getting hired to run the newly established Writing Lab. For four years, he developed extracurricular teaching aids for students, and he embraced technology's promise in writing instruction, spearheading the grant application that jump-started the Computers and Writing Lab. Another lecturer, James Skaggs, did not fit the standard mold. After earning a PhD in English literature from Vanderbilt, he bounced across a few teaching jobs, eventually landing at UT Austin in 1979. Despite his literary background and scholarly record, he became a composition specialist.[72] A third lecturer didn't even have professorial ambitions. Rod Davis earned his master's degree in political science from the Louisiana State University and then enrolled in a PhD program at the University of Virginia. Finding he "just couldn't concentrate," Davis withdrew after one semester. After serving in the US Army, Davis enlisted in radical causes. He took the job at UT Austin so he could draw a stable paycheck, write for partisan magazines, and contribute to local politics. As faculty in the English department, Davis palled around with other leftists on the tenure track, people like the already-famous Marxist, feminist, poststructuralist scholar Gayatri Spivak.[73]

From the start, tenure track faculty had their misgivings. The lecturer positions were not intended to be permanent.[74] Many of the UT Austin lecturers resembled those described in a recent study of adjuncts at early twenty-first-century universities. They were latecomers to the academic profession, enthusiastic but ill prepared and entering a competitive race two legs behind the younger runners.[75] The English department chair acknowledged that the lecturers were "a substantial number of our own new and recent PhDs, persons who have not yet found suitable academic posts elsewhere." He went on to defend the arrangement, citing the "accordion factor." Lecturer labor could expand or contract to meet the unpredictable demand of lower-division enrollments.[76] Convinced by this argument, however discomfited by the situation, the English faculty remained largely complicit with King's solution, and the labor of the lecturers became an instructional staple.

From the day King decided to expand the number of nontenure track faculty, the tenured faculty sought to clarify the lecturers' ambiguous status.

Thus began the departmental troubles with shared faculty governance. During three department meetings in April and May 1980, the faculty struggled with the "composition staffing problem." In mid-April, a few tenured professors showed little empathy for the lecturers, arguing that when they "contract for these temporary positions, they are aware of what they are getting into." Others worried more about the departmental mission, claiming that the last-minute and local search for nontenure track faculty ensured mediocre teaching. However, most of the faculty deliberated with the lecturers' best interests in mind. Most agreed that the lecturers were "underpaid and overworked." Many suggested feasible, though not ideal, options. After noting that the alternative was to hire "fifty" new assistant professors of composition, Wayne Rebhorn suggested a reduction to thirty-five lecturers, so they could provide modest raises and long-term contracts to those who would keep their jobs.[77]

These debates expanded with an all-day meeting of the faculty (lecturers included) in early May 1980 to discuss the recommendations of the department's ad hoc "Task Force on Composition." An "ancillary proposal" of the task force was to reduce the lecturer teaching load from four courses to three per semester. Each of the task force's proposals, including the ancillary proposal to reduce lecturer teaching loads, was passed in June, winning 78 percent of the departmental vote.[78] The following month, the English department chair conveyed the departmental proposals to Dean King. The department chair conceded that "a small number of temporary faculty is a blessing, allowing the English Department a measure of flexibility to meet variations in student demand," but he worried that the situation was unhealthy for both the department and the lecturers. "These teachers comprise a 'second class' cadre in the department—uncertain of reappointment or percentage of appointment, hired late, badly quartered, overworked, devoid of tenure expectations."[79] More than thirty years after these prescient warnings, a national study of the "adjunct underclass" echoed everything that the UT English department chair had said: "When the nation demands college as a necessity for adult life, the system is forced to address raw, cyclical demographics. Adjuncts are the shock absorbers that make the terrain passable."[80] Unmoved by these exhortations, King quickly denied the request for lower teaching loads and higher pay for the lecturers. He swung his managerial fist, shattering the department's efforts to address their logistical problem. Unvexed, in the spring of 1981, the department formed yet another subcommittee.[81] As they studied its edges, the "lecturer problem" swelled. In August 1981, just before the start of a new term, UT Austin allocated $70,000 to hire five additional lecturers to staff composition courses. Just a month later, following what the English department associate chair called an "astonishing" and unexpected increase in undergraduate enrollments, the department hired yet another ten lecturers, raising the total number of part-time and full-time lecturers in the department to sixty-three.[82]

Sensing the urgency, the lecturer committee studied "all major aspects of Lecturer positions in the Department."[83] Their comprehensive report recommended, now for the second time, that the lecturers' teaching loads be reduced from four courses per semester to three. An unnamed lecturer testified:

> By the end of this semester I will have graded 720 essays and 115 tests, prepared 84 lectures and made 168 presentations, and kept 100 office hours. Allowing myself a mere 15 minutes to grade a paper and but two hours to prepare a lecture, I calculate that I make around $7 an hour; a 3/3 load would give 20 minutes a paper and $9 an hour. . . . I respectfully suggest that the students at this university deserve teachers with more than 15 minutes for their work and 5 minutes for their visits. I want to teach as effectively as possible. A 3/3 load is a step in that direction.[84]

Persuaded by such arguments, the English faculty ratified the recommended reduction in the lecturers' teaching load. The report was forwarded to the dean's office in mid-December 1981.[85] In February 1982 in a memo titled "Workload," Dean King again nixed the department's proposal, pointedly noting that the "requirement for 100% appointment as a Lecturer is four (4) *organized* classes."[86]

Twice frustrated, the faculty searched for other ways to ensure quality instruction while both improving employment conditions and maintaining shared faculty governance within the English department. In 1982 they decided to launch a competitive, national search, saying that they sought "improvement of lower-division instruction" and "equal opportunity hiring."[87] The faculty advertised nationally but also determined that the hiring process should give preference to lecturers already under contract.[88] These newer, more qualified candidates expected better treatment, yet they received what one tenured professor called a "guarantee of permanent uncertainty." A graduate student suggested "a multiyear contract for Lecturers," but many faculty began to worry that multiyear contracts might allow nontenure track faculty to serve for six consecutive years, earning de facto tenure, according to the American Association of University Professors (AAUP).[89] The faculty voted narrowly to limit the lecturers to six years of teaching, after which they could petition for appointment as assistant professors. Kinneavy passionately disparaged the six-year limit, saying that "a minority in the department is exploiting a large group of people and depriving them of free speech."[90]

In the fall of 1982, the *Daily Texan* ran a three-part series, giving each installment front-page billing. The initial article reported lecturers' belief that the prominent use of student evaluations corrupted their ability to maintain rigorous standards. Lecturer Rod Davis alleged that "there are lecturers who take students out for beer on the day of evaluations or do other favors solely to get evaluations pumped up."[91] The *Daily Texan*'s second article dug into other concerns, such as late hour appointments. In some cases, the student newspaper revealed, lecturers were not reappointed until the Saturday before the start of fall classes.[92] Lecturers also complained about a ranking system that the Executive Committee kept secret. The English department associate chair defended the process: "To reveal the numerical rankings [of the lecturers] would be 'counter-productive' as it would lead to 'guessing games' among the lecturers as to why one received a fractionally different score from another."[93] The *Daily Texan*'s third article examined the English department's caste system. Davis said that "using lecturers to do the donkey's share of the department's work suggests that lecturers are the migrant farm workers of academia."[94]

The *Daily Texan* then ran a follow-up (fourth) story, reiterating the lecturers' grievances while also voicing their hopes. A new subcommittee had been formed. Led by two lecturers, Jim Skaggs and Sharon Wevill, this committee negotiated with the English department chair and associate chair, as well as the dean's office. One lecturer wrote a memo summarizing their position: "The lecturer 'problem' . . . is not local but national in scope. It follows, therefore, that this English department can assume national leadership by achieving a workable, humanistic, response to this national dilemma."[95] With the benefit of hindsight, Skaggs came to believe that the 1983 subcommittee was just another way to kick the can down the road.[96] The titles "instructor," "lecturer," and even "assistant professor" were intermingled, compounding confusion. Prompted by changes in the regents' rules, the department decided to bring order and some humanity to these titular ambiguities.[97] The subcommittee recommended that the department create three internal tiers (adjunct, lecturer I, and lecturer II) with ascending levels of remuneration and job security.[98] Professor Ruszkiewicz, then director of the first-year writing program at UT Austin, submitted another proposal, which promoted a dizzying hierarchy of lecturers—some with job stability, some precarious, some receiving better wages and honorific titles, others lacking dignity and decent pay.[99] Sledd scorned them all. In his eyes, Ruszkiewicz was just another "boss compositionist" trying to maintain his privileged status while placating the proletariat.[100] This was the sort of reform that Marc Bousquet has roundly criticized, for Ruszkiewicz was clinging to "the desire for control" and eschewing "the reality of collective agency."[101] But when the lecturers did assert collective agency, they asked for less than Ruszkiewicz had proposed and far less than Sledd had demanded. The lecturers rallied behind Susan Rodi (herself a lecturer), who rejected the titular changes and suggested three-year contracts for all nontenure track faculty.[102] Rodi's pragmatism reflects something that scholars affirmed ten years later among nontenure track women teaching in university writing programs. Rodi recognized the system's exploitative nature and accepted that precarity was the price she'd have to pay if she wanted to stay employed at the university.[103] Nevertheless, she hoped to make her situation less uncomfortable. The "pragmatic discourse" that Bousquet attributes to writing program administrators was coming from the rank and file.[104]

Unable to settle the matter internally, the English department sent their emissary, professor Alan Friedman, to petition a higher authority. Friedman asked the University Council to define the lecturer position. He also requested a moratorium on lecturer hiring.[105] The UT Austin vice president skillfully dodged the question: "We appoint Lecturers and Senior Lecturers to fill our needs for instructional service. Lecturers and Senior Lecturers are hired for specific teaching assignments. They are not expected to conduct research or scholarly work or to provide public service."[106] Friedman's request set in motion another series of ad hoc subcommittees—this time at the university level. Two years after the English department failed to find an internal administrative solution to their labor problem, the University Faculty Senate formally recorded its "Report of the Faculty Senate Committee on the Status and Role of the Lecturer," which emphasized that instruction should be carried out whenever possible by permanent faculty.[107] They affirmed the lecturers' contingent status and punted specific policy decisions back to the departmental chairs and committees.

While economic exploitation worried the professors and disadvantaged the lecturers, shared departmental governance proved to be the department's most intractable problem. Starting when the English professors initially deliberated what to do about their growing pool of nontenure track faculty, procedural discussions affirmed that instructors and lecturers appointed on a full-time basis held voting rights in full departmental meetings.[108] As a result, in May 1980, lecturers voted alongside tenure track faculty to reduce their teaching load. In the subsequent fall, the English faculty initiated a routine review of their governance. Among other things, they continued allowing all teaching faculty (lecturers included) to vote on all matters deliberated at full departmental meetings.[109] Since meetings of the full faculty were rare, this provision wasn't radically democratic. More consequential were the reforms to the Executive Committee, the departmental body that handled most budgetary and hiring decisions. The English faculty created two new Executive Committee representatives, each chosen from among the contingent faculty.[110] The tenure track professors quickly realized that they held a minority stake in a majoritarian democracy. Within a year, the Executive Committee's constitution was amended to exclude lecturers.[111] And a year after that, Dean King refused to approve the new constitution unless the department took further measures to de-democratize their governance. Professor Neill Megaw proposed splitting departmental governance between two bodies: an authoritative Executive Committee comprised of tenure track faculty and making major financial and staffing decisions, and a democratic English Department Senate handling day-to-day affairs, such as curricular reform. Lecturers could elect representatives to the English Department Senate but not the Executive Committee. Megaw promised that "an elected departmental senate would provide a stable, democratic, and effective way of making policy decisions that would genuinely represent majority opinion."[112] His solution won the day.

With the new Executive Committee approved, the English Department Senate began its work. This bicameral system was unique at a university where most governance happened within recondite committees behind closed office doors. The English Department Senate met once a month, welcomed all observers, allowed representatives from all ranks (including lecturers), and even kept tape-recorded conversations of their proceedings. The Executive Committee made clandestine decisions, while the English Department Senate hosted raucous meetings. In 1982, for instance, the Executive Committee passed proposals to limit nontenure track employment to six consecutive years and to search nationally for new lecturers. The English Department Senate pushed back against these recommendations, eventually insisting that they be brought before the full faculty where lecturers could vote on their approval. The most heated episodes happened in the spring of 1984. In late March, the Executive Committee issued several recommendations. Among other things, they wanted to limit the number of consecutive semesters that anyone could serve as lecturer. They also wanted to reduce four lecturers—David McMurrey included—to part-time status. The reduction in status would prevent their de facto tenure. Hairston wrote to the English department chair, saying she could "not endorse the proposal" because these long-serving lecturers had "done a good job for us, [and] we still need them to teach courses." Instead of cutting their hours, Maxine Hairston declared, "I think we should ask that they be given tenure and recognized as regular members of the department." She ended with a warning: "The dilemma we have gotten ourselves into is . . . potentially destructive."[113] In this rare moment of reflection, Hairston modeled Donna Strickland's "operative approach" to composition's managerial enterprise. Hairston asked the department chair to "notice and investigate our emotional stances towards our work," and she hoped that this reflection might lead to a conversation about "ethical and political consequences."[114] Others followed Hairston's lead.

Many tenure track professors and graduate students assailed the Executive Committee's proposals. Assistant professor of rhetoric Greg Myers wrote a letter of protest directly to the department chair, arguing that the lecturers deserved better than part-time status after so many years of good service.[115] James Kinneavy and one of his graduate students, David Jolliffe, copied and stuffed their objections into every faculty mailbox. Kinneavy argued that the Executive Committee's policies would "permit hiring of faculty who teach ordinary English classes with no hope of tenure."[116] Jollife contended that the "revolving-door employment policy for lecturers" would split the academic job market, shuttling PhDs from state schools into precarious jobs where they would teach core writing classes, while Ivy League PhDs snatched up the dwindling tenure track posts in literary criticism.[117] Susan Jarratt, a graduate student who later flourished in her own scholarly career, sympathized with the lecturers' plight. She recalled attending one of the decisive English Department Senate meetings: "I have a visual memory of a meeting. . . . And I was present, and a lecturer was present. And he stood up and said, you need to act and give us some clarity, whatever you decide to do. Either fire us all or give us permanent jobs or do something decisive."[118] The lecturer whose name Jarratt did not recall was Rod Davis. He later regretted the moment, feeling that his strident insistence turned away some sympathetic tenure track faculty.[119]

In truth, no one wanted to double-cross or exploit the lecturers. Nonetheless, try though they did, the faculty found no desirable solutions. At the April 4, 1984, meeting of the English Department Senate, Professor Rebhorn (seconded by graduate student David Jollife) moved to put all the lecturers on part-time status. He thought it would be a gift, like a postdoctoral appointment while preparing for an honest run at a tenure track job. This motion and the Executive Committee recommendations were defeated.[120] The department chair called another meeting of the English Department Senate two days later. The Executive Committee now wanted to limit lecturers to six consecutive long semesters (three years).[121] Kinneavy and Megaw both wrote lengthy protest memos, distributing them before the April 6 meeting.[122] When the English Department Senate met a second time, an associate professor of American literature moved to put all lecturers on half-time status. He claimed that the Executive Committee proposal would create a permanent class of contingent labor.[123] This motion and the Executive Committee's revised proposals were defeated.[124]

All these arguments made a certain amount of sense, given a certain set of assumptions. Those contending that the lecturers deserved tenure track employment assumed that the upper administration would hire assistant professors rather than contingent workers. Those arguing that the lecturers should be put on part-time or half-time status assumed that tenure track opportunities were just around the bend. Enrollments weren't falling, and retirements were forthcoming, so many predicted a boom in the job market for humanities PhDs.[125] But none of these assumptions were valid. The mid-century demand for humanities PhDs would never return. Furthermore, to discuss the struggle for academic employment as a "job market" overlooks a simple reality. As Marc Bousquet explains, in the 1980s people applied a "market analogy" to describe a "structural transformation" in academic employment, "the replacement of tenured faculty with managed labor."[126] Put more bluntly: "The job market in the humanities, then, is not a market at all."[127] It is a fiction hiding the purposeful construction of a two-tiered labor system accommodating budgetary austerity and facilitating managerial control. The lecturers at UT Austin in the mid-1980s were among the first to experience this structural transformation, complete with the crushing diminishment of privileges and comforts brought by tenure and earned by professional unions like the AAUP. Already in 1984 it was naive to hope for the days when stable employment could be guaranteed by managerial compromise or achieved with employee action. Within academe, the Reaganite promise of a free market was camouflaging a rigged game.

Three days after the English Department Senate refused to limit lecturers' contracts for the second time, the department chair called them back for another meeting, saying that seventeen professors signed a statement of nonsupport for their actions.[128] In early April 1984 the English Department

Senate met for the third time in a week to deliberate the Executive Committee's recommendations. Neill Megaw moved that the Executive Committee proposals be taken up at a full meeting of the English faculty where everyone (lecturers included) could vote. His motion passed.[129] Roughly a week later, to a packed room, the Executive Committee recommended limits on lecturer employment. Their motion finally and resoundingly failed.[130] Lecturer contracts were still restricted to one year, but they could be renewed indefinitely. No one would be demoted to part-time status. James Skaggs and Rod Davis triumphantly declared that tenure track faculty and contingent lecturers had turned out to vote in the department's most directly democratic assembly.[131] Other tenure track professors began to distinguish themselves as the "regular faculty," petitioning Dean King to deny lecturers' voting rights within the department, while arguing that they themselves held the "*sole* right to make all authorized decisions" regarding the department's future.[132] By this point, King had had his fill of it. He put the department in limited receivership, dissolving the English Department Senate, barring the doors to its general assembly, and giving complete governmental control to the Executive Committee while the faculty worked out a new system of governance.

Newly empowered, English department chair William Sutherland decided to reduce all the lecturers to three-quarters time, ensuring that no one would be able to vote in departmental meetings or claim de facto tenure.[133] Sutherland's effort to neutralize the opposition was foiled by another enrollment boom, which forced the department to rehire most of the lectures at full-time status. Then, in the spring of 1985, the new governance structure eliminating the English Department Senate was proposed. The new Executive Committee would consist of twelve voting members, two appointed by the dean (the department chair and the associate chair), two appointed by the department chair, and eight elected from among the tenured faculty. Megaw formally protested the new Executive Committee, saying it trampled over every imaginable institution of democratic faculty governance. Nonetheless, since the new governing body would be "elected" by a rigged system with limited suffrage, it would "enable the Dean to call the EC a 'representative body.'"[134] Sledd went one step further, calling the new Executive Committee an episode in "organized indecency."[135] He told the general faculty that their new assembly was "blundering university governance from the top down."[136] As Megaw predicted, King approved the Executive Committee and added further managerial provisions.[137] One recently hired assistant professor called it a sign of their "neo-conservative times."[138] He was right about their times but wrong about the "neo."

The Battles of Texas

Faculty governance at American universities had been trending toward authority for decades. By the turn of the nineteenth century, American colleges and universities had created a "semi-autonomous managerial" class.[139] And first-year writing was at the epicenter of modern university managerialism, which consisted of "a complex economic enterprise that has almost from its beginning demanded management as a result of its ubiquity in the ever-expanding American higher education system." Notably, compositionists themselves have typically disliked or denied their managerial roles.[140] Dean King, however, embraced the role, epitomizing the dictatorial administrator as separate from and sometimes even hostile toward the faculty. Holding a master's degree in mathematics and having worked for IBM before returning to earn his PhD in linguistics, he would later recollect, "I did not at all mind the corporate thing, the IBM thing."[141] Academic unions like the AAUP won the tense compromise that most tenured faculty at UT Austin cherished, "the imperfect institutionalization of a corporate ideal within the university" that allowed for a "theoretical free space between absolute autonomy and totalitarian control."[142] The nontenure track faculty didn't care as much for intellectual freedom because they didn't have the time to conduct research or the liberty to design curricula. They just wanted job security. When they demanded it, the upper administration obliterated their every avenue for appeal.

With the governance issue resolved, the upper administration turned its gaze toward Kinneavy's writing-across-the-curriculum program. The department chair approached the dean, admitting the department could not staff all the necessary sections of E 346K.[143] They both then asked the upper administration to cancel the class.[144] A few days later, in February 1985, the English department chair announced to the faculty that UT's vice president had agreed to a moratorium on E 346K.[145] A year later, the class was officially scrapped, along with Kinneavy's three-course writing requirement. The department chair pointed to the logistical problem, saying that they would have to offer 150 sections of E 346K in the fall of 1985.[146] King later recalled that the UT Austin executive vice provost had decided that the lecturers had to go once they began exercising their voting rights in unison.[147] Whether they aimed to reduce the curricular burden or solve the governance problem, the administration's solution was elegantly masked by a circular logic. E 346K was canceled because there was no one to teach it. Fifty lecturers were fired because there was nothing for them to teach.

Salacious stories about the "Saturday Night Massacre of the Lecturers" ignore the faculty's tireless efforts to humanely solve an intractable problem. Many labored to improve the lecturers' situation even after the axe fell. For example, rhetoric professor Steve Witte submitted a report titled "A Comprehensive Solution to the 'Composition Problem'" to the department's Rhetoric Interest Group and the University Faculty Senate. Refusing to accept that Kinneavy's curriculum should be fully scrapped or the lecturers should be fired or permanently remanded to second-class status, Witte acknowledged that this was a "complex problem" warranting a "comprehensive solution."[148] Witte's report is one example of the path chosen by most UT Austin faculty. Another example deserves mention. In February 1985, a literature professor sympathetic toward the lecturers published a survey noting how demoralized, underpaid, and underappreciated they had become.[149]

All these good intentions and honest efforts drown in the clamor of public quarrels. It's easy to see why. The feud between James Sledd and Alan Gribben (then the director of graduate studies and an associate professor of American literature) would be enough to make you forget all the faculty's well-intentioned proposals. Sledd and Gribben first exchanged barbs in front of the University Faculty Senate in early March 1985.[150] Their dispute nearly came to blows a few months later. One late September afternoon Sledd sat on the patio of the Cactus Café, having beers with two graduate students, one of them a Vietnam veteran with a reputation for needling self-important professors, the other Sledd's protégé. The vet loudly invited Gribben, who happened to be passing by, to join their table. Words—their particularities lost to memory, but their tenor easily imagined—were exchanged between Gribben and Sledd. Sledd's protégé rose to defend the honor of his aged mentor. The veteran restrained Sledd's student, pinning him against a wall. Gribben left, shocked.[151] Gribben reported the "assault" to his colleagues and superiors. He sought sanctions against Sledd and the veteran who intervened.[152] Sledd complained to the university president that Gribben was trying to wreck his application for status as professor emeritus.[153] The graduate student who stopped the fight admitted to "intervening in what might have developed into an assault upon a member of the English department faculty." He confessed that he would "probably do it again," if given the opportunity.[154] Gribben withdrew his request for disciplinary action, saying that he considered the matter closed and adding, without a hint of irony, that he hoped the incident would not "mar our sense of unity."[155] The showdown at the Cactus Café captures the worst of 1985 but obscures other matters that deserve to be remembered, for the Saturday Night Massacre would not have been so influential if had it never been so overblown.

In the spring of 1985, with departmental venues now largely stripped away by the new governance structure, the student newspaper became a platform for faculty debate. An exasperated Neill Megaw blurted out, "We... have no other forum than in the *Texan*."[156] On February 20 the editor pleaded on behalf of E 346K, while Kinneavy contributed an article defending the course and Skaggs penned a letter defending his nontenure track colleagues.[157] Three undergraduates also wrote brief letters of support for E 346K.[158] Others among the literature faculty offered solace and confessed impotence. The department chair replied that "the English Department will do all it can to assist lecturers in finding jobs."[159] One professor of English literature said that E 346K was a logistical impossibility, while another assured the quality of undergraduate education would remain high, despite the loss of so many upper-division courses, since writing could be taught within the format of a literature course.[160] An undergraduate, a lecturer, and a former UT Austin alum all contributed short letters defending E 346K.[161] Tenured and nontenure track professors launched personal attacks on one another.[162] Some lecturers set their sights on the department, as did undergraduates.[163] Graduate students also took up arms.[164] When they couldn't place their work in a public venue, some spewed their bile into faculty mailboxes.[165] In early March 1985, the *Daily Texan* turned over its entire editorial page to the intradepartmental dispute, prompting defense of the lecturers' work, explanation of the department's conundrum, and debate about Kinneavy's curriculum.[166] On March 4, 1985, a meeting of the University Faculty Senate exploded over the lecturer controversy. After Gribben and Sledd shouted one another down, Kinneavy traded attacks with the English department chair. This incident was triggered when Kinneavy delivered a report titled the "Decomposition of English," accusing his chair of stacking the deck against E 346K.[167] The department chair said Kinneavy was blindsiding him with personal vitriol. The *Daily Texan* characterized the meeting as a feud.[168]

Kinneavy wasn't the only person stoking the fire. The graduate student who had saved Alan Gribben from certain bodily harm in a masterful facsimile of a Robert Frost poem wrote and circulated "Departmental," full of canine and fecal imagery.[169] Another bitingly satirical piece, "Joe Boggs Goes to the Slaughterhouse"—depicting the lecturers' slaughter as a Friday-night horror flick, the *Texas Chainsaw Massacre (of the Adjuncts)*—soon appeared in faculty mailboxes.[170] By mid-April 1985 the mass firing of the lecturers had become national news in the trade press. The *Chronicle of Higher Education* gave the story a two-page spread topped with the headline "50 Lecturers Lose Their

Jobs in a Dispute over How—and If—Writing Can Be Taught."[171] A sidebar profiling three lecturers told a familiar tale of uncertainty and desperation.[172] At the end was a piece that everyone in the UT English department would agree with, Maxine Hairston's "We're Hiring Too Many Temporary Instructors."[173] Hairston, again, tried to champion an operative approach to management. Her trenchant critique was overshadowed by the feature article, in which Kinneavy repeated his arguments about the "decomposition of English," while the English department chair unabashedly pronounced, "It's an absolutely impossible job for an English department to teach everyone to write."[174] Sledd, as always, gave good copy: "I don't think the face of the world would change a bit if all the English departments simply disappeared."[175]

The departmental culture began to reflect the bitterness and rancor of Sledd's diatribes rather than the sensible critique of Hairston's article or the cautious optimism of Witte's report. Not willing to let the issue die, Sledd made a last stand at a meeting of the University Faculty Senate in late April 1985. He took jabs at his colleagues who, he alleged, had abetted the debacle: "The political issue . . . is the employment of a large number of lecturers whom the dominant faction . . . sees as a threat to the professional status of the literati."[176] Some faculty were no more magnanimous in victory than Sledd was in defeat. One literature professor publicly commented "that the suspension [of E 346K] was requested by the chairman of the English department himself, that most regular faculty support him, and that the only 'inflamed' people in the department are the temporary faculty hired to teach E 346K, who will now have no jobs, and the theorists who invented the course in the first place."[177] An unsigned memo reminded the lecturers that they could apply for unemployment and encouraged them to take time moving out of their offices, for no one would be replacing them.[178] Someone hung a "lecturer scorecard" in the faculty lounge, recording by name those who had landed new gigs and where. In a fit of pique, a literature professor sympathetic to the lecturers' plight tore it down, concerned that the scorecard would exacerbate the already-intolerable departmental division, an impulsive decision for which he later apologized, acknowledging that he "had no right to censure anyone's bitter feelings."[179]

Joyce Locke Carter began her successful academic career one semester after the mass firing. Shortly after she arrived on campus as a new graduate student in the fall of 1985, Kinneavy hauled all the graduate students to an acrimonious faculty meeting, over the department chair's objections. She later called it "quite a stunt . . . an argument to the faculty that 'this is not a frictionless decision we've made. Here are all the people affected, they're going to be graduating from here, and this is important."'[180] Carter's recollection captures the animus. The lecturers' stories remind us of the humanity. By September 1984, Davis could see the writing on the wall. He successfully pitched a story to the editor of *Texas Monthly*, a detailed, scathing article to be written on commission. He documented the history of the labor problem, reviled the abdications of the literature faculty, heralded the champions among the lecturers, and damned those who treated them like expendables. Following Hairston's lead, he even raised the gender-equity issue, for the lecturer cohort was disproportionately female. Heavy on faculty quotes from both sides and thick with detail, Davis's article remains a modern-day broadside. Yet *Texas Monthly* declined to publish. Believing that the English department chair had pressured the *Texas Monthly* editor into quashing the article, Davis had no choice but to submit his work to the *Texas Observer*, where he had previously been editor. He moved on to Texas Christian University, where he suffered a similar series of events—same conflict between tenure track and nontenure track faculty, same indignities, same precarity. Finally, he returned to his journalistic roots, prolifically churning out long-form articles and literary fiction.[181]

In the summer of 1984, David McMurrey realized that he could never expect job stability and he might be demoted to part-time status. He mournfully wrote the department chair to report that "[I am] nearing 40 years of age and [hoping to adopt] one or two children in the next few years. . . . I must seek a position that affords a decent sense of security and permanence and a reasonable opportunity for professional growth and salary increase."[182] If the university could have given him any of these things, even if the offer weren't a tenure track job, he would have considered staying. He wanted to develop software that supported the English composition program. He volunteered to continue working on these projects while employed elsewhere. Valerie Balester, a graduate student at the time, remembered that in 1984 McMurrey had hired a full staff of graduate students for the upcoming year, only to learn in the intervening summer that he would not be rehired for another full-time appointment.[183] At the last moment, McMurrey was offered a full-time contract, but for the last time. In 1985 the Writing Lab that McMurrey had worked so hard to establish simply ceased operations.[184]

The Writing Lab later restarted under the leadership of Light German, a nontenure track faculty member who wouldn't be given a stable contract until 1986 when the department chair finally got the English department's Executive Committee to approve her hiring as a "specialist," not a lecturer or a tenure track faculty member and thus not eligible for promotion or raises but not precarious."[185] Six years later, one of the graduate students who worked with the new Writing Lab Director fervently demanded better job stability for those like her former boss.[186] McMurrey landed on his feet, going to work for no less than IBM, the company that had awarded him ten PC-XTs for use in the Writing Lab.[187] He worked there for eleven years before moving to Austin Community College, where he pioneered the school's online education program.[188] Like McMurrey, after several cycles of summer uncertainty followed by last-minute rehiring, James Skaggs finally found himself on the chopping block in 1985. Slightly older than most of his lecturer peers, Skaggs was outspoken in departmental meetings and public debates. After getting bounced from UT Austin, he floated across a few more nontenure track jobs before finally settling at Western Kentucky University, where he worked through the remainder of his career on the tenure track.[189]

Shortly after the Saturday Night Massacre, James Sledd hoofed it to Wyoming, where he made a big show at a small conference. Many of Sledd's fellow attendees felt guilty about the similarly bad labor situations at their own institutions. Compositionist Edward Corbett recounted a particularly dark night of the soul. Corbett had worked his way through the ranks, beginning his career as a lecturer at Creighton University, teaching five courses per semester, typically a combination of four first-year writing classes and one sophomore literature survey. Then he became an assistant professor and the director of the first-year writing program. He watched the discipline of rhetoric and composition ascend in the 1970s. By the mid-1980s, he had risen himself, enjoying a comfortable, tenured position at Ohio State University, where he taught two courses per semester, mostly to upper-division undergraduates and graduate students. He had published his way into disciplinary prominence.[190] In the summer of 1985, now a full professor, Corbett was a featured speaker at a professional conference. In preparation for his day at the dais, while shaving one morning, he "stuck this big nose of mine against the tip of the nose reflected in the mirror and shouted at the top of my lungs, 'CORBETT, YOU FRAUD.'"[191]

Though the conference was not supposed to feature any discussion of contingent labor, on the first night, at the Vedauwoo National Recreation Park, the professors' talk of precarity flared up like the bonfire illuminating their aggrieved faces. When Sledd finally gave his incendiary talk, the audience was ready for both his fire and his brimstone.[192] He chastised a room full of penitent sinners: "*Research* in composition has indeed become a monstrous industry, with its fully developed professional apparatus of conferences, grants, seminars, institutes, journals and paradigmatic feuds; but the *teaching* of composition in the pattern-setting universities remains a slave-trade.'"[93] The room was stunned into silence; then a graduate student at the University of Washington stood up and asked, "Why aren't you all talking about this?" The session adjourned. As people spilled into the hallways, they spoke of nothing but academic labor and its injustices.[194] The next day, the conference attendees penned the Wyoming Resolution, which demanded that nontenure track faculty receive better salaries, improved working conditions, and a just appeals process. In the following year (1987), the Conference on College Composition and Communication (CCCC) Committee on Professional Standards produced its own guidelines for the ethical treatment of nontenure track faculty. Their "Statement of Principles" called for "tenure track employment of virtually all writing faculty, with no more than 10 percent of classes taught by part-time faculty." Many nontenure track faculty objected that these pie-in-the-sky demands would ultimately hinder the effort "to improve their working conditions and could lead to the elimination of their jobs."[95] In their national professional societies, just as in the hallways at UT Austin, lecturers asked for less than had been demanded on their behalf.

There is no understanding the importance of the Wyoming Resolution or the events at UT Austin that inspired its composition. Two scholars of rhetoric and composition contend that the Wyoming Resolution inspired academic professionals across the nation to seriously consider fair employment practices.[196] The CCCC "Statement of Standards and Principles" has been acknowledged as the "'go-to' document for Writing Program Administrators (WPAs), department chairs, and other administrators and faculty of all ranks as they attempt to create just employment conditions for an increasingly diverse labor pool in a rapidly changing workplace."[197] A leader in the field has called it one of the "heroic moments in the history of the Conference on College Composition and Communication."[198] James McDonald, a UT Austin PhD who witnessed the Saturday Night Massacre, has meticulously documented the series of professional statements inspired by the Wyoming Resolution and the CCCC "Statement."[199] Recently, scholars in the field of rhetoric and composition have called for a new statement, one addressing old problems, such as "inclusive faculty governance" and "vocational values," while also accounting for new dynamics, such as "restrictions on curricular authority" and "assessment driven by accreditation organizations."[200] While there are many differences between the third decade of the twenty-first century and the second to last decade of the twentieth, we can't help but notice one striking continuity. The institutional hunger for efficiency and the ambition toward excellence both form and frustrate writing program administrators, just as these marketized motives directed the UT Austin faculty in the early 1980s.

The question of what is to be done still remains today, and this chapter's saga offers no firm answer. Many of the solutions once proposed are still in circulation, with a few new ideas added to the mix. The American Association of University Professionals and the American Federation of Teachers both push for universal tenure, wanting to eliminate the striated labor system that now characterizes all higher education. The National Education Association lobbies for the better treatment of adjuncts.[201] A nontenure track professor and interim writing program administrator at Oswego State University have together argued in terms reminiscent of Skaggs and Wevill's report: "If [. . .] universities] will allow the creation of teaching substructures at their institutions, especially in composition—then they should be called upon *to make adequate provisions for the fullest possible professionalization of the new faculty communities they have created.*"[202] Like John Ruszkiewicz, many writing program administrators have tried to win this minimal security for their instructors. One associate professor of writing at Syracuse University and a nontenure track instructor in the same program tried to improve the working conditions of their nontenure track faculty, suffering through many of the solutions that Ruszkiewicz recommended, including a series of tiers with ascending pay based on merit.[203] Like Sledd and King, Joseph Harris—one-time director of the Center for Teaching, Learning, and Writing at Duke University—has argued that tenured professors should teach first-year writing.[204] Like Ruszkiewicz, Harris also maintains that colleges and universities should preserve the hierarchy between research and teaching faculty.[205] More recently, those looking carefully at the labor problem in English departments have begun to consider the possibility of reforming graduate curricula, recommending that PhD programs train their graduates for employment outside the university.[206] Their solution, though recently de rigueur, isn't recent. Compositionists have wrestled with employment precarity for the last forty years. Fifteen years after the Saturday Night Massacre, at the end of the twentieth century, a tenured rhetoric professor at The Pennsylvania State University lamented the "McJobbing of the university" and suggested that such "systemic exploitation" might be addressed, in part, by "envisioning alternate employment sites for our PhDs."[207] More than twenty years after that diagnosis, all of higher education is addressing a problem that racked the English department at UT Austin in the early 1980s.

The existing body of scholarship widely acknowledges that writing programs are beset by external economic forces and internal market-like motives. Some soft-pedal this concession by gesturing toward "academia's situatedness in larger socioeconomic developments."[208] Harris bluntly states the matter when he says, "We are indeed workers in a corporate system."[209] Both perspectives admit that some complicity with exploitation may be the coin in the writing program administrator's Faustian bargain for professional and departmental status. Like this chapter, these competing solutions and this common concession indicate how freighted the labor problem in higher education has become. This chapter pushes back against simple stories that pit villainous provosts against heroic workers, with a craven class of complicit middle managers in between. Nevertheless, monochromatic caricatures and Manichaean narratives persist. Sledd called his rhetoric colleagues "a bunch of seniors maneuvering to win recognition as Generous Patron." And he righteously demanded—with "the full expectation that it will be hard, dangerous to some careers, and probably unsuccessful in the short run"—a long march toward tenure track employment for all.[210] More than thirty years later, Marc Bousquet said that writing program administrators who advocate for anything short of Sledd's collective long march are "heroic WPAs," cloaking themselves in disciplinary glory, obsequiously accepting "some form of (marginal) respectability and (institutional-bureaucratic validity)," while unwittingly serving "upper management by legitimizing the practice of writing instruction with a revolving labor force of graduate employees and other contingent teachers."[211]

As this chapter illustrates, Sledd's and Bousquet's allegations are undeniably true, but their critiques overlook many specifics. We offer another approach and a different vantage. By telling a story at the ground level and trying to capture the administration's imposing demands, the faculty's complex motives, and the range of local variables, we offer the "institutional history" necessary to "prepare ourselves for the future."[212] Those contributing to the discipline of critical university studies commonly argue that we need "institutional histories of scholarly research, of tenure, of academic status, and, perhaps most important, of the ever-changing college curriculum."[213] We agree, and to that list we add one more element, something borrowed from the discipline of writing program administration studies. Institutional histories should account for not only national trends in higher education but also the specific contingencies at particular places. This story about the Saturday Night Massacre at UT Austin models an institutional history that accounts for both the national trends and the institutional peculiarities. This story also demonstrates what happens when writing program administrators fail to account for their national and local context. In this chapter's story, Kinneavy and Sledd aren't craven calculators but romantic crusaders. Their quest for the bygone days of full tenure track employment and inclusive faculty governance failed to account for the national trends in academic labor and precluded compromise with the university's managerial upper administration, contributing to a slaughter of the innocents.

3

The Battle of Texas

The Battle of Texas is the most famous episode in UT Austin's epic march through the 1980s, a culture war fracas that drove three tenured professors out of the English department, wrecked two efforts at university-wide curricular reform, inspired one fated bill in the Texas state legislature, ruined several friendships, and scarred countless careers. It instigated unthinkable episodes, such as one cartoon published in a student-run newspaper. Racist by any standard, titled "The New E 306," featuring a byline that reads "Can't Teach This," and referring to a proposed revision to the first-year writing curriculum, the cartoon depicted a Black figure, an absurdly dressed caricature of a 1980s rapper, dancing in front of the UT Austin tower and holding up signs that say "Rhetoric" and "Composition."[1] These egregious incidents inspired the Texas humorist Molly Ivins to declare, "What a squall, what an uproar, what a mighty brouhaha. Such grandiose posturings and eschatological pronouncements—and all over a plan to change an English course."[2] Confronted with such theatrics, we are tempted to open with the low blows and the high dudgeon. But a race to the drama would distort the episode, simplifying a complicated and multilayered story about academic disagreement, administrative maneuvering, American politics, public argument, and personal attack. At its core, the Battle of Texas is about the politics of diversity that arose from the 1970s rights revolution in higher education, not faculty infighting or the media circus. To avoid any simplified fixation on the most dramatic episodes, we tell the story as it deserves to be retold—in unfolding layers and interacting episodes, beginning with the decision to revamp the E 306 curriculum.

In 1989, thanks largely to the Saturday Night Massacre, the first-year writing course at UT Austin (E 306) was suffering from four years of neglect. The graduate instructors who taught the class were inadequately trained, the program underfunded, and the students dissatisfied. So the faculty committed to a full overhaul.[3] This renovation would prove possible but also challenging because of a fundamental disagreement. Competing within the UT Austin English department were three dominant approaches to first-year writing pedagogy. Justifying all three were two tacitly opposed assumptions about literacy. On one side were current-traditional rhetoric and process pedagogy, which both implicitly suggest that literacy is a decontextualized skill offering academic and professional success. On the other side was neoclassical rhetoric, which explicitly proclaims that literacy is a historically situated practice with both professional and civic applications. These sparring pedagogies and their dueling assumptions were championed by different professors.

Professor James Duban studied literary criticism but loved syntax. He told his students that anyone could master "the sort of writing that they must undertake during the next four years of college—and beyond." His approach to the subject was formal, grammar heavy, and technically minded, aiming to impart "a basic understanding of the mechanics of writing and a systematic approach for editing their work."[4] Both students and administrators thought him a transformative teacher.[5] Nevertheless, as pioneers of process pedagogy, Maxine Hairston and John Ruszkiewicz flatly rejected Duban's current-traditionalism. Instead of lecturing on paragraph coherence, they taught drafting, peer review, and revision.[6] Despite their different pedagogies, Duban would have agreed with Ruszkiewicz and Hairston, for all three assume that writing is a technical skill that can and should be taught without concern for historical context or political agenda. Since good mechanics are the same in all cases and at all times, and the writing process is necessary to address all occasions, writing pedagogy (and the literacy that it aims to impart) should be historically and politically innocent.

Several scholars in the field of composition studies have argued that neither current-traditional rhetoric nor process pedagogy is so anodyne. Current-traditional rhetoric, as mentioned in chapter 1, drafted humanistic instruction into the Cold War by promising to impart the skills necessary in an industrialized economy and teaching students the virtues associated with a liberal democracy. One historian of education explains how this midcentury socioeconomic exigence called forth an instrumental view of literacy, not unlike the one shared among Duban, Ruszkiewicz, and Hairston: "Freshman [sic] English, then, assumed general goals as a capsule liberal education and as an introduction to political and professional discourse. Given these goals, the content of the course—reading and writing—becomes instrumentalized. Reading becomes the means to getting at what is important in substantial subjects; writing becomes the expression of the content one has learned."[7] Beneath this instrumental view of literacy is a larger ideology assuming that good writers should "display an original, honest self, yet at the same time conform to rigid (and usually tacit) notions of the qualities that an original self must display in academic discourse."[8] Duban revived current-traditional rhetoric's explicit formalism while ignoring its implicit politics. He voiced no anxieties about Sputnik, nor did he spout any patriotic paeans. Instead he told his students that they would "acquire a foundation of editing skills necessary for success in other courses . . . and in numerous vocations."[9] His formal instrumentalism did not go unchallenged. Two decades prior, in the 1960s, a generation of compositionists had abandoned both Cold War civic education and current-traditional formalism, ushering in a surge of radically contextualized and playful writing pedagogies, a congeries of possibility that a leading scholar in the field has called the "cultural spirit of the liberation of language."[10] At the 1968 Conference on College Composition and Communication, we can see evidence of the avant-garde composition classroom, but we must also note "the conservative reaction."[11] Process pedagogy was about to end the efflorescence of the 1960s.

Process pedagogy resembled the situated and playful pedagogies blossoming a decade prior because students could choose topics that interested them while practicing the writing process. As one historian of rhetorical pedagogy points out, focusing on the writing process "offered teachers a . . . way to respond to students' insistence on 'relevance' in their courses." Process pedagogy didn't burden instruction with ideology or history. Teachers could focus on skills, which were no longer defined in terms of syntax and form but now described in terms of drafting and revision.[12] They say politics makes strange bedfellows. So do pedagogies. Even though they thought different skills were at the core of literacy and composition, Duban, Hairston, and Ruszkiewicz were brought together by their common dismissal of sociopolitical context and their shared instrumental view of literacy. Their approaches to the writing classroom jibed nicely with the 1980s neoconservative emphasis on "outcome-based education" because both current-traditional and process pedagogies emphasize "what students produced," be it error-free prose or a proper course of peer review and revision.[13] Among the UT Austin rhetoric faculty, Lester Faigley later explained that the country's neoconservative political agenda "initially benefited college composition because it created widespread interest in the teaching of college writing that helped to open up new faculty positions and new sources of funding."[14] In this national political environment, process pedagogy bolstered the writing program and won institutional support for the writing faculty by preserving an instrumental view of literacy.

Nevertheless, not everyone jumped on the process bandwagon. James Kinneavy hid neither his political motivations nor his ideological assumptions. Kinneavy's writing-across-the-curriculum program was explicitly premised on the civic mission of rhetorical education. Echoing the ideological commitments of midcentury higher education, Kinneavy wanted to train citizens who could deliberate in a healthy democracy. E 346K tried to weave vocational literacy into civic training, suggesting that to be good citizens students must also become good professional-class workers. Kinneavy's connection of democratic citizenship and professional ability has a long and troubled history, as chronicled by those attentive to "how language proficiency became connected to other civic habits."[15] Throughout the twentieth century, the equation of democratic citizenship and professional competence excluded many, especially immigrants, nonnative speakers of English, and members of marginalized communities with their own distinct discursive patterns. While disenfranchising a host of people, midcentury English classes "made themselves relevant to the citizenship-building concerns of the time" by promising to teach marketable skills.[16] By promising professional dividends on an academic investment, "university-oriented literacy" spoke to "a burgeoning middle class."[17] James Kinneavy—for better or worse—participated in this equation of instrumental literacy, democratic citizenship, and professional employment.

But in the latter decades of the twentieth century, people began to question the formula in part because this chain of equivalences was exclusionary but also because it was anachronistic. Kinneavy offered civic literacy for the Cold War era, unsuited to a pluralistic democracy or a postindustrial economy. So, from the 1960s onward, many argued that the commonplace assumptions about literacy and citizenship needed to be radically rethought. One well-regarded scholar, for example, contended that writing-across-the-curriculum programs and process pedagogy both contributed to the instrumentalization of discourse, detracting from language's most important civic function, "the shared sense of a 'world.'" This "disappearance of the public vision" led to "mutual incomprehension and distrust." Many called for "a revitalized public discourse, a conversation open to every person, and to every discipline, dialect, and tradition."[18] Already invested in a civically oriented and classically informed rhetorical pedagogy, Kinneavy heeded closely this renaissance of civic literacy. He braided its principal contributions into the 1987 syllabus for E 306. Instructors in every required writing course at UT Austin ruminated on language's "relativistic" and "ideological" character. They taught their students that "the reader is enabled to create meaning by prior knowledge of the conventions governing text formation in a given discourse community." They furthermore explained that language ideologically unites communities by "embodying a shared set of cultural values." Finally, they defined language as "an instrument of political repression and domination." In the 1987 E 306 syllabus, this critical approach to literacy was explicitly tied to a "developing [scholarly] interest in the social context of writing."[19]

Following a cutting-edge trend among compositionists and literacy specialists, UT Austin writing teachers envisioned the university as a community held together by a peculiar set of reading and writing habits. They tried to help students form "transition groups," collaborative networks of shared support and encouragement, to enable everyone to "reacculturate themselves by working together."[20] They encouraged multiplicity, treating it as a resource that might help students traverse the "zone of proximal development" between their many home languages and a privileged academic discourse.[21] They also worried that the transition into the academic discourse community was politically fraught. Reading the scholarly literature cited in the 1987 syllabus, new writing teachers at UT Austin learned about discourse communities and realized that any discourse community can become "a way of regulating who has access to resources, power, even to discourse itself."[22] They acknowledged the plurality within every community and the potential for community reformation.[23]

Just as Kinneavy thought classical rhetoric could offer critical tools for interrogating every discourse community by empowering without indoctrinating, some scholars in the field of composition studies argued that "the academic community's importance to our culture lies in its ability to be a community with a relatively high tolerance for frequent debate over what the community knows."[24] But others wondered how one privileged notion of academic discourse can suit the "storm of rights-based, identity-group introspection and political action" that gave birth to "the current-day idea of diversity."[25] Many composition teachers therefore abandoned Kinneavy's monological rhetorical pedagogy and its assumption that "students should necessarily be working towards the mastery of some particular, well-defined sort of discourse." They decided instead to encourage "a kind of polyphony—an awareness of and pleasure in the various competing discourses that make up their own" languages.[26] They celebrated the habits conforming to academic literacy and the abilities deriving from students' home languages, seeing "not two coherent and competing discourses but many overlapping and conflicting ones."[27] Once they fully acknowledged the relative and ideological qualities of language, all of these scholars jeered at the assumptions implicit in Duban's current-traditional and Hairston's process pedagogies. They also rejected the singular commitment to academic discourse exhibited by Kinneavy's rhetorical pedagogy. Instead of a guiltless exploration of grammatical forms or writing processes or a uniform examination of argumentation and style, they wanted their writing classes to be "public space[s] or zone[s] of contact."[28] In line with the rights revolution that shook American politics and changed university landscapes, the scholarly conversation about writing instruction was trending toward "post-process" pedagogy, a loose agglomeration held together by a few assumptions: "The writing act is public, thoroughly hermeneutic, and always situated and therefore cannot be reduced to a generalizable process."[29] The 1987 E 306 syllabus, heard as one contribution to a scholarly conversation about writing instruction, reveals that Kinneavy was trying to revive rhetoric's civic mission without resuscitating Cold War prejudices. To pull this off, he needed a partner, someone younger and more in line with the scholarly turn toward diversity politics.

In the summer of 1983 at a seminar hosted by the University of Pennsylvania, James Kinneavy befriended Linda Brodkey.[30] Five years after their initial encounter, he wrote to the chair of the UT Austin English department, recommending Brodkey for a position at the rank of associate professor with tenure. He described her first book as "a superb example of a sociology of writing."[31] That monograph contributed to the relatively new subdiscipline of literacy studies, which builds on qualitative sociological analyses of how people learn language habits (including reading and writing practices). Early work in literacy studies employed rigorous ethnographies and sophisticated sociolinguistics to study multiple communities and their "literacy events." When writing specialists first took up literacy studies, they added the insights of process researchers. They tried to marry process pedagogy's "cognitive" view of literacy to the "social" explanations favored by sociologists.[32] But shortly after its beginning, literacy studies veered away from cognitivist approaches and toward contextualized views. Looking at the "situated nature of literacy" allowed scholars to see "the ideological dimensions ... the politics by which reading and writing preferences of elite groups get installed as the measure against which other versions are deemed inadequate or undesirable."[33] A committed participant to the discipline of this emerging subdiscipline, Linda Brodkey saw literacy as neither a technical skill nor a decontextualized capacity. For Brodkey and her like-minded intellectual community, literacy was a set of communally situated practices, ideologically and politically freighted, empowering some while excluding others.

Brodkey's intellectual dedication to literacy studies complemented her political commitment to defining college education as a right. Like those advocating for women's studies and ethnic studies programs because they think the traditional Western curriculum excludes women and people of color from higher education, Brodkey saw current-traditional and process pedagogies as a hindrance to underrepresented students.[34] She also questioned the Cold War association between democratic citizenship and professional literacy, the same association underpinning James Kinneavy's rhetorical approach to writing instruction. Brodkey wanted to liberate her students from the "middle-class illusions of meritocracy." She endeavored to teach them that "freedom is only meaningful if the citizenry is literate. Not just functionally literate. Literate. Not just fluent. Literate. Literacy is not just skills, nor is it abilities. Literacy is an attitude, entitlement, the entitlement that middle-class privilege masks in prescriptions but that writing lays bare in the sheer force of the desire to see and to get readers to see what can be seen from where the writer stands."[35] Brodkey's rights-based perspective implicitly challenges any instrumentalist pedagogy that "surreptitiously calibrates all writing to middle-class notions of literacy, and then installs a middle-class version of fluency as the *exclusive* standard."[36] She believed that if students were taught any kind of "prescriptivism" or given any formal instruction in grammar, any lock-step march through the writing process, any uniform approach to argumentation, the result would be "devastating and pernicious."[37] In the spring of 1990 when she was appointed to chair the Lower Division English Policy Committee at UT Austin, Brodkey brought this rights-based perspective to E 306. Like others in her field, she wanted to "make the idea of difference, its meaning and implications, a theme for extended discussion."[38] Borrowing from contemporary scholars at other universities, she hoped for "a dialogic pedagogy that recognizes individuals as real players in the social game, conscious agents who are never altogether powerless, unaware, or passive in their relations with others."[39] She acknowledged the plurality of discourse, experimenting with language and interrogating the power relations established when any literacy is privileged as the "norm" or the "ideal."[40] She titled her new, rights-based syllabus for E 306 "Writing about Difference."

One hundred and seventy-two pages long, the "Writing about Difference" syllabus features sample readings by contemporaneous argumentative theorists. Also included are sociological articles about race, class, gender, and disability. Additionally, the "Writing about Difference" course packet showcases Supreme Court cases such as *Sweatt v. Painter*, a famous allegation of discriminatory admissions policies at the University of Texas Law School. Most important, the packet includes assignment prompts for an ambitious amount of student writing. Ten short writing assignments ask students to summarize key arguments and define important terms. Building on these short papers, six substantive writing prompts ask students to hone both their analytical and their argumentative skills. Students had to analyze the main reasons, the evidence, and the assumptions that support an academic article or a court decision; then they had to review, evaluate, and apply the arguments found in an academic article; finally, they would research, define, and critique a widespread stereotype. Each of the essay assignments builds on the work required by at least one of the ten short writing assignments. All this writing and reading rockets toward the same end. Brodkey wanted students "to conduct civil discussions in class as well as identify and explore argumentative possibilities in the works they read and write."[41] "Writing about Difference" is built on Brodkey's assumption that critical content is an integral part of literacy instruction. Because this robust curriculum suited the political exigencies of its era and echoed the scholarly conversation in Brodkey's field, when the "Writing about Difference" course packet finally went up for final departmental approval in the fall of 1990, the English faculty voted overwhelmingly in its favor, 46–11.[42]

According to present-day scholarly evaluations, "Writing about Difference" itself is a public pedagogy. Tyler Branson, for instance, contends that Brodkey's syllabus "disrupted dominant public perceptions of writing and writing instruction."[43] Irvin Peckham describes Brodkey's approach to critical literacy as a "social strand of critical thinking . . . a dialectic between thinking and acting, the self and the world."[44] Brodkey's syllabus effectively disrupted the instrumentalist consensus that informed process and current-traditional pedagogy. Her syllabus also challenged Kinneavy's uniform approach to argumentation and his equation of democratic eloquence and vocational acumen. But Brodkey wasn't the only person and literacy studies wasn't the only discipline challenging the midcentury intellectual agreement on topics such as education, history, politics, and culture. This Cold War consensus was steadily crumbling. Commenting on a number of 1980s intellectual disputes, the historian Daniel Rodgers explains that "in political and institutional fact and in social imagination, the 1930s, 1940s, and 1950s had been an era of consolidation. In the last quarter of the century, the dominant tendency of the age was toward disaggregation."[45] If historians in the 1980s couldn't agree about the nature of progress, literature professors in the same era couldn't agree about the Western canon, and economists at the same time couldn't agree about the value of macroeconomics, why should we expect writing specialists to agree about the nature of literacy?

Before anyone contested her vision, administrative initiatives and campus incidents emboldened Brodkey. The College of Liberal Arts had a new dean. Standish Meacham was good friends with Robert King, but they were an odd couple. King came from humble origins in the Deep South. Meacham was born to money and privilege in the Northeast. King earned his PhD from the University of Wisconsin. Meacham went to Yale. King was a linguist, Meacham a historian. King was conservative, Meacham liberal. While King saw himself as a problem-solver, Meacham imagined himself as a visionary. Newly risen to a high perch in the university administration, surveying the distant horizon, Meacham saw disquieting clouds. UT Austin was homogeneous in faculty and curricula, yet the student body was increasingly diverse. Contemporaneous proponents of multiculturalism in higher education were noticing that US immigration policy in the 1970s had brought in a wave of Latin and Asian denizens, all hungry for opportunity, many looking to higher education for their chance at the American dream.[46] A predominantly white faculty and an overwhelming Western curriculum could never connect with Chinese, Mexican, Guatemalan, or Filipino students. So, Meacham promoted diversity hiring among the faculty and "multicultural" offerings in the course catalog. His curricular initiative echoed a national trend. By the early 1990s, nearly half of all colleges and universities had added a multiculturalism course to their general education requirements. Most famous among such efforts is the "Michigan Mandate" (1990), issued by the flagship university's president, James Duderstadt.[47] Equally celebrated, though not as successful, was Stanford University's 1988 replacement of a core course in "Western Culture" with a class that introduced a range of cultures, identities, and traditions. Meacham appointed a faculty committee to identify existing possibilities and develop multicultural courses. He also encouraged students to take one such multicultural class instead of a standing requirement in American history and government.[48] It would take years to get Meacham's multiculturalism requirement through the requisite faculty committees. So, while making the long march toward structural reform, Meacham spied the terrain for other opportunities. That's when the new English department chair and the newly appointed director of first-year writing knocked on his door.

Linda Brodkey suggested that E 306—the only universally required course on campus—could bring multiculturalism to the masses. The new version of E 306 would feature a recent book, *Racism and Sexism: An Integrated Study* (1987) by Paula Rothenberg and others. Brodkey believed that "the new E 306 curriculum will require, at least in the first couple of years, a standardized curriculum, which I've agreed to write this summer." James Kinneavy had promised to help.[49] Dean Meacham was reluctant at first, thinking that the idea was "ill-conceived and without much merit."[50] But he agreed, nonetheless. Inside Parlin Hall the English faculty calmly considered Brodkey's proposal. Outside the building's limestone walls, on and around campus, racial animus flared. Two UT Austin fraternities had been caught selling T-shirts emblazoned with racist images. To make matters worse, these same fraternities had spray-painted racist epithets on cars in the area. Anti-racist protests erupted around campus. The April 1990 incidents inclined Dean Meacham and the other English professors toward Brodkey's idea.[51] They needed an "inclusion bureaucracy," a set of reforms that could channel student demands through institutional programs capable of diffusing the most radical proposals.[52]

And so in the spring of 1990, nine English professors slumped lazily around a conference table in room 202 of Parlin Hall to discuss Brodkey's proposal for a multicultural curriculum in E 306. They didn't have much to go on—just a one-page memo and a book recommendation. Brodkey called the meeting to order at 1:00 p.m. sharp. Her overflowing enthusiasm cut through the circumstantial tedium. She gushed about her curricular vision. E 306 would focus on Supreme Court cases tried under Title VII of the Civil Rights Act (1964). Students would read judgments and dissenting opinions that dealt with discrimination on the basis of race, religion, ethnicity, sex, age, and disability. They would write "exploratory" papers, an anchor point in Kinneavy's rhetorical theory.[53] But the committee wasn't interested in any of that. Instead, they briefly deliberated the Rothenberg book.[54] Then they endorsed Brodkey's idea and her proposed text. One member of the English department's Lower Division English Policy Committee, James Duban, had missed the April 3 meeting and subsequently wrote a calm letter of dissent to the other members. He assured everyone that he valued the "cordial tone of their discussion" and wanted "more discussion" about a matter that would affect many teachers and even more students. He worried about the Rothenberg book and suggested an alternative. John Ruszkiewicz, another committee member who had been absent, wrote his own letter expressing similar reservations. He agonized about the administrative process and the Rothenberg book: Since E 306 was a required course, its revision should be handled methodically and by committee; since E 306 was taught by a variety of instructors, it should allow a variety of content, never forcing an inexperienced teacher to handle controversial issues; since the Rothenberg book was not "balanced," the committee should consider other anthologies on the same topic. Ruszkiewicz suggested that instead of uniformly assigning the same text, graduate instructors might choose from a list.[55]

When the Lower Division English Policy Committee reconvened one week later, Brodkey gave Ruszkiewicz the floor. He began by stating that he did not object to an elective multicultural writing course. He did, however, worry about a required multicultural curriculum. He mainly objected to the critical approach to literacy instruction that Brodkey's curriculum implied. The main subject of E 306, he argued, must be writing and argumentation, as stipulated by the university-approved course catalog. He worried that the Supreme Court cases—requiring substantial background knowledge—might distract from basic writing instruction. Ruszkiewicz's objections reveal the core distinction between his process pedagogy and Brodkey's critical literacy. He saw literacy as a skill that should be taught absent social and political context. He worried that extraneous content would interrupt skill acquisition. In sum, if literacy is defined in instrumental terms, then a course dedicated to Supreme Court cases about discrimination is not a writing class. It's a sociology or a legal studies class. The committee discussed Ruszkiewicz's objections and then adjourned.[56] Three days later, an award-winning teacher in the English department publicly endorsed Meacham's multiculturalism initiative.[57] A few days after that, the University Faculty Senate approved Meacham's recommendation for a multicultural requirement in the core curriculum.[58]

When Ruszkiewicz recommended that they pilot Brodkey's proposed course in a few summer sessions, he was offering a way for process pedagogy to coexist alongside critical literacy. The consensus about literacy may be fractured, but that disagreement didn't have to result in immediate civil war. With a departmental majority in her pocket, a sympathetic dean in her corner, and popular sentiment on her side, Brodkey decided against all compromise.[59] The Rothenberg book would stand along with the standardized curriculum. She scheduled another Lower Division English Policy Committee meeting and hammered out a memo defending her position: "Writing about Difference" would meet the requirements stipulated by the course catalog; piloting the curriculum would not reveal anything about the learning outcomes; *Racism and Sexism* was not a biased anthology but a critical text. Ruszkiewicz hastily scrawled comments in the margins of her memo: "Note, focus is not on writing" and "Still a topics course."[60] On April 17, when the committee met for the third time in as many weeks, the air was electric. Ruszkiewicz charged in, making four motions: (1) The "Writing about Difference" syllabus should be developed as planned but piloted in select sections of E 306 during the 1990–91 academic year; (2) the course syllabus should allow for multiple approaches to writing instruction; (3) the instructors should be able to use the 1987 E 306 syllabus and course packet if they did not want to teach the new "Writing about Difference" curriculum; and (4) the committee should rescind their endorsement of *Racism and Sexism*.[61] Every motion was discussed and then voted down, 4–2, with Ruszkiewicz and Duban dissenting.[62]

Hairston shared the dissenters' reservations, which she communicated directly to Dean Meacham. She emphasized the pedagogical question at the heart of the E 306 debate: "What kind of required writing course will best prepare freshmen [sic] to enter into the academic life of this university?" She repeated Ruszkiewicz's worry that a heavy addition of politicized content would hamper writing instruction by intimidating students: "Because of their fear of grades, freshmen [sic] are usually reluctant to express their opinions," especially on controversial issues. How could they practice the writing process if they were afraid of writing at all? She cautioned that the graduate instructors didn't know enough about the law or sociology to responsibly teach Supreme Court cases. Hairston assured Meacham that she was on his side: "The University should be moving quickly and firmly towards promoting cultural diversity throughout the entire curriculum." But E 306 was not the answer. To be a good writing class, E 306 had to remain "a course that encourages students to explore ideas freely through writing in an open classroom," a place where students could become "independent thinkers and confident writers."[63] In order to acquire instrumental literacy, students could not be distracted or cowed by extraneous content.

Hairston, Duban, and Ruszkiewicz voiced their concerns internally to the department and to the dean. Meanwhile, rumor of a politically subversive writing course had spread around campus. Deans in the colleges of engineering and natural science and the business school were appalled. In response, they began planning their own first-year writing programs where instructors would not have to follow Brodkey's syllabus or use Rothenberg's book.[64] Within the College of Liberal Arts, several departments were similarly aghast.

Faculty in the psychology department, led by Joseph Horn, an associate dean of liberal arts, complained that the Rothenberg book was "one-sided, egregiously propagandistic, and lacking in scholarliness and objectivity." They worried that such a "biased" text could only exacerbate racial strife.[65] Many English professors brushed such concerns aside. Several volunteered to teach the new syllabus—a remarkable show of support, given that E 306 was taught almost exclusively by graduate instructors.[66] In late May, Brodkey asked the university bookstore to stock eight hundred copies of Rothenberg's *Racism and Sexism*.[67] Come late June, she had to cancel the order. The extradepartmental controversy had inflamed the intradepartmental disagreement.

In late July 1990, the upper administration pressured Dean Meacham, and Meacham pressured the chair of the English department. "Writing about Difference" would be delayed until the 1991–92 academic year. Meacham assured the English faculty that he would "continue to support strongly . . . the concept of English 306 as a rhetoric and writing course with a unified curriculum centered on the themes of diversity and difference." Nevertheless, they needed to "address concerns and misunderstandings about the course, expressed within the University community."[68] Meacham hoped for calm deliberation among the faculty. Instead, he got complaints from outside and conflict from within. The press had begun following the intradepartmental dispute. President William Cunningham was receiving letters from students, faculty, and influential donors, all wanting to weigh in on Brodkey's syllabus. Dean Meacham organized a special meeting of the Liberal Arts Advisory Council. For a day and a half, the main topic of discussion was E 306 "Writing about Difference." Meacham was always skeptical about the curriculum, and Cunningham was leery of its premise. In early July, they considered piloting a few sections with the new syllabus, but by month's end, all this unwanted attention had forced their hand. Cunningham pressured Meacham into delaying implementation of Brodkey's plan. Thereafter, Cunningham would broker no further compromise.[69] This wasn't a postponement. It was a pocket veto.

The English department faculty, as yet unaware of how recalcitrant President Cunningham had become, tried to salvage the curriculum. First, they voted to support the uniform implementation of "Writing about Difference" in every E 306 classroom. Then they appointed a subcommittee to revise Brodkey's work. But the upper administration was so chary of "radical indoctrination" that they wouldn't green-light anything remotely resembling the original syllabus. In February 1991, after repeatedly having their work rejected by upper administrators, all seven of the faculty appointed to revise

Brodkey's work resigned in protest.[70] Ruszkiewicz suggested new guidelines for the E 306 curriculum.[71] In March, the English department chair threw in the towel, asking James Kinneavy to produce an E 306 syllabus that the upper administration would tolerate. The English faculty met in early May 1990 to deliberate Kinneavy's suggestions.[72] He had assembled a grab bag of pedagogical options and curricular suggestions. Instructors who wanted to focus on the writing process could do so. Instructors who preferred to emphasize argumentation or grammar could have their fill of it. Instructors anxious to bring critical literacy into the classroom could scratch that itch. Kinneavy admitted that this capacious curriculum tolerated his "traditional" approach to classical rhetoric, letting students pick their topics and focusing on the argumentative modes of discourse.[73] Hairston remarked that Kinneavy's syllabus "gives the student and the teacher lots of choice in what they want to teach." The readings, Kinneavy confirmed, covered a "wide range of topics."[74] The faculty, Brodkey included, voted to approve, 36–0.

In January 1991, for reasons unrelated to Brodkey's fated syllabus, Dean Meacham resigned. In February, a Democratic Texas state legislator who feared that Meacham's absence would jeopardize the push toward a multicultural curricular requirement filed a bill requiring all students at publicly funded colleges and universities to complete a course on racism and sexism.[75] The bill, like Brodkey's curriculum, never made it out of committee. Later that spring when Meacham's multicultural requirement came up for a vote before the general faculty assembly, President Cunningham manipulated the process, putting the matter to a silent, mail-in ballot.[76] Under the cover of anonymity, the general faculty voted against Meacham's multicultural addition to the core curriculum. From an outsider's perspective, it looked like an internal, academic disagreement about the nature of literacy had spiraled outward into the wider university. But the UT Austin faculty saw things a bit differently. They didn't blame the campus controversy. They blamed the media. Ruszkiewicz said reporters had misrepresented the departmental disagreement. Kinneavy thought the pundits failed to offer any productive solutions. One of the professors contributing to the development of E 306 "Writing about Difference" alleged that his colleagues used the newspapers to fight a proxy war.[77] Brodkey echoed these sentiments, saying that conservatives "control the story." She was shocked by how "uncritically the media fell for it."[78] And she was right. The internal, intellectual disagreement about literacy had morphed into a public controversy about politics. Were it not for this public controversy, Cunningham may have remained open to the curriculum. Meacham may have continued to support its implementation. When public complaints advanced, the upper administration retreated. But the UT Austin English faculty were not entirely innocent victims of media misrepresentation. They played a precipitating role in their tragic plot when they decided to go public about their dispute.

James Kinneavy was born too late. When talking about rhetorical education, he often invoked what the sociologist Michael Schudson calls "democracy writ small," the practice of deliberation in communal assemblies and local media, a Progressive era ideal developed in the first decades of the twentieth century and reaching its apotheosis between the two World Wars.[79] Kinneavy said that literacy "has to be concerned with the polis, has, in some sense, to be political."[80] In the 1960s and '70s, the rights revolution had inaugurated a new style of politics, which Schudson associates with the Civil Rights Movement, a politics characterized not by deliberation but by litigation, protest, assertion of individual right, and appeal to an outside power.[81] These tactics and the associated style of politics characterize the faculty's extradepartmental actions during the Battle of Texas. Rather than talking to one another at key moments, they decided to "go public" with their arguments about literacy.[82] All of them—left, right, center, process pedagogues, current-traditionalists, and critical literacy advocates—turned to their professional societies and political interest groups. In the fall of 1990, for instance, English faculty who favored Brodkey's syllabus petitioned the American Association of University Professors and the Modern Language Association, arguing that the guarantee of academic freedom should prevent outside organizations and administrators from interfering in curriculum development. Those who opposed "Writing about Difference" similarly looked for outside support, like an associate professor of American literature who petitioned the University Faculty Senate and the University Council to examine and vote on the completed course packet.[83] When these intra-institutional appeals fell on deaf ears, he turned to an outside political organization, the Liberal Arts Foundation Council, telling them that the "English department should be placed in receivership indefinitely."[84] Serving as a senior administrator in the College of Liberal Arts, Joseph Horn appealed to his fledgling and partisan professional association, the National Association of Scholars (established in 1987).

The most alarming instance of a faculty member pleading for outside support happened toward the end of the Battle of Texas when John Ruszkiewicz began to correspond with Lynne Cheney, conservative firebrand and chair of the National Endowment for the Humanities (1986–93).[85] Thereafter, in her diatribes against tenured radicals, Cheney cited information that Ruszkiewicz provided. In *Telling the Truth* (1992), a famous assault on the humanities in higher education, she cites Ruszkiewicz's evidence, and in their correspondence she personally thanks him for his assistance.[86] This wasn't Ruszkiewicz's first appeal for outside support during a departmental controversy. After the Saturday Night Massacre, he wrote to Ted Koppel, a UT graduate and the anchorman of a popular television news program, *Nightline*. Ruszkiewicz told Koppel that UT Austin's "large-scale dismissal of non-tenured faculty underscores a national problem with instruction in writing." He enclosed several articles about the controversy, suggesting these clippings might give Koppel additional "insight" into "the political dimensions of America's literacy crisis."[87] When reaching out to both Koppel and Cheney, Ruszkiewicz was hoping to inspire outside agitation that would pressure the university into a change of policy. In the summer of 1990, long before anyone contacted Cheney, those favoring "Writing about Difference" went public in the exact same way.

Fearing a popular backlash and preempting administrative reaction, Linda Brodkey decided to submit press releases to local and national newspapers. The department chair joined her in this effort. The *Austin American-Statesman* published articles in late May and early June 1990, the first casting Brodkey's curricular innovation in a positive light and the second praising her efforts as "progress" that might help to "eradicate the racial and cultural tensions on campus."[88] The *Daily Texan* contributed an equally glowing front-page article, followed by an opinion column, exalting Brodkey to the high heavens and congratulating her for "bringing the ivory tower back to the streets."[89] Shortly thereafter, the *New York Times* published a favorable article that described Brodkey's plan and ended with reservations expressed by the dissenting faculty. These reservations emphasize a line of argument that had been present but largely latent in the intradepartmental debate about literacy. Instead of explaining that the addition of critical content might detract from practical writing instruction, Brodkey's critics worried that a mandated and uniform syllabus emphasizing civil rights cases might impinge on instructors' academic freedom.[90] Thereafter, the faculty's public arguments about E 306 privileged political concerns about academic freedom over academic debates about literacy. Those who favored "Writing about Difference" insisted that professors had a right to teach whatever they wanted, while detractors rejoined that graduate instructors and E 306 students had a right to instruction and education free from any ideological agenda. Looking closely at the faculty's arguments in the UT Austin student newspaper, we can see how these rights-based appeals competed with and eventually overtook the arguments about literacy and pedagogy.

In his only substantive contribution to the public controversy about E 306, James Duban defended instrumental literacy while voicing his concerns about academic freedom. In an opinion piece for the *Daily Texan* published in August 1990, he described the instrumental literacy taught in his classes: "My 17 years as a teacher of writing lead me to conclude that the teaching of basic writing skills is the only legitimate subject matter for a freshman-level [sic] writing class."[91] This article was reprinted in the *Austin American-Statesman* a few weeks later.[92] Duban principally worried that "excessive focus on expressly social, political and legal topics can interfere with the teaching of basic writing skills."[93] Ruszkiewicz followed with his own *Daily Texan* article, similarly defending instrumental literacy. But, instead of Duban's "intensive" instruction in grammatical style and argumentative form, Ruszkiewicz wanted the writing class to focus on the "processes of composing that make . . . [students] competent to handle the rhetoric of various academic assignments." He believed that an experienced professor could balance the writing process and the critical content, but an inexperienced graduate student would likely flounder. E 306 was taught by inexperienced graduate students, who would not balance the time requisite for political topics with the attention needed for the writing process. Toward the end of his editorial, Ruszkiewicz added concerns about students' right to academic freedom: "I think students are less likely to write significant and challenging pieces when they find themselves constrained by a subject matter that seems to hide a political agenda."[94] A couple of UT Austin English professors, appreciating Ruszkiewicz's reasoned pedagogical argument, slipped handwritten letters of support in his faculty mailbox; one said that Ruszkiewicz's *Daily Texan* editorial was "the best thing that has been written on the E 306 mess."[95] Another complimented his studious attention to writing pedagogy, the "care in constructing an analysis sentence by sentence."[96] Though neither of these supporters mentioned Ruszkiewicz's appeal to students' academic freedom, Duban noticed and repeated it: "At stake is academic freedom for students and teachers."[97] Duban and Ruszkiewicz agreed that if "Writing about Difference" were to be mandated, students and graduate instructors who disagreed with its "political agenda" would have to suffer the curriculum.

Linda Brodkey and her collaborator on the E 306 curriculum, John Slatin, published two articles in the *Daily Texan*, systematically refuting the pedagogical and the political arguments made by Ruszkiewicz and Duban. They dedicated the first article to the political claim that their syllabus violated students' and instructors' right to academic freedom. If anything, they argued, students and instructors would be liberated by their newly honed critical literacy, for "people who cannot tell the difference between what they believe and what someone else believes are ripe for indoctrination." The new curriculum, they contended, would enable truly free and critical inquiry, "guiding students to discover that *every* position is subject to critique."[98] In their second article, Brodkey and Slatin systematically addressed the pedagogical argument, explaining that critical content would improve, not preclude, writing instruction: "An emphasis on content is not inconsistent with the previous emphasis on the writing process.... The [new] syllabus strengthens the commitment to teaching the writing process by linking those processes more closely to content."[99] They meticulously listed the writing assignments that students would have to complete, demonstrating that the writing process would be taught alongside formal argumentation and critical analysis. They concluded their second article by returning to the political question, alleging that Duban and Ruszkiewicz were smuggling in "*their* political views" under the guise of an ostensibly "neutral," instrumental literacy. If Duban and Ruszkiewicz were sneaky ideologues, then Brodkey and Slatin were the honest defenders of students' intellectual liberty. Their curriculum would not violate anyone's academic freedom because no one would be required to argue one side of any issue: "There is nothing in the syllabus to require that either instructor or student adopt a particular point of view or a specific stance."[100]

Maxine Hairston publicly supported Meacham's curricular reforms, wanting the university to mandate two multicultural courses rather than the one suggested by the University Faculty Senate.[101] But she also worried that politicized content would jeopardize students' exposure to and practice with the writing process. As the basis of a now-famous *Chronicle of Higher Education* article, Hairston offered a choice: teach instrumental literacy through the writing process, or teach politics by exposing students to heady content. To her fellow writing teachers, she pleaded, "We are not missionaries; we're educators."[102] The following year, she defended her position in a scholarly article published in a prestigious academic journal, *College Composition and Communication*. She repeated the (arguably false) dilemma: "We must teach ... [first-year writing] for the students' benefit, not in the service of politics or anything else."[103] Unlike Ruszkiewicz and Duban, Hairston focused on the pedagogical argument in her public writings. But in her private correspondence, she voiced a political anxiety about students' academic freedom. Responding to the *Chronicle of Higher Education* article, one instructor at Northern Arizona University challenged Hairston's dilemma, saying that discussing political content facilitated her ability to teach writing, for "writing about social and political issues ... has given a place for students to voice concerns." Echoing Brodkey, Hairston's correspondent explained that her students were liberated, not indoctrinated, by critical literacy. Hairston cordially replied that she was not opposed to students writing about politics. Instead, she believed that "topics such as racism and sexism should [not] be *mandated* in such courses; students should not be *forced* to write about them. . . . If they *choose* to write about such topics, fine."[104] When her pedagogical argument faltered, Hairston resorted to the political claim.

There is good reason to believe that the faculty had to go public to defend their curricular ideals. Culture war battles over higher education demand response because, as Ryan Skinnell points out, academics "consign ourselves to mere spectatorship in national and regional ... struggles over what counts as literacy," if we confine ourselves to departmental deliberations.[105] There is also good reason to insist that the public argument about E 306 required Hairston, Brodkey, Slatin, Ruszkiewicz, and Duban to pair their pedagogical arguments about literacy with political arguments about academic freedom. Virginia Anderson, also examining the public controversy over E 306, explains that the arguments about pedagogy failed to persuade the public because they appealed to "insiders" who were themselves aware of literacy studies, rather than to "outsiders" who worried about professorial indoctrination and authoritarian censorship.[106] Finally, there is every reason to believe that the faculty's appeals to academic freedom carried substantial risk because their rights-based arguments invited other rhetorical devices that proved far more volatile, igniting what Tyler Branson has called a "moral panic" over E 306 "Writing about Difference."[107] Three other rhetorical moves consistent with the politics of appeal fomented public outrage. These are the arguments about victimhood, viewpoint diversity, and the appeal to identity, which soon overwhelmed the deliberation of pedagogy. When Brodkey, Slatin, Duban, Ruszkiewicz, and Hairston went public, they made arguments about academic freedom and writing pedagogy. When others publicly debated "Writing about Difference," they focused on the appeal to rights, altogether abandoning the discussion of literacy.

In 1991, Evan Carton was a tenured professor of American literature at UT Austin deeply invested in both nineteenth-century romanticism and twentieth-century politics. During that same year, Dinesh D'Souza, having finished a brief stint as a policy adviser to President Reagan (1987–88), returned to his career as a conservative journalist and published his first book, *Illiberal*

Education. D'Souza believed that the culture war raging on American college campuses was really a "victim's revolution." In the name of "diversity, tolerance, multiculturalism, [and] pluralism," campus protesters became oppressors when claiming that their status as victims warranted their abuse of others.[108] Or so D'Souza maintained. Carton saw things differently. He published a rejoinder in *Tikkun* magazine claiming that those complaining about "'The Victims' Revolution,' 'Thought Police,' or 'the P.C. Front'" were not really engaging "the distinct issues raised by professors whose progressive or radical political commitments openly inform their teaching." Instead, wrote Carton, conservative detractors were trying to "conflate all such activism and to reduce it to a generalized principle of subversion that may be rhetorically saturation-bombed."[109] Not long after their tussle in the print media, on October 28, 1991, Carton and D'Souza debated on the stage of Southwestern University in Georgetown, Texas.

If he had been present a year earlier on July 28, 1990, when fifty students gathered in the sweltering Texas heat to support Brodkey's E 306 curriculum, D'Souza likely would have said that these protestors, though claiming to act "on behalf of minority victims," were really victimizing Brodkey's critics.[110] Many of the speeches made that morning in the shadow of the UT Austin tower would have caught D'Souza's attention. A member of the student organization Todos Unidos said that President Cunningham's recent decision to exclude students from a multiculturalism workshop was "as racist as any slur." Alerting the crowd to the "academic death squads on our campus," a UT Austin professor of ethnic literature said the administration's suppression of Brodkey's syllabus violated English professors' academic freedom. Undoubtedly, both of these speakers presented themselves as victims. But Carton didn't. Instead, he noticed that students were already affected by the politics of race and class, already members of the university community, already wanting to debate the issues relevant to their lived experience: "The new 306 would have been—and I hope will still be—a politicization of the entering freshmen [*sic*] and their curriculum," engaging students "immediately in their first year, in the polis."[111] Carton was repeating a point that Brodkey had made to the English faculty when she declared, "If students don't begin exploring racism and sexism in college classrooms, then I can't imagine where else in this country anyone is likely to learn how to broach these complex and critical issues."[112] Neither Carton nor Brodkey postured as victims. Instead, they celebrated literacy defined in broad civic terms.

But this appeal to civic literacy, redefined for the rights revolution in American politics, drowned in the rhetoric of victimhood, an argumentative tactic that Carton identified when comparing the conservative assault on multiculturalism to the simultaneous American military operations in Kuwait: "Free speech . . . is the great shibboleth of Operation Campus Storm." And Carton was onto something, for those who most readily donned the mantle of "free speech" also vociferously complained that "multiculturalism . . . deprives the white majority" of this essential right.[113] D'Souza and his political ilk said the advocates of multiculturalism threatened free speech by overperforming their victimhood in order to collect undeserved rewards and tyrannize their imagined oppressors. The real victims, according to D'Souza's "antivictimist" argument, were those who suffered from the multiculturalists' slings and arrows, the "victims of victimism," good traditionalists silenced by multiculturalists, upstanding citizens cowed by protestors, decent faculty calumniated by those who gathered in late July 1990 to advocate "Writing about Difference."[114] D'Souza believed that a few student-run newspapers were waging a righteous campaign against those who threatened free speech with their victimist vitriol. But by his lights, most student journalism in the late 1980s toed the multiculturalist line, endeavoring to silence all dissent by wantonly accusing the dissenters of oppression. To be sure, D'Souza's antivictimist crusade responded to arguments about conservative censorship and its multiculturalist victims, but D'Souza's crusaders were no ornery band taking on a tyrannous army. Rather, on the UT Austin campus, the (liberal) multiculturalists were scrappy and underfunded, while the (conservative) antivictimists were legion and loud.

Scott Henson was an undergraduate and a *Daily Texan* columnist. So was with his friend, roommate, and collaborator, Tom Philpott Jr., the son and namesake of a firebrand UT Austin history professor. Henson had grown bored with his economics major and even more bored by the student newspaper's formulaic content. He and Philpott were inspired by people like Dinesh D'Souza, Jonathan Karl, and Laura Ingraham, pundits who launched their careers by assaulting the academy or winning internships at conservative think tanks. Henson and Philpott wanted to do the same, but with a liberal slant. They ditched the *Daily Texan*, learned investigative tactics, and founded the *Polemicist*, which they published out of their apartment, funded by advertising revenues and keg parties. At its peak the freely distributed *Polemicist* circulated an astounding ten thousand copies per issue.[115] Its white-hot prose traveled all the way to San Francisco, where a UT Austin alumnus and former E 306 instructor read about those supporting "plurality" and those opposing "ideology" in the E 306 classroom.[116]

The high point of his maverick journalistic adventure might have occurred on September 17, 1990, when Henson attended a meeting of the University Council. Once given the floor, he grilled President Cunningham about the delayed implementation of Brodkey's "Writing about Difference" syllabus. Henson knew that wealthy donors had pressured the university administration into delaying Brodkey's curriculum. Here was victimhood, plain as day, a professor censored by political interests and dark money. Annoyed but still poised, Cunningham laid the decision to cancel E 306 squarely at the feet of Dean Meacham.[117] Shortly after Henson's cross-examination, the *Polemicist* went to press, dedicating much of their next issue to the E 306 controversy. In three separate articles, they told a lurid tale: conservative legions had besieged, sacked, and burned Brodkey's curriculum. She was the victim of a rabid "smear campaign."[118]

The day before Henson grilled Cunningham in front of the University Council, one conservative columnist pilloried "Writing about Difference" in the pages of the *Washington Post*.[119] Shortly thereafter, the *Daily Texan* inveighed against the E 306 revision.[120] Henson wanted to champion the underdog, to "let Linda Brodkey say her piece." He admired her curriculum, though he didn't quite grasp her critical approach to literacy. Instead, he thought the Supreme Court cases would be "more relevant to a freshman [sic] English" student.[121] Though they wanted to support Brodkey, Henson and Philpott saved most of their artillery for Alan Gribben, an associate professor of American literature who initially and vocally opposed Brodkey's syllabus. They also went out of their way to allege that James Duban had attempted to intimidate a female colleague, threatening her with a libel lawsuit in a confrontational Friday-evening phone call to her home number.[122] And they called out by name a fellow undergraduate journalist at the *Daily Texan* for scheming on behalf of the conservative National Association of Scholars.[123] In a later article, Henson and Philpott accused top administrators—specifically, Vice President Fonken and President Cunningham—of squashing E 306. They revealed that "the backlash against . . . [Brodkey's E 306 syllabus] has a carefully crafted political agenda."[124] They had followed the money trail left behind by the conservative National Association of Scholars, whose local affiliate, the Texas Association of Scholars, had funded some of the opposition to Brodkey's syllabus. Altogether, their story overflowed with conspiratorial musings, malicious actors, and innocent victims.

In the *Daily Texan*, several of Brodkey's supporters followed Henson and Philpott's lead, turning their attention away from curricular matters and toward the topics of conservative censors and right-wing conspiracies. The

Daily Texan editor criticized "dyspeptic traditionalists" who accused Brodkey of "thought control," concluding with the false binary of social justice versus racist bigotry and saying that additional deliberation would allow everyone to witness an honest debate over whether "the University wants to make its curriculum honest and inclusive, or whether it will perpetuate its dated Anglocentrism."[125] Other arguments published in the student newspaper similarly wandered away from the debate about literacy. Some attacked Gribben. A UT alum accused him of "bitching for bitching's sake."[126] Branding themselves "the Howlers" and assaulting Gribben's "garbled use of the language of politics and economics," a group of feminist graduate students celebrated "women, people of color, lesbians and gays . . . the real beleaguered minority."[127] And some defended Gribben. A graduate instructor in the English department declared: "Anyone who knows Alan Gribben will find your characterization of him . . . laughably absurd."[128] Gribben, who received fan mail praising his appearance, and another UT professor of philosophy were featured together on a public access TV program where they fought to "prevent the politicizing of E 306."[129]

While some fixated on Gribben when hurling invective or singing panegyrics, others repeated the *Polemicist*'s allegation of a right-wing smear campaign. Two English professors who admitted to having no part in E 306 and little knowledge of its curriculum published an article alleging that right-wing blowhards unfairly maligned Brodkey by spreading "deeply illogical, even absurd," and "chilling echoes of innuendo" across newspapers and television programs.[130] Forty professors in the English department published a "Statement of Academic Concern" claiming that Brodkey and her syllabus had been unfairly tarred by conservatives, who lobbed "*ad hominem* attacks and misrepresentation at the expense of genuine intellectual debate." Those who signed the statement further alleged that the assaults on Brodkey's syllabus were a violation of "the principle of academic freedom."[131] In response to this fixation on Brodkey's intellectual freedom, many of her detractors claimed that she and her fellow travelers were the real censors. One tutor who regularly worked with UT students wrote to Gribben directly, saying that undergraduates, already suffering intolerant instructors, "believed they were having an ideology pushed upon them" in their writing classes. The tutor confided in Gribben, "Such [radical, indoctrinating] instructors were not few in number."[132] In the *Daily Texan*, an associate professor of government called Brodkey's curriculum "indoctrination in bigotry."[133] When the *New York Times* reported on the class's postponement, they quoted Gribben, who demanded a "freshman [*sic*] writing course free of indoctrination."[134]

During the summer and early fall of 1990, this evolving rhetorical ecology, characterized by an invasive political argument and a diminished curricular concern, allowed an especially caustic claim to thrive. Antivictimist arguments positioned UT Austin students and Brodkey's critics as the true victims of power-hungry radicals. Such antivictimism ran rampant in another student-run newspaper. The *University Review* included on its board of advisers a slate of conservative firebrands, including a conservative *Dallas Morning News* pundit, a Republican National committeeman, a former Texas House of Representatives speaker, and the chairman of the Texas Republican Party. The first issue (September 1990) opened with a two-page screed about E 306 arguing that the multicultural revolution justified attacks on innocent white men with hypocritical appeals to victimhood, asking, "How can a course be a beacon for diversity and tolerance when its originally proposed text defined racism as something capable only of whites and sexism capable only of males?"[135] This was followed, in the same issue, by another three-page assault on English department "radicals" who had become "increasingly intolerant of traditional scholars." Offering a bizarro mimicry of Henson and Philpott's right-wing conspiracy among university administrators, the *University Review* described a left-wing takeover of the English department: "They often pack hiring committees and curriculum committees. They attend all departmental meetings and are vociferous. . . . Much of their success is due to their bullying behavior."[136]

A month later, the *Review* invited Gribben to write a guest column defending his stance on E 306. Gribben rebutted the claim that he had led a right-wing assault. Instead, he alleged a left-wing coup: "The debate at the meeting [where the English faculty voted to approve Brodkey's syllabus] became almost a charade, so predetermined seemed the outcome." Gribben argued that he was the true victim of Brodkey's "proponents [who] prefer to rail about the purported menace of a national conspiracy."[137] Soon, the local media was parroting Gribben's self-portrayal. A conservative *Daily Texan* columnist called Gribben "the victim of a fierce political battle" who was abused "because he opposed a group of intolerant ideologues."[138] A conservative columnist for the *Dallas Morning News* (who was also an adviser to the *University Review*) depicted Gribben as a culture warrior Pyrrhus, winning his fight against the "new McCarthyites" but sacrificing his reputation and his peace of mind in the process.[139] In the spring of 1991 as Gribben was departing Austin for another tenured position, the *Dallas Morning News* published a two-page feature article describing him as a 1970s radical so dedicated to racial equality that he married an Asian woman—a man unfairly drummed out of his job and home by a series of protests beginning with the late July 1990 rally in front of the UT Tower.[140] The *Austin American-Statesman* published a shorter but no less sympathetic feature article repeating Gribben's claim that he was "forced out by the 'politically correct' fundamentalists" and quoting Gribben's account of his last, sad days in Austin: "Here I am putting my house for sale in a soft market, uprooting my family from a community they love."[141] The most elaborate antivictimist tale was spun by a conservative provocateur in a book-length tirade describing Brodkey as someone whose victimist rhetoric asserted that teaching standard English would "maintain the domination of society by the dominant group."[142] By contrast, Alan Gribben was presented as a man "shunned in hallways, uninvited to parties, the target of at least one campus demonstration [and] persistently labeled a 'right-winger' in campus publications," the true victim of Brodkey's victimism.[143]

Gribben's retelling of his story and the media coverage about his saga are eerily similar to another potboiler told by Dinesh D'Souza—a tale of another "true victim," a Princeton University English professor pilloried for his opposition to a women's studies program in the early 1980s.[144] And both sagas resemble the journalistic saga about James Duban, who also left the UT Austin English department not long after the Battle of Texas concluded. Like Gribben, Duban was presented as yet another true victim of multicultural victimism. In September 1991, the English department chair removed Duban from his long-occupied post as chair of the honors program. A *Dallas Morning News* commentator alleged it was a political hit job. Duban's successor was a "supporter of the multiculturalist approach," while Duban vocally opposed Dean Meacham's multicultural curricular proposal.[145] The *Austin American-Statesman* published its own sympathetic portrait of Duban, presenting the English department chair's action as retribution for Duban's dissent during the victim's revolution.[146] The *Daily Texan* lamented Gribben's fate ("the unfortunate victim of a political war"), saying that the English department administration had made another example out of Duban while trying to strong-arm the rest of the department into supporting Dean Meacham's multicultural agenda.[147] A UT Austin classics professor called Duban a "victim of politics."[148] The continuity among these stories demonstrates that antivictimist rhetoric and its characteristic claim of "true victimhood" pervaded 1980s debates about multiculturalism on college campuses. These antivictimist narratives overwhelmed Henson and Philpott's story about Brodkey's academic freedom and replaced her arguments about critical literacy. Furthermore, the rhetoric of true victimhood is still alive and well, still prevalent in controversies about campus politics, as Kiara Walker's recent scholarship demonstrates.[149] We might not be fighting the same culture war on twenty-first-century campuses, but many people are using the same rhetorical artillery that battered Linda Brodkey and her supporters in the late 1980s.

In the late 1980s, Geoff Henley left West Texas to become an undergraduate at UT Austin. He decided to take a survey of world literature, which happened to be taught by a Canadian, feminist, Marxist professor with no intention of teaching the "Western canon." Sitting in an auditorium on the first day, Henley expected to receive an anthology that featured "the Greeks, the Romans . . . the epic of Gilgamesh and just everything." Instead, he was handed a reading list filled with contemporary works. When he voiced his concerns, the professor suggested that he take another class with a more traditional instructor, recommending a few alternatives. Henley took her advice, switching to a British literature class with a more conventional professor. Looking back on that early college experience, he griped: "If you're stripping [Mark Twain and Voltaire] away from undergrads . . . you're just essentially imposing a Maoist view of the world without giving them any context. You are doing them a profound disservice." A couple years after his first encounter with UT Austin's tenured radicals, Henley won an open tryout for a position as a regular columnist for the *Daily Texan*. He later advanced to the editorial desk, an elected position. Henley imagined himself as an embattled minority, one of the newspaper's "two or three" politically conservative staff.[150]

At the student newspaper, Henley was hardly an ideological minority. He was one of several conservative *Daily Texan* columnists who took aim at Brodkey's curriculum, and he often repeated antivictimist arguments. Unlike the rest of his literary coterie, Henley took his activism to the streets. One late October evening not long after Brodkey released the "Writing about Difference" course packet and syllabus, President Cunningham stood before a large congregation of eager parents, ready to gush about the undergraduate experience at UT Austin. Outside the assembly, Henley was handing out flyers pillorying Brodkey's syllabus. Streaming into the auditorium, parents read that "Students Advocating Valid Education [SAVE] seeks to remove political ideology from the classroom." During the Q&A after Cunningham's talk, one parent asked about E 306. Cunningham, unprepared for this line of questioning, struggled to diffuse the situation.[151] A few months later, Henley published a lengthy investigative article discussing the E 306 controversy without ever saying anything particular about the syllabus except that it initially featured the Rothenberg book. Rather than discuss pedagogy, Henley spewed personal attacks vaguely aimed at "advocates" who, he said, practiced "intellectual dishonesty and contempt for academic inquiry."[152] Many English faculty publicly protested Henley's style of journalism, saying he specialized in personal attacks.[153] The English department chair took special umbrage, calling Henley's writing "scummy."[154]

Henley's most significant contribution to the debate about E 306 was his demand for viewpoint parity. In an article published not long after his October stunt, Henley complained that Brodkey's curriculum was "unbalanced," failing to represent anything but leftist perspectives. He demanded that the course include "legal and expository writings from other such [conservative] partisans" to "balance" Brodkey's curriculum.[155] Henley's call for viewpoint diversity bolstered the antivictimist rhetoric already overtaking the E 306 debate. If conservative voices were silenced by victimist radicals, then the solution must be fair representation of both sides. Recent analyses reveal that "such advocacy does not promote substantively diverse social and political perspectives." Instead, viewpoint parity, when attempted nowadays, is often "disastrous." In the twenty-first century, the demand for equal representation provides cover for unscientific arguments that obscure the main issues under debate in campus controversies. In the 1980s, though he wasn't demanding that students consider racist polemics about genetic superiority, Henley was leveraging "diversity polemics" by assuming that "racial and gender parity" has been achieved in higher education, so the real "discrimination" on college campuses is against "communities with conservative worldviews."[156] In his eyes, Henley became a victim when professors like Brodkey did not actively feature his viewpoint in their classes. Albeit not as reactionary as twenty-first-century demands for viewpoint diversity, Henley's appeal was just as effective. To those who argue that women, the queer community, and students of color are harmed by widespread university institutions, viewpoint diversity advocates of the 1980s and today have countered that they, cultural conservatives, are the true victims.

The antivictimist call for viewpoint diversity is absurd on its face. If one class does not privilege or represent a conservative viewpoint, then a conservative student's rights will not necessarily be infringed. Every student, as Brodkey often pointed out, can still assert their beliefs by talking back to the curriculum. Every student can still take other classes where they might learn about, in Henley's words, "the Greeks, the Romans . . . the epic of Gilgamesh and just everything." In the late 1980s, Henley was living proof that he wasn't victimized by multicultural curricula any more than his fellow students would have been abused by "Writing about Difference." When he found one survey of literature wanting, he took another class reflecting his own political biases. Additionally, despite all the influence some leftist professors had on the UT Austin curriculum, Henley freely voiced his opinions in the student newspaper. Nonetheless, though the appeal of viewpoint diversity deflates when punctured by the slightest interrogation, it proliferated during the E 306 controversy because it complemented the antivictimist rhetoric already in circulation. When another undergraduate claimed that a public access television show about the E 306 controversy did not give fair time to his conservative perspective, he parroted Henley's arguments not in the interest of advocating viewpoint diversity but rather in an effort to claim true victimhood.[157]

The politics of appeal invited demands for rights and claims to victimhood, which together inadvertently incited the demand for viewpoint diversity and the rhetoric of true victimhood. Combined, these arguments constituted a rhetorical shift from policy to identity following a pattern described by Patricia Roberts-Miller: "If policy is purely a consequence of identity, then there is never any reason to debate policy."[158] This declension from policy-oriented deliberation to identity-obsessed shouting was well underway during the summer of 1990, nearly two months before Brodkey would release the syllabus and course packet. In early July, using funds from the conservative Texas Association of Scholars (an affiliate of the National Association of Scholars), associate dean Joseph Horn paid for an advertisement in the student newspaper while submitting a similar ad to the *Austin-American Statesman*.[159] The *Daily Texan* "Statement of Academic Concern" appeared on July 18 glittering with signatures from fifty-six UT Austin professors and ornamented by a list of conjectures ending with the claim that Brodkey and her allies were a "biased" group of ideologues who would impose a "single hegemonic view" on UT Austin undergraduates.[160] From that moment onward, before anyone could make specific pedagogical arguments about Brodkey's syllabus, the public debate trended away from the complex academic debate about literacy and the related departmental disagreement about pedagogy. The public debate further transmogrified and simplified when the faculty appealed to higher authorities to assert their right to academic freedom. And the matter was completely distorted once journalists penned exposés about right-wing conspiracies and true victimhood. Out of this multistage rhetorical distillation emerged the opposed identities most commonly associated with the 1980s culture wars: the intolerant leftist ideologue versus the censorious right-wing curmudgeon. In trade journals, a similar recipe yielded equally strong liquor.

The November 1990 issue of *Radical Teacher* published a chronology of the crisis, prefacing these materials by saying that "ultra-conservative faculty members and alumni" had infringed on "the right of the writing program administrators to design curricula and syllabi."[161]

Identitarian arguments about E 306 may have reached their nadir in the spring of 1991, but the culture war controversies at UT Austin had been drawn into this orbit three years prior when Alan Gribben voted against a proposed graduate concentration in ethnic studies and third world literature. Thereafter, his colleagues gave him the side-eye. Maxine Hairston noticed the professoriate's "special sort of cruelty." Dean Robert King commented, "Alan wasn't sent to gulag perhaps, but he was certainly sent to Coventry." Feeling estranged, Gribben happily received a call from an opinion columnist for *Texas Monthly* magazine.[162] He corroborated a rumor about radical English professors burning books (among other things) at a department party. He even provided a juicy quote to embellish the story.[163] Then a conservative columnist for the *Dallas Morning News* called to ask about tenured radicals who unconscionably politicized their classrooms.[164] Gribben soon extended these identitarian accusations to the E 306 controversy. In a June 18, 1990, letter to the *Daily Texan* editor, Gribben accused Brodkey and her allies of a plot to "grade students on 'politically correct' thought."[165] Seven days later, shaken by these accusations of political bias, the English department dropped the Rothenberg anthology altogether, thinking they would defuse the curricular controversy by removing the objectionable content.[166] They were mistaken, for the public controversy was primarily about identity, not pedagogy. On the same day that Brodkey told the university bookstore to cancel their order for the Rothenberg book, the *New York Times* repeated all of Gribben's allegations, intimating that the Rothenberg book was the only required text in the "Writing about Difference" curriculum.[167] Less than two weeks later, in early July 1990, the *Dallas Morning News* repeated the false claim about the Rothenberg book while painting Alan Gribben as an "un-ideological" victim of radical intolerance.[168]

The editorial staff at the *Daily Texan* called Gribben an intolerant curmudgeon.[169] Gribben shot back, accusing the *Daily Texan* of "intimidating faculty dissenters" who demanded to see "the 'mystery packet' of [E 306] readings."[170] Gribben's comment is revealing, for the E 306 syllabus had not been released, thus precluding any substantive debate about pedagogical policy. The same thing happened in the national press. A commentator for the *Washington Post* alleged that leftist E 306 professors wanted to subordinate "instruction to political indoctrination."[171] A pundit for the *US News and*

World Report compared Brodkey and her supporters to the religious leaders of Iran, "the academy's new ayatollahs."[172] A talking head bloviating in the *Washington Post* labeled Brodkey's syllabus "a consciousness-raising indoctrination in politically correct attitudes."[173] *Z Magazine* attacked the National Association of Scholars, accusing Gribben and others of censorious intolerance.[174] *Voice* magazine published an article claiming that a conservative cabal was trying to indoctrinate students by silencing professors.[175] Occasionally, the possibility of a debate about pedagogical policy glimmered in the local press. In early September 1990, for instance, a *Houston Post* editorial made specific reference to the "Writing about Difference" syllabus.[176] But these embers were quickly extinguished in the flood of identitarian accusations.

While the Battle of Texas raged in the media, the Persian Gulf War (1990–91) stormed into Kuwait. Commenting on the latter event, the French philosopher Jean Baudrillard provocatively claimed that the megaton bombs, the hundred thousand dead, and the ignited oil wells never took place. Baudrillard rightly noticed that the media spectacle began before the fighting. The war's simulacrum took the place of the actual carnage. Something similar can be said about the E 306 controversy, for the public debate began in June 1990 shortly after Brodkey broadcast her intent to revise the curriculum but long before late August when she revealed the course packet and syllabus. Prior to the syllabus's release, the only thing anyone knew about the class was that it might feature Paula Rothenberg's *Racism and Sexism*, and even this wasn't true because the committee designing "Writing about Difference" removed the textbook from their plans shortly after the initial public backlash in June. Before Brodkey ever released her syllabus and a substantive public debate about pedagogical policy could be had, fever dreams about a new McCarthyism and a cadre of tenured radicals were, in Baudrillard's words, "blocking up the screen hole through which escapes the substance of events."[177] Once identity supplanted policy, there was "no interrogation into the event itself or its reality."[178] Applied to the E 306 controversy, Baudrillard's speculations are less about media and more about "artful substitution."[179] In Kuwait, carefully selected videos of smart bombs effortlessly displaced the actual explosions. In Austin, identitarian arguments took the place of critical literacy. In both cases, the simulacrum preceded the event since chuckleheads started to describe the war before any shots were fired and pundits started crying about McCarthyite censors and Marxist professors before Brodkey's syllabus even existed.

This identitarian simulacrum was so intoxicating that even the UT Austin English professors abandoned their grounded discussion of writing pedagogy in their private correspondence and personal interactions. Hairston told Ruszkiewicz that they were fighting an outspoken gang of "radical" leftists. She warned that Brodkey and company would bring about a new "McCarthyism."[180] On the opposing side were statements no more high-minded. Addressing the entire university faculty, Dean Meacham said a "McCarthyite class" of people (many associated with the National Association of Scholars) had frustrated his curricular initiatives.[181] In a memo to James Kinneavy, Linda Brodkey sorrowfully sang that the National Association of Scholars held "the University of Texas hostage to the agenda of the most reactionary political association in the academy."[182] Addressing like-minded academics outside UT Austin, Brodkey's ally and fellow proponent of the new E 306 curriculum, John Slatin, maligned nefarious right-wing organizations and their professorial enablers, saying this insidious conspiracy had stymied his valiant effort at correcting the "gay-bashing, sexual harassment, and similar nastiness" prevalent among UT Austin student fraternities.[183]

Commenting on the "role of claims as performances of group identity," Patricia Roberts-Miller observes that "there are certain political issues that appear impervious to persuasion." Once people start making public arguments to "signal group loyalty" rather than address policy, they are inclined to hold firm "regardless of discomfirming evidence."[184] Since many of the identitarian arguments chronicled in this chapter predate the release of the "Writing about Difference" syllabus, the most incendiary student journalism appeared shortly after Brodkey released the course packet, and the student journalists made no specific mention of the course syllabus itself, even though they reviewed its contents, we have to wonder whether Brodkey's curriculum was ill-fated before the public debate about pedagogy ever began.[185] Convulsed by identitarian attacks, contorted into claims about true victimhood, and crippled by demands for viewpoint diversity, the pedagogical conversation that Brodkey, Ruszkiewicz, Hairston, Duban, and Slatin wanted to have in late August 1990 could never take place. Shot down before it ever took the field, the opportunity to deliberate critical literacy's merits was the greatest casualty of the Battle of Texas.

Among the fallen also lie several friendships. James Berlin was a scholar of rhetoric and a supporter of Linda Brodkey. He and John Ruszkiewicz, though politically at odds, had become close in the mid-1980s when Berlin was a visiting professor in the UT Austin English graduate program. At an academic conference in the spring of 1991, his voice "breaking with emotion," Berlin told a packed room that Maxine Hairston's *Chronicle of Higher Education* article about the E 306 controversy was "dogmatic."[186] Berlin's characterization wounded Ruszkiewicz, who conceded to Berlin that "there were excesses on both sides of the controversy," while hoping that they might learn "to deal with . . . [their differences] more civilly."[187] A year later, all such hope was lost in the mayhem of an identitarian scrimmage. In June 1992, Ruszkiewicz attended a seminar hosted by the conservative Heritage Foundation. At the close of a heady week, Ruszkiewicz addressed his fellow seminarians, saying that his quondam friend could only be described as a "scholar" if using "the term loosely." Ruszkiewicz then speculated that Berlin might learn something from his conservative companions if the lesson were assisted by "a stout cudgel."[188] It's fair to say that Ruszkiewicz didn't truly want to beat sense into his one-time colleague. But it's also fair to say that Ruszkiewicz believed Berlin beyond the point of rational, policy-oriented debate. And it seems most fair to say that, in 1992, Ruszkiewicz himself had strayed far past the earshot of sweet reason. In a year's time, he and many others—including Hairston, Brodkey, Meacham, and Slatin—had completed the journey from pedagogical disagreement to partisan vitriol, from pedagogical policy to identitarian accusation, from an academic debate about literacy to a violent war over rights. Along the way, all of them sacrificed friendships, lost face, damaged reputations, and doomed a curriculum. And they didn't make this journey alone. Others beyond the UT Austin campus followed. Ten years after the Battle of Texas ended, an accomplished scholar in the field of literacy studies declared that "Brodkey was censored in the tradition of dictators who censor those who speak out."[189] Brodkey's syllabus was dead, and the UT Austin debate about critical and instrumental literacy had been buried. Yet the simulacrum of identitarian accusation, untethered from its precipitating academic disagreement, marched on.

The Battle of Texas is a cautionary tale about a typical culture war progression from academic scrimmage to public skirmish and then national scourge. The historian Daniel Rodgers notes that many intellectual disagreements within the 1980s academy were similarly "amplified in the more polarized" environment beyond the ivory tower.[190] To this broader narrative, our story about the Battle of Texas offers a close analysis of the rhetorical and political steps toward carnage. This progression's contemporary relevance is hard to miss. At the moment in the field of literacy studies, the application of critical race theory to composition pedagogy flirts with the identitarian arguments that ultimately doomed Brodkey's syllabus. April Baker-Bell, for example, has recently appealed to students' rights while demanding aggressively critical approaches in the classroom. Baker-Bell contends that allowing and even encouraging students to alternate between their home language and the discourse of standard edited English is inadvertently harmful because even as such pedagogical "code-switching" extends respectability to Black English, it "doesn't seriously acknowledge what Black students give up when they give up their language."[191] Though Baker-Bell doesn't fall into identitarian argumentation, confining herself to the academic terrain of sociolinguistics and composition pedagogy, her detractors rush toward concerns about "identity politics." In a new twist on the rhetoric of victimhood, Erec Smith says that Baker-Bell's anti-racist pedagogy will harm students of color by denying them the opportunity to "forego intellectual accountability and well-reasoned responses to inquiry simply by virtue of being marginalized groups." According to Smith, Baker-Bell delivers "disempowerment" and "infantilization" rather than access to critical thinking or higher education.[192]

Neither Smith nor Baker-Bell make antivictimist appeals or allow identitarian concerns to supplant pedagogic discussion. But it's not hard to see how such an internal, academic debate about literacy might cascade into a public feud over students' right to education free from indoctrination and professors' right to academic freedom. In 2022, the Texas state legislature relied on such public arguments to support a failed legislative effort at banning any critical race theory from publicly supported college classrooms. Senate Bill 16 promised to protect "intellectual diversity" and prohibit violations of "academic freedom," recalling Henley's demand for viewpoint parity and D'Souza's concerns about censorious victimists. The university's response—repeating the language of academic freedom—was based on a template that has informed similar resolutions across the country and throughout the state of Texas. As we retread the course of the 1980s culture wars, the Battle of Texas teaches faculty and administrators about the risks of going public and the dangers lurking in rights-based arguments. Most important, the Battle of Texas demonstrates the corrosive potential in arguments about true victimhood, viewpoint diversity, and, above all, identity.

But for the writing program administrator, the story told in this chapter also recollects a point made by many academics who suffered through the 1980s culture wars. These political conflicts over academic freedom and students' rights damaged American higher education's reputation, justifying managerial control and forgiving fiscal austerity at colleges and universities across the country. Recent public commentators have said something similar about the twenty-first-century revitalization of culture war attacks on higher education. A pundit for the *New York Times* recently contends that "the point of this [new culture war] . . . is to undermine public education through a thousand little cuts, each meant to weaken public support for teachers and public schools, and to open the floodgates to policies that siphon funds and resources from public institutions and pump them into private ones."[193] It would be hard to find nationwide evidence of such foul conspiracy. Nevertheless, the repeated concomitance of fiscal discipline, managerial imposition, and political turmoil suggests something more than coincidence. And at UT Austin we can find direct evidence proving that the 1980s culture war provided cover for managerial encroachment on the writing program by hiding marketized reforms behind partisan motives.

Once the political quarrel was over, the reconstitution of the writing curriculum resumed. While some professors were fighting over E 306 "Writing about Difference," others were quietly rethinking the first-year writing program from the bottom up, attempting one more time to address the budgetary problems caused by higher enrollments while struggling to resolve the governance issues created by nontenure track faculty. In 1992 as the Battle of Texas ended—after the last desultory shots rang out, but before the smoke cleared—the president of the university announced a complete overhaul of the English department, a bold move made possible in part by his promise that an independent writing program offering an elective curriculum would prevent another public political fight over first-year writing. President Cunningham's final statement on his decision to create a new writing division suggests that he was wrestling simultaneously with the twin problems of diversity and austerity. To Cunningham, an autonomous writing program that was separate from the English department and divorced from its tenured radicals would kill two birds with one stone: "I felt that we had made a great deal of progress just avoiding the implementation of a radical multicultural course. . . . However, the fundamental issue still existed—how to teach English 306 effectively to a large number of undergraduates."[194] Cunningham's curricular and institutional reforms aimed principally to answer the latter question, though they were justified by the former concern.

The Battle of Texas is a tragic story of protagonists, like John Slatin and Linda Brodkey, who tried to swim against the prevailing political tides and drowned in the undercurrent. To understand why they suffered such a tragic fate, we have taken a page from the university studies playbook, situating the tale of institutional policy in a larger context that includes national politics and postmodern media. But even this story, with its panoramic backdrop, fails to do what Lester Faigley suggested not long after the Battle of Texas ended. Looking back in the early 1990s, Faigley concluded that "the narrative of Right versus Left may be misleading for our understanding of the present."[95] In order to get beyond the culture war narrative, we nest the Battle of Texas between the demise of James Kinneavy's professional writing program (recounted in the previous chapter) and the creation of an independent writing program with an elective writing curriculum (retold in the next chapter), suggesting that political conflict and fiscal austerity combined in the 1980s to create a volatile circumstance in which higher education could rapidly and radically change. This, we propose, is the most important lesson for writing program administrators. Conservative detractors may have defeated E 306 "Writing about Difference," but their success made possible another unintended achievement. The tragic tale of Brodkey's "Writing about Difference" syllabus is a prelude to another story in which phronetic actors could exert their agency as writing program administrators. The backlash against Brodkey's syllabus cleared the ground for something no one foresaw and few thought possible: curricular changes and administrative restructuring in direct response to the upper administration's demand for austerity.

4
Revision and Division

The history of twentieth-century US higher education comes in different keys. In one ear, we hear a pounding economic symphony about the industrial revolution, the demand for professional-managerial workers, the rush of students, their hope for higher status, the federal investment in universities, the growth of scientific research, the reduced price of attendance at midcentury, the diminished state funding in the later decades, and the rapid rise in tuition that resulted thereafter. This is the background music for the Saturday Night Massacre, a crescendo of economic factors resulting in a climax of labor exploitation. In the other ear, we listen to a political hymn about increasing diversity among college students, their demands for access and inclusion, the struggles—both in the Supreme Court and on innumerable campuses—over admissions policies, curricular standards, and, above all, students' rights. This solemn chorale accompanies the march to access and equity. It is the anthem of diversity and the score for the Battle of Texas.

One can easily find books about the marketization of higher education and the influx of private actors and innovative technologies as if these trends were exclusive of the demand for just admissions policies or the insistence on inclusive campus institutions. And likewise, several scholarly studies focus on the politics of diversity and the rights revolution without regard for the creeping austerity that shaped higher education at the close of the twentieth century.[1] This scholarly division of the political from the economic recalls the consensus of those who lived through the last decades of the twentieth century. In 1987, Allan Bloom published *The Closing of the American Mind*, a now-famous culture war screed against diversity in higher education. Bloom complained about "students who come [to college] hoping to find out what career they want to have."[2] He didn't point to or even mention rising tuition rates, which undoubtedly pressured students to focus on vocational majors most likely to help them pay back their student loans. Instead, he blamed multicultural curricular reforms, which had enervated "liberal education" and resulted in "an intellectual crisis of the greatest magnitude, which constitutes the crisis of our civilization."[3] Bloom's contemporaries at UT Austin similarly dissociated economic pressures from political struggles, believing that the Battle of Texas had little or nothing to do with the Saturday Night Massacre. James Sledd, for example, believed that the culture war fight over the first-year writing curriculum at UT Austin distracted people from the unrelated marketization of higher education. Toward the end of the E 306 controversy, he cried out, "Instead of befouling itself with arguments about an introductory textbook in sociology, the UT English department should take steps to end its customary dependence on underpaid, overworked, ill-prepared" nontenure track instructors.[4] Just as Bloom wouldn't acknowledge that the rising cost of tuition contributed to the decline in liberal arts majors, Sledd couldn't imagine that the struggle over multicultural curricula might allow administrators to address the problem of contingent labor.

Unlike those who lived in the moment, focusing their attention on either budgetary pressures or culture war conflicts, in this last substantive chapter, we layer the economic dynamics and the political conflicts together into one fugue about the revolutionary circumstances that reshaped higher education and upended the writing program at UT Austin. We do so by examining concomitant and interacting trends: increased enrollment, accommodating institutions, diversity politics, economic austerity, and administrative managerialism. None of these alone should be labeled an underlying disease. Rather, they are all symptoms of a larger and longer historical etiology, inclusive of austerity and diversity, finally resulting in a feverish pace of rapid change. The combined economic and political crises over employment and curriculum—the Saturday Night Massacre and the Battle of Texas—razed the first-year writing program and made possible fundamental changes to the teaching and the administration of its classes. Many scholars and public figures have shined their lights on the century's last decades, illuminating their revolutionary potential. In 1984, the economist Michael Piore and the legal scholar Charles Sabel published *The Second Industrial Divide*, a prescient description of the information economy that would soon sweep industrialism aside. In 1987, US President Reagan challenged USSR President Gorbachev to remove the wall separating communist East Berlin from the capitalist West. In 1990, still in the throes of such enormous change, the cultural critic Fredric

Jameson argued that the Western world was entering "a transitional period between two stages of capitalism in which the earlier forms of the economic [were] in the process of being restructured on a global scale." The industrial era and the Cold War were ending. Something new, "taking forms we cannot yet imagine," was emerging.[5] In this chapter, by narrating the fallout of both the Saturday Night Massacre and the Battle of Texas, we similarly attend to the last two decades of the twentieth century as a transitional moment by showing how economic and political developments interacted to reshape higher education and make possible the institutions and the curricula that persist today.

Sterling Morrison's greatest accomplishment began in 1965 when he became lead guitarist for the Velvet Underground. He toured the world and launched the indie rock movement. Morrison's second great act began in 1971 when he enrolled in the English graduate program at the University of Texas at Austin. Joseph Kruppa's greatest accomplishment happened in 1971 when he recognized Morrison's name among a stack of graduate school applications. A professor of contemporary literature and twentieth-century culture who had successfully lobbied Lou Reed to visit one of his classes, Kruppa put Morrison's application at the top of the pile, actively recruited him, and called personally to say he had been accepted. By 1986, Morrison had finally earned a doctorate of philosophy. He left Austin to become a Houston tugboat captain.[6] Kruppa stayed behind, chairing a 1985 committee that would effectively abolish an industrial era mainstay in higher education, the universal first-year writing requirement.

To some in the English department, the drive toward abolition had nothing to do with postindustrial austerity in higher education. Instead, abolition looked like another assailment in the long-standing war between literature and rhetoric. So it had been for a century.[7] So it appeared in 1985. Some, like John Ruszkiewicz, would always see the effort to abolish E 306 as one big yank in an extended tug of war over the "English department's center of gravity."[8] James Sledd similarly described this episode as an epic battle between "the empire of rhetoric and the empire of literature."[9] However, there are good reasons for doubting their story about an interdepartmental civil war. To begin with, literature professors later reported an affection for the rhetoric faculty, a respect for their discipline, and a love for writing instruction.[10] Larry Carver, a British literature specialist, said that he respected James Kinneavy deeply and was "very fond of teaching composition."[11] Carol MacKay, an award-winning teacher and scholar of Victorian literature, earned her PhD from the University of California, Los Angeles (UCLA), where she helped to direct the first-year writing program and worked with area high school teachers. She wrote a textbook for the writing classes at UCLA. She was interviewed by Maxine Hairston, who advocated for her hire. She married one of the lecturers. Though she would be the first to admit that there were "literature people with a capital L," MacKay primarily identified with Hairston and company.[12]

In addition to the often collegial relations between literature and rhetoric faculty, there is another substantial reason to doubt that abolitionism resulted from interdepartmental strife. Long before the 1985 push to remove the first-year writing requirement, people were promoting abolition without reference or allegiance to their warring disciplinary kingdoms. Abolition had loomed over the required first-year writing course since the early 1980s. At first, two oddly allied reapers jointly stalked E 306. Sledd was committed to the writing requirement, yet he believed that the faculty and the administration never really cared about writing instruction. He accused his fellow English professors of inventing novel ways to let students off the hook. And the dean's office, Sledd alleged, was helping. Only 25 percent of those taking the English Composition Test scored high enough to claim credit for E 306, yet the dean's office reported an exemption rate of two-thirds or better. How could 66 percent claim credit when only 25 percent tested out? He admonished the English faculty for its "irresponsibility" and the dean's office for its chicanery.[13] Alongside James Sledd was James Vick, who had no faith in the requirement and wanted students to set foot on campus with writing already mastered. Vick believed that "students with sufficient high school preparation should be able to obtain credit for E . 306 by advanced placement."[14] For different reasons, with no allegiance to the realm of rhetoric and no obeisance to the lords of literature, both Vick and Sledd agreed that the university might as well give up on E 306 altogether.

Adding to these long-standing doubts about one class at one university, animus toward all required writing classes burned across the nation, a sentiment fueled by talk of "remediation." In the national conversation, two talking points menaced courses like E 306. First, people said that writing can't be taught. The skill, they claimed, emerges when ability encounters opportunity, so good teachers should simply give talented students the chance to improve their capacity. Second, many claimed that writing requires technical mastery of surface-level mechanics, something that's easy to teach and so best left to lower-level teachers.[15] One associate professor of British literature claiming to represent the "overwhelming majority of the [UT Austin

English] department's . . . faculty" repeated these arguments when he suggested that if writing can be taught, then it is, at best, remedial instruction. In this professor's eyes, Kinneavy's E 306 syllabus offered "simplistic generalizations about the 'forms' of writing before [tackling] the problem of having something substantial to write about." To those who shared these sentiments, Kinneavy's rhetorical pedagogy looked like "trade school education." They hungered for the "cultivation and expression of an attitude towards knowledge," not Kinneavy's "arbitrary . . . writing formulas."[16] The director of the Humanities program was pioneering an alternative to E 306, HMN 303, where students could focus on "content," not "mechanics"—folklore, philosophy, literature, and history. Soon, 26 percent of UT Austin students received credit for E 306 by taking this new, content-heavy class.[17]

By 1985, the rhetoric of remediation had permeated the institution. In 1981, a music professor sitting on the University Faculty Senate wondered whether E 306 was a "pre-college" course.[18] Around that same time, a prominent member of the tenured English faculty told the University Council that high schools, not the university, should bear the responsibility of remedial writing instruction.[19] Two years after these remarks, in 1983, the undergraduates were parroting his claims. A student representative to the University Council told his professors that "E 306 is not regarded as a highly intensive educational course; it is regarded primarily as a remedial course." He requested a "hard-nose course" with rigorous content, perhaps something more like HMN 303.[20] In a candid moment, dean Robert King told the rhetoric and composition faculty that "E 306 is not a university-level course. It is not quite a remedial course, but it almost is." And besides, "probably the top half of . . . [UT Austin's students] exempt out. And roughly 50% of UT's students don't graduate . . . [so] what this means is that we're teaching 306 to people who don't graduate from UT."[21] Disdain for "remediation" dripped from the mouths of the most humble undergraduate and the most adulated administrator.

In addition to these early reservations about the required course glommed on to national opposition to all such "remedial" classes and piling atop the campus-wide belief that E 306 was insubstantial, the staffing problem endangered the writing requirement. In fact, the staffing problem contributed most to abolitionism at UT Austin. The English faculty commonly believed that E 346K had to go because they couldn't staff the class without temporary faculty. E 306 would have to be another casualty in the Saturday Night Massacre, starved once austerity claimed the writing program labor supply.[22] Evan Carton added that the lecturers teaching E 306 had brought internal tension to the department. He recalled a deep resentment from those who had been vetted for the tenure track and toward those who had been hired through a much less rigorous process for nontenure track employment. To become a tenure track literature professor, Carton had earned his PhD from Johns Hopkins, published in academic journals, and suffered through a multistage interview process. He would later recall, "Those of us who had been hired on the basis of national searches thought that there was a discrepancy between the kinds of credentials that we had and the credentials of this increasing group of lecturers who were hired locally, often without the same kind of scrutiny." When the lecturers claimed equal departmental status, the tenure track professors took umbrage.[23] Since the lecturers taught E 306, the tenure track professors thought the curricular requirement should be terminated with their employment.

But the most convincing proof that the UT Austin abolitionists acted in good faith—without acrimony toward their rhetoric colleagues and in the hope of solving the labor problem—comes from Joseph Kruppa himself. While the rhetoric of remediation and the rumors of civil war blew like a bad wind through Parlin Hall, Kruppa tried to ignore it all and focus on his mission. His committee had to "re-evaluate E 346K."[24] They had to build a writing program that could be staffed by a reduced coterie of graduate instructors.[25] This was a financial problem—the result of external austerity, not internal strife. They had to consider all options. Maybe reduce the number of required writing courses from three to two. Maybe exempt more students (with lower test scores) from E 306. Maybe send E 306 to University Extension at UT Austin, a distance-education wing of university instruction where curricula were delivered, at that time, through video lectures and workbook exercises, all graded by underpaid adjuncts.[26] Kruppa defended his holistic and practical approach, saying, "Lecturers make a department unworkable after a while." They had to reexamine E 306: "You can't look at one part of [the writing program] without looking at all of it."[27] Dean King, anxious to solve the labor problem, liked all of Kruppa's ideas. Abolition of the required writing course is not "a radical proposal," King declared, adding, "I think it would take pressure off liberal arts courses."[28]

In August 1985, with the dean's support, Kruppa's committee delivered their proposal to the department. They opened by staking out practical goals: maintain the nine-hour writing requirement, remain a leader in writing instruction, and, above all, remove any incentive to hire lecturers. His committee report boldly insisted, "We must staff our courses with faculty and graduate students without hiring additional temporary faculty." The pool of lecturers would not be refilled. The English department had to make due with present resources. Kruppa's committee offered three proposals: (1) remand E 306 to University Extension, effectively relieving the burden of instruction but not relinquishing curricular design; (2) offer a suite of writing classes, some focusing on literary content, others on rhetorical skill—E 346K would be an elective, but so would two new courses, E 316 (advanced sophomore literature) and E 309 (advanced sophomore writing); (3) reaffirm the importance of advanced writing courses already offered within the department, such as John Trimble's E 325.[29] The English faculty voted for the proposal, 3–1. Kruppa rejoiced, boasting that they had spoken with a "very strong and clear voice" in favor of abolition.[30] He predicted that, by 1988, E 306 would be sufficiently diminished and completely exiled.[31]

Flush with victory, Kruppa spent the next few months championing his proposal. Echoed by others on his committee, he assured the student newspaper that E 306 taught through University Extension would maintain its quality. Most important, the shift to University Extension would take pressure off the English department's labor pool. One of Kruppa's committee members explained, "It is difficult for one department to handle all the students."[32] Kruppa guaranteed that the new writing class (E 309) would offer students a classroom experience more "sophisticated" than the remedial E 306.[33] Another English faculty member agreed, saying that E 306 was "flatly designed" but E 309 allowed professors to be "more creative and teach the things in which they are interested."[34] Kruppa's proposal did not survive unscathed, however. E 316, the new sophomore-level literature class, was supposed to be taught in small seminars.[35] Without a legion of lecturers to staff small classes, the "Masterworks of Literature" course had to be offered in lecture halls packed with two hundred to three hundred students. Graduate instructors facilitated discussion groups. With this amendment in place, Kruppa's proposal earned the university's blessing. Dean King expressed hope for the eventual abolition of E 306 and the creation of E 309: "The writing course that the Department plans to offer will be a fully developed composition course with at least as much writing as is now required in English 306. . . . I think it is a noble goal, and I think it is attainable."[36] Echoing the national rhetoric of remediation, the new president, William Cunningham, agreed that E 306 should be shuttled to University Extension because writing skills "really ought to be taught" in high schools.[37]

But not everyone supported Kruppa's proposal. Some of the rhetoric faculty were especially critical. Ruszkiewicz said, "It would be irresponsible to suspend or replace the successful E 306 course simply because a few people in the department don't like it."[38] Hairston told Kruppa that his efforts to reconceptualize the writing program should focus on improving, not eliminating, lower-division instruction.[39] Kinneavy told the University Council that the instructors working for the University Extension program would be just as exploited as the English department lecturers, for they, too, were contingent faculty.[40] Ruszkiewicz told the student newspaper that by allowing most students to test out of E 306, Kruppa's proposal would teach students "examsmanship," not writing. Hairston sparely commented, "I just don't agree with it."[41] While reviewing its spring 1986 implementation, Kinneavy said of E 316 (the new lecture-hall literature course), "The course is basically not a composition course."[42] Ruszkiewicz wrote President Cunningham directly to explain that E 306 was a "well-honed, well-proven, and . . . remarkably popular course," not remedial education but rather "college-level" instruction.[43] But their flailing and multipronged attack was beaten back at a University Council meeting in February 1986 when President Cunningham said the English department and the dean's office had already decided to move forward with abolition.[44] Not long after, standing at the podium in front of the University Council, Kruppa repeated his claim that if they kept E 306 on campus, then they wouldn't be able to staff it without lecturers.[45]

Ruszkiewicz, Hairston, and Kinneavy maintained their opposition in part because they believed that abolition was another front in the war between literature and composition. By the early 1980s, the profession had become so embroiled in this interdisciplinary strife that the Modern Language Association created a special council to investigate the tension.[46] In 1984, while serving on the investigative committee, Kinneavy collected surveys from rhetoric and composition faculty around the country, a chronicle of resentment. Some compositionists reported that relations within their departments were "admirably equitable." Others, like an anonymous respondent from UT Austin, described open hostility: "I realize that what I have said is definitely 'us vs. them.' However that adequately expresses the various attitudes within the department."[47] The rhetoric professors had heard Kruppa boldly declare: "We are a literature department," not a writing program.[48] The UT Austin faculty had read a Miltonic pasquinade, written by a member of Kruppa's committee, in which God pontificates about his expertise in rhetoric, yet Satan makes the better argument.[49] To Kinneavy and his like-minded colleagues, these were neither benign statements nor harmless jokes. They were salvos. And abolition was the first assault. Foreshadowing later scholarly arguments, Ruszkiewicz explained how Kruppa's proposal was really an assault on rhetoric by the literature faculty: "Many faculty members use imaginative literature in writing classes to avoid teaching writing." Furthermore, said Ruszkiewicz, "To impose literary studies upon writing courses is to distort the nature of an introductory writing class."[50] After a member of Kruppa's committee became department chair, Kinneavy publicly warned that under William Sutherland's new leadership, "the literary course will replace the composition course."[51] He made more pointed accusations while sitting across from the English department chair in the University Faculty Senate, alleging that the administrators of E 346K had tried to convert his writing-across-the-curriculum class into a "course in discourse analysis, a sub-species of literary criticism." Now they were coming for E 306. "The writing program at this university is being systematically dismantled at almost every level, and an attempt to replace composition courses with literary courses is underway."[52] In professional journals, Hairston recounted the "recurring fracases with the literature people." She resented their "elitist mindset." She believed that "the scholar-critics in most departments don't believe in teaching writing as a discipline." She called them "Mandarins."[53] She wanted them out.

One episode in the summer of 1985 demonstrates the sense among some of the rhetoric faculty that in the aftermath of the Saturday Night Massacre, their discipline and its curricular kingdom were under siege. Ruszkiewicz, still director of the first-year writing program, hired a mercenary. He invited a mentor from his graduate student days at Ohio State, an eminent academic, to speak at the English department's graduate instructor orientation. Edward Corbett's scholarly talk would prove that people like Hairston, Kinneavy, and Ruszkiewicz could make a scholarly contribution equal to that of literary studies. Before Corbett championed the discipline of rhetoric and composition, Ruszkiewicz defended E 306, rebutting the rhetoric of remediation while advising the new graduate instructors: "To teach writing well, you need an accurate assessment of the discipline [rhetoric and composition] itself. . . . If you believe in a golden age when English teachers did nothing but teach literature because the high schools were doing their job properly, you are simply indulging in mythology."[54] Then, shortly after Ruszkiewicz's remarks, Corbett soporifically lectured about the continuous tradition of language arts education from the ancient Greeks to the mid-1980s.[55] Just before skipping town after his lecture, Corbett wrote a note on hotel stationery to Ruszkiewicz obliquely referencing the interdepartmental turmoil: "I hope things work out well for the writing program, and I also hope that time may heal the wounds that were suffered and inflicted in this last year."[56] In August 1985 while Corbett stood under the Holiday Inn portico hailing a cab to the Austin airport, the English faculty was preparing not to bandage wounds but to twist the knife.

Kruppa's appeal to financial necessity convinced most of the English professors to remand E 306 to University Extension. The rhetoric of remediation convinced faculty outside the English department to support this decision. And the literature-versus-rhetoric narrative persuaded Kinneavy, Ruszkiewicz, and Hairston that they were being blitzed. None of these stories accurately represent the root cause of the UT Austin abolitionist movement. Not disdain for remediation or a haughty assertion of literature's superiority but instead economic austerity had besieged the first-year writing requirement. But, just as defeat seemed imminent, the cavalry arrived. An entirely different line of argument had incensed the undergraduates. The student newspaper began regularly reporting on the Kruppa proposal in September 1985, not long after the English faculty had approved it.[57] Student journalists worried (accurately) that E 306 taught through University Extension would cost students more than residential instruction.[58] In the spring of 1986, they resumed their coverage, publishing the second article in a two-part series on the abolition of E 306.[59] Students voiced their opposition immediately and consistently. Against the rhetoric of remediation, students positioned their own rhetoric of irresponsibility, a *deus ex discipulis* as unexpected and powerful as any *deus ex machina*.

In September 1985, the *Daily Texan* complained that "if E 306 is required for graduation, it must be an important course. The least the English department can do is teach it."[60] An English major said the faculty in essence had declared, "If you can't write, it's not our problem."[61] A junior majoring in psychology accosted the English faculty with similar imputations: "How can the university expect us to know what they haven't taught us?"[62] A high school senior wrote the *Austin American-Statesman* asking, "How is it that they can require a course but not teach it?" The *Statesman* advice columnist replied, "If all course requirements could be satisfied without having to put a bunch of noisy, loutish young people in a classroom and teach them, the university could get on with its real business."[63] Kruppa's patient explanation that they had to solve the lecturer problem by looking at all the administrative options drowned in the din of undergraduate outrage. Ruszkiewicz contributed his voice to the heckler's veto, telling a reporter for the *Daily Texan* that E 306 taken through University Extension would cost more than taking the course residentially, "$24 in the regular terms versus $108 in extension."[64] Hairston, Trimble, Ruszkiewicz, and Kinneavy wrote and circulated a lengthy critique of Kruppa's proposal. They included Ruszkiewicz's concerns about cost, but they also repeated Kinneavy's claims about quality and labor. E 306 offered through University Extension would be a bad class taught by forty-five to fifty lecturers, they alleged. And they added a concern about the English graduate program. To prepare for their future careers in academe, graduate students needed to apprentice in first-year writing classes.[65] Kinneavy told the University Council that the Kruppa proposal would turn UT Austin's writing program into an "embarrassment."[66]

University administrators must have heard these complaints. They certainly noticed when the local press began to repeat the undergraduates' rhetoric of irresponsibility. In May, *Texas Monthly* ran an extended article comparing UT Austin to its rival, Texas A&M, asserting that UT Austin faculty had a deep antipathy toward undergraduate education. In a scathing review filled with humiliating details, the article emphasized UT Austin's poor writing instruction and a "lax credit-by-exam policy" that allowed many underprepared students to test out of E 306.[67] Some of the literature faculty expressed concern about their public image.[68] So the upper administration began to change its tune. In February 1986, James Vick, a once-upon-a-time abolitionist, did an about-face, saying that moving E 306 to University Extension would leave the university with the "weakest possible English requirement."[69] In February, despite Hairston's recriminations and Vick's volte-face, Vice President Fonken still supported Kruppa's proposal to abolish E 306.[70] By May, Fonken, like Vick, could see that the tide was turning against abolition, so he assured everyone that E 306 was not going to University Extension. It would be offered on campus for years to come.[71]

But it wouldn't. E 306 hadn't been saved, only given a reprieve. The course wouldn't be sacrificed on a public altar, but it would die of a thousand cuts. After suffering a loss in the court of public opinion, the English department leadership realized that they could not eliminate the first-year writing requirement de jure, but financial austerity remained, as did the ban on contingent labor, so they decided to abolish E 306 de facto. First, they removed the writing program from the rhetoric faculty's hands. In March 1986, as public outrage about the abolition of E 306 swelled, the English department chair removed Ruszkiewicz from his position as director of the writing program.[72] Ruszkiewicz was replaced by a literature professor. Lance Bertelson came to UT Austin in 1978 after earning his PhD with a concentration in eighteenth-century British literature from the University of Washington. Thin expertise qualified him for this newfound position. For a year while in graduate school, he had assisted the director of first-year writing. Now recently tenured, Bertelson had to "calm things down." After the lecturer massacre, Bertelson pledged to "be nice" and not to "come up with anything controversial—at all."[73] He kept his promise, directing the writing program for two uneventful years. In 1988, Bertelson handed the reins over to a cultural studies scholar. The first-year writing program was also placed under a new suzerain. Wayne Rebhorn became chair of the Lower Division Policy Committee, which oversaw two subcommittees, one focused on sophomore-level literature classes and the other managing first-year writing classes.[74] The "acting director" of the first-year writing program did not invite Kinneavy, Slatin, Faigley, or Hairston to present at the new teacher orientation. Only Ruszkiewicz spoke, and then briefly.[75] Later, Ruszkiewicz accused his successors of replacing Kinneavy's compendious guide to first-year writing instruction (the 1987 E 306 syllabus) with a thirteen-page handout suggesting that new graduate instructors choose among avant-garde critical theories.[76] This episode of scandalous negligence resulted in the disarray that Linda Brodkey inherited when she became director of lower-division writing in the fall of 1989.[77]

Departmental neglect starved E 306 of engaged faculty. As more students tested out of the writing requirement, enrollment attrition robbed the classes of matriculants. Seventeen percent of UT Austin's students tested out of E 306 in 1978.[78] By 1986, that number had risen to 40 percent. Once transfer credits were taken into consideration, only one of every three students took their required first-year writing course on campus.[79] In 1988, 45 percent of entering students tested out of the class. Undergraduates continued to pressure the faculty with charges of irresponsibility. A first-year student told the *Daily Texan* that a "90 minute multiple choice exam" could not "possibly take the place of the eight to 10 papers required of E 306 students."[80] Others outside the university similarly groused. In 1991, numerous Austin high school English teachers wrote Vice President Fonken to complain that half of all UT Austin students received credit for E 306 through transfer or by taking the English Composition Test.[81] The steady exodus of students continued for the next three decades. In the 2014–15 academic year, 7,539 new students enrolled at the university, but only 1,133 took the required first-year writing course in residence.[82] In less than thirty years, the enrollment in E 306 fell from 83 percent to 25 percent of the incoming first-year class. The writing requirement was never formally abolished, but it was thoroughly diminished. Composition instruction would not burden the university with staffing problems. Austerity had quietly claimed the universally required writing class—an industrial era mainstay of American higher education—even while the class remained on the books of the university catalog.

The first-year writing requirement, by then a century old, was a product of a century-long expansion of higher education, an effort to accommodate students who were underprepared for college-level work. Recent scholarship has documented how cruel and belittling this requirement could be, especially when students were made to take remedial writing classes where their skill levels were linked to personal failings and inherent attributes.[83] This flawed but well-intentioned effort to open higher education's doors persisted as long as the student population grew in tandem with state support. When public funding no longer kept pace with enrollments, the requirement faltered. At UT Austin starting in the 1980s, fiscal austerity bled E 306 so much that it might as well have been sacrificed. The concomitant disagreement about what constitutes American citizenship and proper civic education would similarly challenge the uniform curriculum taught in UT Austin's required writing classes.

Unlike James Kinneavy, Maxine Hairston, and John Ruszkiewicz, Lester Faigley had been an active member of the Kruppa committee. When the proposal to abolish E 306 was put before the English faculty, he seconded it.[84] He admitted that abolition was difficult, but he believed that students would benefit more from a different sort of writing class. Standing right next to him in solidarity was American literature professor Evan Carton.[85] When Kinneavy asked the University Council to stop the sinister plot against E 306, Faigley championed abolition.[86] But Faigley wasn't a turncoat. Rather, he was a pragmatist trying to resolve an internal dispute. On the one side were those who wanted to read challenging works of literature and philosophy. On the other side were those who encouraged civic engagement and technical skill. One of Kinneavy's acolytes, a graduate student committed to midcentury civic literacy, marched with the latter camp, stuffing a mimeographed defense of E 346K and E 306 into all the faculty mailboxes. He said some professors harbored a narrow view of "humanism" that led them to push for writing instruction featuring great books and big ideas. In contrast, he proposed a "civic" and "activist" definition of humanism that was achievable in E 306.[87] In his classes, he had been asking students to write letters to the editors of local newspapers, believing that the goal of literacy education is "citizenship," a universally democratic value.[88] Opposite this viewpoint was an assistant professor who advocated for literature and philosophy in the writing curriculum. She opposed teaching civic literacy in a required first-year course because a remedial emphasis on "narrowly technical" skills could not address "portentous social issues." Of course, she wanted "civic responsibility and civic action." Her class, titled "Technology and the Self," would respond "civically to the special emphasis on this campus on technology and business."[89]

This electric disagreement charged several heated departmental exchanges. In the summer of 1985, for example, Ruszkiewicz wrote one of Faigley's abolitionist conspirators to defend E 306 and E 346K. Like Kinneavy's graduate student, Ruszkiewicz defended any writing pedagogy that put "language and writing at the center of undergraduate education."[90] His opponent, another tenured faculty member, replied, "Writing courses [must be] based on significant readings, so that students will learn to write, to think, and to *be* better."[91] In March 1986 when Kinneavy made his final stand, pleading with the general faculty to preserve E 306, Faigley allied with Ruszkiewicz's opponent, suggesting that the English department replace two required writing courses (E 306 and E 346K) that imparted practical literacy with two content courses (E 309 and E 316) that served the faculty's disciplinary interests. Ruszkiewicz objected, saying that the English professors aimed to trade a successful writing class for "a literature course." Hairston similarly balked, saying their "state-of-the-art composition program ... put together and run for the past fifteen years by professional specialists" was being tossed out. In its place was a literature survey assembled by "faculty whose expertise is not in composition studies." But the English department chair got the last word. He reminded Kinneavy and company that writing pedagogy emphasizing "intellectual content" had recently been featured in one of the major research journals dedicated to rhetoric and composition, *College English*.[92] E 309 would replace E 306.

Faigley and his allies wanted to obviate the struggle between literature specialists and compositionists by simply erasing the uniform curriculum. They recommended the English department replace the required first-year course with a rigorous elective whose content and pedagogy varied according to the instructor's interest. Five years earlier at a University Council meeting, a government professor had originally pitched this idea: "Let us call it E 309, Advanced Rhetoric and Composition, to be taken at the lower-division level before the taking of the Masterworks of Literature."[93] Unlike E 306, E 309 would allow each instructor to choose their topic, select their readings, and teach in their preferred manner. Most important, unlike E 306, E 309 would not be required for all majors or part of the core curriculum. In between this prescient suggestion and Faigley's subcommittee recommendation, several other English faculty cozied up to the elective banquet. James

Sledd, for instance, wanted to replace the defunct E 346K with a slate of elective lower-division writing classes, and Neill Megaw agreed wholeheartedly.[94] John Slatin, then a recent hire with expertise in modernist literature, similarly suggested a buffet of lower-division "foundations courses," all taught in different ways, with varying content and pedagogies.[95] They were all looking for a compromise. Sledd explained, "From a full range of electives, a set of requirements might emerge," but in the meantime, an elective curriculum might allow some departmental detente, "with nobody losing face or violating conscience."[96] Slatin echoed Sledd, explaining, "All of us, 'literature people' and 'composition people' alike, need to acknowledge that we teach composition *all the time*, although we do it in different ways."[97] Faigley, similarly looking for a practical compromise that would address faculty infighting and administrative austerity, wanted to prepare a lower-division feast with philosophical fare and rhetorical fodder.[98]

Faigley's compromise proved revolutionary. Those wanting to teach practical proficiency and civic literacy could have students write letters to the editor. And those wanting to read literary masterpieces could assign heady tomes and analytical essays. E 309 tolerated multiple approaches. Other, extradepartmental factors ensured the elective curriculum's success. Faculty across the university still refused to teach writing classes in their home departments. As a result, students couldn't find the six hours of upper-division writing coursework recommended by the Vick report and required for most majors. In the late 1980s, the upper administration yielded to the faculty's recalcitrance. In April 1989, the Education Policy Committee of the University Faculty Senate proposed that any writing course (lower or upper division) might fulfill a student's six-hour writing requirement.[99] Taking Kinneavy's advice into consideration, the University Council eventually passed a set of revised recommendations that excepted E 306 and E 316 but allowed all other lower-division writing classes to satisfy the two-course mandate.[100] Thus was born UT Austin's "substantial writing requirement." Instead of a lockstep curricular march through civic literacy and professional skills, students could choose any two courses (lower or upper division) featuring writing as a significant part of the classroom instruction. Since everyone needed to find six hours of substantial writing coursework beyond E 306/E 316, and faculty outside the English department were unwilling to offer substantial writing courses, E 309 sold to a hungry market.

Between the spring of 1988 and the fall of 1989, the College of Liberal Arts offered a feast of 228 classes with a substantial writing component per semester (on average), most of them in the Department of English. By comparison, students pecked at a paltry thirty-three writing classes per semester (on average) in the College of Communications—the second-highest number of substantial writing component classes.[101] In the School of Social Work, students starved on their meager ration of two courses with a substantial writing component per semester. A report from the University Faculty Senate Curriculum Committee concluded that most colleges and schools were either barely sustaining or horribly depriving their undergraduates. Only the College of Liberal Arts, thanks to the English department, offered more writing courses than its students needed. One hundred and fifty-five writing classes per semester would have satisfied the graduation requirements of liberal arts majors, yet their college offered 278. When students outside the College of Liberal Arts couldn't find writing classes in their departments, they gorged at the E 309 buffet. The variety of topics and approaches to writing instruction offered in 1989—most under the banner of E 309—paraded before the students' bulging eyes: "The Construction of Gender," "Rock and Roll/Cultural Criticism," "Writing about Failure," "Writing about the Social Construction of the Self," "Writing in Context," "Thinking and Learning," "Culture and Society."[102]

While an interdepartmental disagreement about first-year writing pedagogy provided the immediate exigency for Faigley's elective first-year writing curriculum, an intellectual undercurrent carried E 309 to the UT Austin campus. Experts in the field of writing studies were disputing the nature of literacy, so they questioned the uniform curriculum required at the time in most first-year college writing classes. Faigley was among the "new abolitionist" intellectual vanguards "arguing from their scholarly as well as their practical knowledge of writing issues that students are not as well served by the required . . . [first-year] course as they could be by other kinds of writing instruction."[103] Faigley and others wanted to remove the uniform curriculum and its Cold War presumption of universal literacy.[104] This first fissure would become the intellectual fracture that culminated in the Battle of Texas. Leading scholars in the field asserted that the universal requirement promoted a cultural uniformity suited to the ideological climate of mid-century America.[105] They spared no one in this critique. By neo-abolitionist lights, the neoclassicists, like Kinneavy, tried to impart literacy with a "unity and transferability" that never existed.[106] In neo-abolitionists' eyes, process pedagogues purported to teach a singular depoliticized skill to a psychically whole writer. But in reality, they inculcated industrial era dispositions, such as hard work, democratic ideals, and a utilitarian mindset, and always failed to impart the "practical skills" promised on every syllabus. Shattering the instrumentalist consensus that held Kinneavy, Hairston, and Ruszkiewicz together, these theorists made bold statements challenging the foundation of any uniform curriculum. They proclaimed, among other things, that "there is no such thing as 'the academic essay.'"[107] Based on this momentous theoretical revelation, they proposed abolishing the universal curriculum in favor of an elective writing program.[108] If literacy is fragmented, then writing classes should be plural.

Advancing with the neo-abolitionist battalion, Faigley skewered the intellectual foundation of Kinneavy's *Theory of Discourse*, mortally wounding the uniform curriculum that Kinneavy had imposed on every section of E 306. Faigley explained that "a coherent consciousness capable of knowing oneself and the world" is a modern mirage. He went on to illustrate that composition studies had fractured into two competing views of the subject, (1) the high modern and psychically integral composer, and (2) "the postmodern 'free' individual of consumer capitalism: one who can change identities at will because identities are acquired by what one consumes."[109] He reviewed a range of approaches to writing—linguistically informed, politically radical, grammatically technical—finding beneath every one a presumption of "coherent textual unity that reflects liberal consensus . . . only as long as the *author*-ity of the author as a rational, knowing subject is maintained."[110] In his scholarly writing, Faigley shatters the Cold War consensus about universal instrumentalist literacy. In his successful proposal for an elective writing curriculum, he challenged the uniform writing curriculum, a pedagogical institution that had been in place at nearly every college and university since the beginning of the industrial era.

One year later, Linda Brodkey's effort to impose a uniform curriculum on all sections of E 306 was the last attempt to realize any singular vision of civic literacy and writing pedagogy at UT Austin. After that fiasco ended, no one would dare try to impose the same pedagogy on every UT Austin writing class. Intellectual fracture, diversity politics, and culture wars erased the midcentury pedagogical consensus about literacy and its correlative curricular uniformity. Postindustrial consumerism invited an elective curriculum that allowed students to choose a writing class according to their individual fancy. With the universal requirement winnowed thanks to fiscal austerity, and the uniform curriculum erased due to intellectual fracture and diversity politics, all that was left for a complete transformation was an administrative overhaul of the English department.

Lester Faigley wasn't the only person favoring an elective over a uniform writing curriculum. Motivated by fiscal austerity, interdepartmental disagreement, and intellectual fracture, some of the rhetoric faculty walked another road to Jerusalem. In April 1985, Stephen Witte presented a report to the University Faculty Senate emphasizing three intertwined problems: the labor problem, the departmental problem, and the philosophical problem. The labor problem had been debated as a "logistical" concern since the late 1970s—too many students, not enough money. The departmental problem arose from the competing interests between literary scholars and rhetoric practitioners. And the philosophical problem manifested in the competing approaches to first-year writing instruction. Witte fixated on the departmental and philosophical problems, saying that literature professors with no scholarly credentials in writing pedagogy claimed authority over first-year composition: "This university has traditionally viewed published scholarship as the only basis for claiming expert knowledge in a field."[111] John Ruszkiewicz repeated the sentiment when complaining about the literature faculty's "uninformed" approach to writing instruction.[112] Maxine Hairston likewise contrasted the "state-of-the-art" curriculum in E 306 with the retrograde approach found in some E 309 courses.[113] Witte didn't defend the E 306 requirement or reassert the need for E 346K. Instead, he offered a "comprehensive solution": "Accord writing, the study of writing, and the teaching of writing independent status as a discipline, to create a separate department of literacy complete with an undergraduate and a graduate program, in a college with a dean who will respect it as a discipline."[114] When they turned away from pedagogical arguments about remediation and departmental disagreements about disciplinarity and instead started to proffer practical solutions to the twin problems of contingent labor and faculty dissensus, the rhetoric faculty got the administration's attention. Dean Robert King called John Trimble into his office to say that he was already promoting, on the sly, an independent writing division.[115] Trimble also learned that, unlike the rhetoric faculty, King singularly cared about labor. Witte's departmental and philosophical conundrums were minor diversions. King needed a solution to what he called the "fundamental problem" of "enrollments" that could not rely on more than fifteen lecturers and should seriously consider remanding E 306 to community colleges.[116] The rhetoric faculty saw an opportunity to trade abolition for autonomy.

The rhetoric faculty wanted to solve the departmental problem by giving autarky to two regions (rhetoric and literature), both within the English department's kingdom. This new division of composition would also solve the philosophical problem by giving the literature faculty complete control over lower-division classes designated as literature classes (such as E 316) and giving the rhetoric faculty control over lower-division classes designated as rhetoric classes (such as E 317 and E 310). Finally, the labor problem would be solved by altering E 306. The rhetoric faculty wanted the course to remain residential but not required. They believed that students would voluntarily recognize their need for a first-year writing course, so enrollment would drop but not completely disappear. Since enrollment in E 306 was already in a free fall, this decision to make the class an elective did not seem like a major concession. In place of the first-year writing requirement, they suggested a panoply of writing classes ranging from E 306 (a standard introduction to college-level writing) to E 317 (a technical writing course suited to sophomores in engineering and the applied sciences) to E 310 (an intermediate writing course for students majoring in business and other applied studies) to E 325 (an upper-division course for those wanting to improve their creative nonfiction) to E 346K (a junior-level writing-across-the-curriculum course). They concluded their report by addressing Dean King's outstanding concern. Without a universal requirement, the English department would only schedule as many classes as it could staff with professors and graduate instructors. This, of course, was the same advantage offered by Faigley's successful proposal for an eclectic curriculum offered under the banner of E 309.[117]

The rhetoric committee submitted their proposal to Dean King in May 1985 just as the Kruppa committee was beginning its work. Three months later when the English department began to consider the Kruppa proposal, Kinneavy asked the English professors to consider his suggestions. In September, the *Daily Texan* ran a full-page investigative article detailing the two competing curricular overhauls. Kruppa and Kinneavy appeared beneath the masthead, staring one another down in separately aggressive profiles.[118] This presentation made high drama out of a foregone conclusion. The English faculty flatly refused to consider Kinneavy's report, though they discussed Kruppa's proposal at length. An associate professor of Irish literature called the question, and the faculty voted overwhelmingly in favor of Kruppa's proposal.[119] Kinneavy subsequently tried to get the University Council to intervene, but to no avail. When his complaints reached the council's agenda in May 1986, King told the general faculty that this was a matter for the English department to decide, and they had decided it back in September.[120] King didn't care if the writing requirement and the uniform curriculum were replaced by Faigley's E 309 or Kinneavy's suite of lower- and upper-division classes since both equally addressed the problems of fiscal austerity and faculty dissensus. Since most of the English faculty favored Faigley's proposal, Dean King threw his weight behind it.

The Kruppa and the Kinneavy committees responded to the same exigencies and arrived at similar solutions. The logistical problem of contingent labor led them all to accept the effective abolition of the first-year writing requirement. The intellectual fracture among the faculty prompted their acquiescence to an elective writing curriculum. Faigley and Kruppa wanted to remand E 306 to University Extension and institute E 309, a course that varied as much as the instructors who taught it. Hairston, Trimble, Kinneavy, and Ruszkiewicz threw out universal requirements altogether, instead offering what Kruppa called a "cafeteria" of options.[121] Both committees and both proposals were following national trends. The scholarly field of rhetoric and composition had been steadily turning away from universal requirements for some time.[122] Unfortunately, in 1985, while there was much incentive to replace the required first-year course with an elective writing curriculum, there was no institutional motive to create a separate academic unit. After the controversy over Brodkey's "Writing about Difference" syllabus, Dean King and President Cunningham realized that an independent division of writing might obviate embarrassing public scandals about writing pedagogy. The labor problem had imperiled the universal writing requirement, while intellectual disagreement had poisoned the uniform writing curriculum. The culture war's risorgimento of civic literacy, now artfully retrofitted for the politics of diversity, finally provided an excuse to administratively overhaul the English department.

In a greenish, low-slung, rambling building a few blocks north of the UT Austin campus, Trudy's Texas Star serves up gut-busting Tex-Mex cuisine. Here, in late November 1991 after the public battle over Linda Brodkey's E 306 syllabus, Elizabeth Cullingford and John Ruszkiewicz sat across from each other, sharing chips and salsa, wanting to "mend fences." Cullingford, at that time, was an associate professor of literature, Ruszkiewicz an associate professor of rhetoric. She admitted that their peace mission may be "an impossibility." After ten years of controversy, some professors nursed too many grievances. Others hid too many skeletons. The chasms dividing them seemed innumerable and unbridgeable: a literature scholar and a writing teacher, a political liberal and a moderate conservative, an Oxford alumna and an Ohio State graduate.[123]

But Cullingford was a charming Pollyanna with a lilting British accent. She was also in Paris during the Brodkey affair. So she seemed impartial.

She confessed that she did not support the "Writing about Difference" syllabus. She thought the course's proponents were in a "highly emotional, highly political mood." Besides, she confided, the course would never fly in Texas. Toward the end of the conversation, she turned to the subject of Robert King, who had recently been reappointed dean of the College of Liberal Arts, this time in an "acting" capacity. When their lunch concluded, Ruszkiewicz left the table with a full belly and an unsettled mind. Though he thought their conversation "candid," he didn't find much common ground "beyond the notion that we shouldn't act so uncivilly toward one another."[124] A little more than a decade later, the separations between them would extend from scholarly and political matters to administrative responsibilities. Not long after their lunch, Ruszkiewicz joined a new, independent unit in the College of Liberal Arts. Cullingford would remain in the English department, ultimately becoming its chair, while Ruszkiewicz eventually served as director of the Division of Rhetoric and Composition.

On June 1, 1991, after Standish Meacham's untimely abdication from the dean's office, Robert King returned to his regal post—this time for an interregnum.[125] As acting dean, King's first order of business was the (again unruly) issue of English department governance. He felt that the Executive Committee—which he had favored in 1985—gave too much authority to a small coterie of radical professors. The E 306 controversy provided an opportune pretext for his managerial imposition. He demanded a new governmental structure, an Executive Budget Council consisting of full professors. Geoff Henley sided with King, proclaiming in his *Daily Texan* column that the Executive Budget Council was a democratic assembly able to thwart those totalitarian Leftists and their Marxist curricular agenda.[126] In late June when the department chair heard of King's machinations, he called a meeting of the full English faculty. Then he wrote to King, complaining about the Executive Committee's possible dissolution.[127] Other conservative culture warriors at the *Daily Texan* threw their weight behind King, likening the English department's Executive Committee to the Soviet Union's Communist Party.[128] Now writing for the popular left-wing press, Scott Henson accused King of tyranny.[129] In October, an associate professor of English lobbied to reassemble the local chapter of the American Association of University Professionals, claiming that King's efforts threatened the long-standing tradition of shared faculty governance.[130] But this counteroffensive was short-lived. In December, the English department gave in to King's demands, agreeing to a modified Executive Budget Council: nine full professors, five associate professors, and two assistant professors, all elected.[131]

The Battles of Texas

Dean King's next initiative began in the winter of 1992. In January, an ad hoc University Council Committee on the Undergraduate Experience issued its report listing a series of proposals. It was a mélange of possibilities reflecting the politics of diversity and the rights revolution that dominated higher education in the latter decades of the twentieth century: a dorm for students who wanted more multicultural relationships, a center for students seeking opportunities to volunteer, a "Teaching Institute" offering incentive and funding for curricular innovation. Under the larger heading of possible "actions to improve instruction in writing," the committee mentioned "a Division of Rhetoric and Composition." This new unit would be "established in the College of Liberal Arts" and "responsible for the administration, staffing, and teaching of first-year and advanced composition courses." The proposal for a new academic unit dedicated to writing instruction was out of place among these other initiatives. Alongside more elaborate and grandiose suggestions, like a "University Honors Program" and an annual festival celebrating Texas diversity, and subordinated beneath a tedious subheading, the Division of Rhetoric and Composition might easily go unnoticed.[132] But it caught King's eye because reorganizing the English department would allow him to address fiscal austerity and the politics of diversity. He could fix the lecturer problem and diffuse the culture war with a grand top-down putsch.

When delivering his report to the general faculty in January, the committee chair recommending these policies explained that the general faculty would deliberate some, while the upper administration would mandate others.[133] The following May, Dean King convinced the provost (Gerhard Fonken) and the president (William Cunningham) to take up the suggestion for a new Division of Rhetoric and Composition.[134] Dean King wouldn't risk this initiative by exposing it to faculty debate or popular vote. This government by fiat elicited complaints from the English department. The department chair grumbled that administratively separating the writing program from the English department would be a "bad idea."[135] But outside the English department, the proposal for a new division was heralded. Geoff Henley, among others, celebrated. As Henley saw it, the English department had behaved irresponsibly. It was time for the adults to take charge.[136] Other *Daily Texan* columnists agreed that a new administrative unit would reduce departmental infighting, so faculty could focus on undergraduate education.[137] Meanwhile, behind closed doors, the president, the dean, and the provost discussed the proposal's feasibility. In early August, King tipped his hand to Ruszkiewicz, asking for a budget.[138]

Both Dean King and President Cunningham would later claim credit, with King calling the creation of the Division of Rhetoric and Composition "my finest accomplishment."[139] They met with Provost Fonken on August 31, 1992, Cunningham's last day as president. Cunningham wanted to ensure that undergraduate writing classes would be staffed by dedicated teachers, not research professors. He worried that if they didn't address the matter then and there while King held the reins, then it would never be settled. He was convinced that the "only way to solve this problem once and for all was to create a separate division . . . apart from the English department and under the direct control of the dean's office." In all writing classes, Cunningham wanted "professional full-time teachers," many with PhDs but none on the tenure track. He turned to King: "The stars are aligned. If we don't do this and do it today, it will not happen. Bob, if you will recommend it to Gerry [Fonken], and, Gerry, if you will recommend it to me, I will approve it."[140] He promised that the new division would be "a great step forward in the continuing improvement of the undergraduate educational experience." The author of the report initially proposing an autonomous writing program predicted that the new division would reduce the tension between literature and rhetoric faculty, allowing professors to properly focus on the classroom. Ruszkiewicz agreed: "In the long run, we'll end up with one of the best writing programs in the country."[141] The day after creating the Division of Rhetoric and Composition, William Cunningham resigned as president and ascended to the chancellor's office in the University of Texas system.

With a new president at the helm, Dean King stayed onboard to implement the old president's decree. In September, the English department chair circulated King's plan.[142] He revealed that King didn't want a fully independent academic unit; the dean wanted to appoint the division's director, and the director would make curricular and staffing decisions, which were all subject to the dean's approval. Many professors believed King was seizing control of the writing program. This was managerialism as its most egregious. So the English faculty pushed back. Several objected that the process for creating the new administrative unit violated long-standing practices of shared faculty governance. Professors who had disagreed bitterly with Kinneavy during previous moments of departmental crisis now allied with him to oppose King's administrative overreach. One of Kinneavy's erstwhile enemies complained that President Cunningham's actions showed "no attempt . . . to consult with those of us who have shown a lifetime commitment to teaching writing." Kinneavy added that the division's director and the college dean would exercise complete control over staffing.[143] The newly appointed director of the English graduate program circulated a petition to hold an English department meeting about King's proposal. If English graduate students were shut out of teaching the new division's writing classes, what activity would subsidize the graduate program in literature?[144]

The English faculty met in late September. Kinneavy told the fifty or so professors in attendance that he did not believe a new unit would improve the quality of writing instruction. He told others privately, "The members of the Rhetoric group are not straining to get out of the department."[145] Faigley, Slatin, and Trimble all agreed. Only Ruszkiewicz voiced his full-throated support of the new academic unit.[146] The rhetoric faculty—Lester Faigley, John Slatin, John Trimble, John Ruszkiewicz, and Linda Ferreira-Buckley—decided to form their own committee so they could discuss and respond to Dean King's proposal.[147] Though she supported the new division, Maxine Hairston did not join their committee because she had recently retired. Kinneavy similarly absented himself, though for different reasons. Despite his promotion of a similar restructuring seven years prior, Kinneavy now had reservations about an administrative reorganization. Faculty outside the English department shared his concerns. John Durbin, a professor of mathematics and an influential member of the University Council, wrote the new president to voice his reservations.[148] In mid-September, the University Council met for the first time to deliberate King's proposal. Provost Fonken fielded questions. Then he suggested that King hold court at the next meeting of the general faculty.[149] At the October 19 meeting, King explained that his plan was not set in stone, but the need could not be ignored. The Division of Rhetoric and Composition would open its doors in June 1993, though its governance, staffing, and place within the college might differ from the original proposal. The university president told the University Council that the matter was settled.[150] Carton had campaigned against programmatic independence, claiming that the English department was doing a fine job with writing instruction. He said that instead of taking the writing program from the English professors, the rest of the university should follow the English faculty's good example.[151] He soon became chair of an unwieldy English department committee that had to design the new unit, which he had opposed. Faigley, now aware of the curricular potential in the new division, joined Carton's committee, diluting their animus toward King's proposal.[152]

In his plan for the Division of Rhetoric and Composition, Dean King followed the example set by other colleges and universities where administrators severed their writing programs from their English departments. In 1993, two other independent writing programs, at the University of Arkansas Little Rock and San Diego State University, were similarly commanded into existence. In all three places, the upper administration placed the writing program directly under the dean's control.[153] In the years prior and those since, many deans, provosts, and presidents have similarly liberated rhetoric and composition faculty from English departments, claiming to advance educational excellence through administrative intervention.[154] When President Cunningham announced the new division, he repeated the typical promises: "The establishment of a Division of Rhetoric and Composition would bring about a new and valuable focus to the improvement of writing skills."[155] King elaborated, claiming that the division would improve education by "employing and training teachers comfortable with their mission," "target[ing] its instruction to serve more students," and being "directly accountable" for undergraduate success.[156]

To most of the faculty within the English department, Dean King's plan seemed frighteningly managerial. One director would lord over a collection of contingent faculty, hiring and firing at will. If this composition czar chose to appoint any tenure track professors, they would have to come from other units, so they could be removed from the division and returned to their home departments by individual command and without appeal. Realizing that such managerial control might endanger his proposal, King assured everyone that the division's director and associate director could hire good teachers, design quality courses, and come up with innovative responses to student demand and the job market. He promised better coordination between the lower-division courses (taught primarily by graduate instructors and contingent faculty) and upper-division courses (taught largely by tenure track professors). He vowed that new and exciting efforts, like the Writing Center and the Computer Writing and Research Lab, would be better managed and administered. He explained that lower-division instruction would particularly improve because the division's associate director could focus attention on writing courses without the distraction of literature courses.[157]

Dean King promised that his new division would be pedagogically nimble, responsive, and innovative. When Ruszkiewicz defended King's proposal before the English faculty, he compared it to the Saturn auto manufacturer, which similarly promised to implement a new management strategy allowing for greater innovation and market sensitivity. They could change their managerial "culture" to allow the rhetoric faculty to "think faster, smarter, better" and "strive for real excellence."[158] But the rest of the faculty saw no such potential. To their minds, the new writing division would extend King's old managerial control. King's plan exemplified the administrative oversight now common in market-oriented colleges and universities. One academic dean at the DeVry Institute of Technology explains that administrators in for-profit higher education see faculty governance as a hindrance to pedagogical innovation.[159] At for-profit schools, pedagogical change happens at the top. Teaching faculty deliver but don't develop curricula.[160] King's director of the Division of Rhetoric and Composition, similarly, would hire teachers and mandate curricula. King hoped that tenure track faculty would teach a few token upper-division writing classes. He admitted that lecturers and graduate instructors would teach the lion's share of the division's offerings.[161]

While Ruszkiewicz analogized Dean King's plan for the Division of Rhetoric and Composition to the just-in-time management practices at the Saturn corporation, just up the road at Texas A&M University, another rhetoric professor painted a dystopian picture of a "Suzuki" composition program. Where Ruszkiewicz saw pedagogical potential in the Saturn model, Jan Swearingen saw managerial control.[162] She was awed by the same dystopian vision that nowadays captivates those who criticize the marketization of higher education: managerial imposition, the end of small classes, the erosion of tenure, the onslaught of digitized distance education, employment precarity for the professoriate, institutional collapse for the humanities. While recently indulging such a dark fantasy, one commentator emphasizes, "I do not believe this bleak picture is inevitable."[163] The experience of the rhetoric faculty at UT Austin likewise lends hope for a different future. Sharing such hope, Ruszkiewicz and his cohort refused King's all-powerful director, opting instead for another system of faculty governance. They reached toward what Clyde Barrow has called a new university management paradigm characterized by institutes and centers: "Unlike a heavily tenured department, institutes and centers . . . respond to uncertain funding opportunities by maintaining a small permanent nucleus of flexible specialists, supplemented by an ever-changing satellite faculty."[164] Five tenured rhetoric professors would serve as the flexible specialists. A fleet of graduate instructors, a few lecturers, a couple of para-academic administrators, and one "specialist" would be the satellite faculty. No all-powerful director would determine curricula. The core professors would set a curricular example by teaching their own classes and training the graduate instructors. The satellite faculty would contribute their expertise and ability.

While the English department committee worked out the division's governance, the University Faculty Senate formed another committee intended to scrutinize Dean King's plan.[165] Their suggestions were taken up and approved by the University Council in mid-November.[166] Provost Fonken didn't appoint the University Council committee until February 1993, essentially neutering its ability to influence the division's design because the committee members wouldn't begin meeting until the academic unit had opened its doors. No longer able to criticize its inception, they decided to help the new division achieve its mission.[167] Lester Faigley, recently appointed to serve as the division's first director, became a leading voice on the committee.[168] In October 1994 when the University Council committee finally submitted its recommendations, the Division of Rhetoric and Composition was fully operational. The committee recommended that UT Austin, not departmental coffers, fully fund a writing center that operated under the Division of Rhetoric and Composition's control. They also recommended additional support for writing classes across the university.[169] The rhetoric faculty further developed a suite of lower-division classes and lobbied for a series of tenure track hires. Faigley worried that without a substantial addition of faculty, the rhetoric faculty wouldn't be able to realize the division's mission. No leadership in writing pedagogy, no assistance to the substantial writing program, no pioneering efforts in tutoring or digital literacy would be possible without more tenure track professors.[170] King agreed. The division would soon add three more professors to the cadre of flexible specialists. After ten years of disagreeing about the abolition of E 306, Brodkey's syllabus, US politics, and the need for an autonomous writing program, Faigley and Ruszkiewicz finally agreed that they would not be part of a "service department."[171] The additional tenure track faculty, fully funded centers, and emerging elective curriculum guaranteed that they would get their wish.

The rhetoric faculty met with Dean King on October 5, 1992. They focused on the new initiatives that King had mentioned in his proposal: the Writing Center, the Computer Writing and Research Lab, the division's leadership in the substantial writing program, the new classes that the flexible specialists would develop and the satellite faculty might teach. They also talked about the money required to make all of this happen.[172] They had everything they wanted. They began to meet independently to develop their own vision for the new division. Lester Faigley, John Ruszkiewicz, John Slatin, and Linda Ferreira-Buckley (hired in 1990) got together weekly. Writing pedagogy was their first priority. They aimed to develop their elective lower-division writing courses (E 309), build a first-class writing center, and integrate technology into writing-studies research and instruction. They wanted to build "computer classrooms." They wanted to recruit more core faculty.[173] A few days after the rhetoric faculty's first weekly meeting, King made their membership on Evan Carton's committee official.[174] As Carton's committee developed its proposals, Faigley, Ruszkiewicz, Slatin, and Ferreira-Buckley provided most of the intellectual content. In his mid-December progress report, Carton ticked off the same wish list that the rhetoric faculty had discussed with King in early October: a writing center, computers in composition classrooms, better training for new instructors, new faculty lines. They requested an advertisement for a new faculty member specializing "in rhetorical theory or history, discourse studies, and/or composition theory and practice."[175] They would not achieve everything requested. Slatin, for instance, went so far as to suggest that no more than 10 percent of the division's classes should be taught by contingent faculty.[176] All these items had been hashed out in the informal meetings and practical compromises.[177]

While making their demands, the rhetoric and composition professors were careful to promise that their new division would solve long-standing labor problems. A two-tiered faculty would permit them to add or reduce the workforce depending on the students' demand and the university's budget. A waning first-year writing requirement would allow the division flexibility in difficult economic straits.[178] During the summer of 1993, they turned to the curriculum and wrote up a list of their proposed courses. Susan Rodi, one of the few lecturers who survived the 1985 massacre, was now full-time in the newly formed Division of Rhetoric and Composition. She imagined a suite of elective, lower-division writing courses: E 309K (Writing about Literature), E 309K (Writing about Popular Culture), E 309L (The Writing Process), and E 309M (Thinking and Writing). John Slatin further suggested that E 309M focus on writing with technology. Linda Ferreira-Buckley cautioned that E 309K courses should emphasize writing, not literature—skills, not content. John Trimble asked that all the lower-division writing classes address some of the technical, stylistic matters that he taught in E 325 (Advanced Writing).[179]

By the summer, the division's priorities became clear, crystalized in their curricular proposals. They cared about their new classes, bold centers, and innovative programs. The *Daily Texan* gushed about the elective, lower-division curriculum.[180] The UT Austin alumni magazine similarly heaped praise on the Writing Center, the Computer Writing and Research Lab, the curriculum, and the instructor training.[181] In May 1994, nine months after the Division of Rhetoric and Composition officially opened, Maxine Hairston wrote Dean King, bragging about their accomplishments. She looked forward to an undergraduate major and a graduate program in rhetoric and composition. She thanked King for making "a plan that I've championed for so long . . . finally become a reality."[182] James Sledd, emeritus gadfly, saw the division as just another instance of tenure track professors feathering their nests at the expense of good education and to the detriment of contingent faculty. Sledd called Ruszkiewicz, Slatin, Faigley, Trimble, and Ferreira-Buckley "careerists," sneering that they had earned for themselves "new opportunities" while creating "new frustrations for a minority of serious composition teachers."[183] But Sledd failed to see what the rhetoric faculty saw: functional governance, effective teaching, curricular innovation, and creative centers. By cutting up the English department, implementing an elective writing curriculum, and effectively eliminating the required first-year writing requirement, they abandoned the institutions, curricula, and pedagogies that had characterized industrial era writing programs. They built something new.

The 1980s were a stormy decade battering higher education with financial austerity and political discord. In the fall of 1993 when the Division of Rhetoric and Composition opened its doors, Hairston believed that this new academic unit could sail these tumultuous waters. Since then, other writing programs across the country have similarly reconfigured their workforce, reconnoitered their curricula, and reformed their administration, with some electing institutional autonomy, others an elective curriculum or a reduction in the first-year writing requirement, and others still looking for their own way to navigate the swells. There is no single passage through this storm. Everyone working today in higher education wonders when the clouds will break and what the new sky will reveal. No clear or complete answer can come from one study of an academic unit during a decade now forty years past. Maxine Hairston and others saw great potential in administrative autonomy, as evidenced by the optimistic conclusion to this chapter's story, but their sunny outlook does not reflect the final outcome. Since 1993, numerous writing programs have attained administrative autonomy, only to find that the problems of the contemporary university do not vanish under new management. Three volumes of essays chronicle numerous independent writing programs, their titles reflecting a progression from Hairston's optimism to pragmatic pessimism: *A Field of Dreams: Independent Writing Programs and the Future of Composition Studies* (2002), *A Minefield of Dreams: Triumphs and Travails of Independent Writing Programs* (2017), and *Weathering the Storm: Independent Writing Programs in the Age of Fiscal Austerity* (2019).

The labor issue exemplifies the recalcitrant challenges facing any academic unit in contemporary higher education. A survey of thirty-four independent writing programs collected roughly ten years after the formation of the Department of Rhetoric and Composition (ca. 2001), revealed that all but one such program relied on contingent labor; tenure track faculty taught first-year writing in only 40 percent of these programs; nontenure track faculty directed 17 percent of the programs; and, overall, tenure track faculty taught only 10 percent of the writing classes offered by all thirty-four autonomous writing units.[184] An associate professor in the Department of Rhetoric and Writing Studies at San Diego State University put the matter bluntly when stating that writing program administrators, like Hairston, often assume that departmental autonomy will alleviate "the continued inequitable material conditions in which we academic professionals labor. . . . We imagine that creating a department of our own will be the answer. I can assure you it's not."[185] Echoing this sentiment, the writing program directors at the University of Winnipeg declare that "independence was no panacea" for their labor problems; for when the writing program left the English department, they maintained "a two-tier system of instructors and professors that held the potential for duplicating inequities."[186] Finally, twenty-five years after the Department of Rhetoric and Composition opened its doors, professors working in the independent writing program at the University of California, Santa Barbara, announced that two of the issues vexing Hairston continued to trouble them: "the relatively new status of writing studies as a discipline and the tenuous status of the non-tenured instructors who do the majority of the teaching, in our program and nationally."[187] We must therefore concede that the writing program at UT Austin offered no sure-fire solutions, exportable best practices, silver bullets, or safe bets for future academics.

With that concession made, the history of the Division of Rhetoric and Composition does nonetheless suggest that the future does not have to be a tempest of exploited professors, administrative mandates, and political squalls. We won't bring back the midcentury public funds or the Cold War political consensus. We can't escape the economic straits or the cultural conflicts. And we don't want to. State funding for higher education brought with it national expectations about civic literacy that clashed with contemporary diversity politics and the rights revolution. Political controversy reflects changing demographics and results from the enduring need to address students' diversity. We live in interesting times. As the history of the writing program at UT Austin from the mid-1970s through the mid-1990s proves, faculty caught between the evolving student body and the imposing upper administration are not helplessly drifting through stormy waters. Writing program administrators have a role in the future of higher education. The history of the writing program at the University of Texas at Austin teaches not the glory of administrative autonomy but the efficacy of phronetic administrators.

Conclusion
Memory, Responsibility, History

Like most universities today, the University of Texas at Austin pays a shocking sum each year to market itself to prospective students, the public at large, alumni donors, an often skeptical state legislature—anyone who will listen. Televised advertisements in recent years have been quite consistent: images filtered through a burnt-orange gel; a baritone Texas drawl extolling the virtues of the university, its researchers, its students, its storied legacy; aerial shots of a pristine campus, with sunsets framing the university skyline and panoramic sweeps of its limestone majesty; and then the marketing slogan, "What Starts Here Changes the World." Indeed, UT Austin regularly ranks highly in national and international appraisals of research universities. But it hasn't always been so. In the 1970s UT Austin was not the elite institution that it is today. UT Austin's writing program was indistinguishable from others around the country, teaching the same current-traditional rhetoric developed in the late nineteenth century. A regional school with big ambitions, the University of Texas was home to an energetic group of rhetoric and writing faculty who set out to change writing instruction.

Wider political, cultural, and economic developments contributed to this metamorphosis. Anticommunist fervor waned as US soldiers died in faraway countries fighting military insurgents. The Civil Rights Movement inspired the politics of appeal and the demands for justice: the right to fair pay for women, the right to social tolerance for the LGBTQ+ community, and the right to a college education for everyone. Adding to these political and cultural factors were demographic and economic pressures. Between 1949 and

1979, college enrollments nationwide grew by almost 400 percent, with most of that growth happening in the 1970s.[1] As enrollments grew, public funding dwindled. During the 1950s and '60s, the US federal and state governments funded higher education, seeing it as public good. But then came the taxpayer revolt of the 1970s, which began in California and spread to the Eastern Seaboard.[2] Universities had to find their own revenue in an increasingly competitive environment. At UT Austin, efficiency and excellence—marketized motives if ever there were—grew from institutional ambition. Additionally, access and inclusion—ideals inspired by diversity politics—led to curricular innovations and encountered political roadblocks. Finally, austerity—the result of reduced public funds despite rising enrollments—imposed restrictions that at times seemed unbearable.

In these changing times, industrial era justification for a universal writing requirement with a uniform curriculum—the effort to increase access, the promise of professional skills, the hope for civic edification, and the attempt to shape liberal democratic citizens—faltered, for the universal requirement required too much labor, and the uniform curriculum invited too much controversy. The ideal of what even constitutes a "democratic citizen" became a contested notion. The faculty, stumbling their way through back-to-back crises while trying nonetheless to build a world-class writing program, fell on two innovations: an autonomous writing division and an elective writing curriculum. The autonomous writing division addressed the labor crisis by adopting a flexible administrative structure and diminishing the first-year writing requirement. The UT Austin rhetoric faculty also implemented an elective writing curriculum that appealed to students as consumers, sidelining the civic mission that James Kinneavy and Linda Brodkey championed, while embracing what Lester Faigley called "the postmodern 'free' individual of consumer capitalism."[3] The elective curriculum had the added advantage of accommodating intellectual diversity among the professoriate while avoiding political controversy in the wider public sphere.

In this book, we have offered a close and detailed explanation of how transitional times led to institutional and curricular changes. Though the historical contribution is easy to repeat, the ethical argument requires explicit mention. In telling this story, we have emphasized tragic, romantic, and phronetic characters, suggesting that the latter are best suited to moments like the 1980s and our decade. The tragic protagonists are easy to spot: James Kinneavy as Oedipus, trying to forego the dissolution of a robust writing program, yet only contributing to its abolition; James Sledd as Cassandra, futilely warning about consequences that are inevitable despite his foresight; Linda

Brodkey as Orestes, desperately dodging an interdepartmental imbroglio yet harried back into its entanglement by the media furies. The romantic protagonists similarly stand forth: James Kinneavy (again) as Childe Harold, exalting midcentury civic education despite an institutional push toward professional accreditation; James Sledd (again) as Don Quixote, tilting at tenure track windmills in the managerial university; Maxine Hairston as Captain Ahab, chasing process pedagogy into a disastrous culture war; John Ruszkiewicz as John Galt, uncompromising in his values. Tragic and romantic protagonists dominate the middle chapters of our narrative. Phronetic characters emerge in the first and the last chapters. These are the compromised but effective middle managers attending "to local, material conditions rather than overhauling the intellectual superstructure of our field," making "logistical" proposals rather than "exhortatory" demands, dealing with "long-term contracts, caps on enrollments, and the authority of teachers over the design of their own courses" rather than calling for full employment or advocating absolute rights.[4] They are Maxine Hairston and James Kinneavy, who engineered a composition revolution in the late 1970s, and John Ruszkiewicz and Lester Faigley, who negotiated an autonomous writing division and an elective curriculum in the early 1990s. Notice that our characterizations of tragic, romantic, and phronetic protagonists are not deterministic. Many of the principals—notably, Kinneavy, Hairston, and Ruszkiewicz—occupy different roles at different moments of institutional tumult. Our narratologically presented claim, though, is that the phronetic writing program administrator, the fox, by seeking out compromise, seizing opportunity, and shying from absolutism is not only a more effective writing program administrator but also a more ethical one. Empowered by a willingness to compromise and unencumbered by purist idealism, the phronetic administrator offers us a model of how to navigate the choppy seas of austerity amid storms of political fracture. The phronetic disposition does not give us an exact chart through such troubled waters, but it does indicate what sort of captain we want at the helm making decisions in reaction to changing conditions.

We support our historical argument about one writing program in an age of austerity and diversity and our ethical argument about the importance of phronesis in transitional times with careful citation of primary source data, mindful interviews with participants, and continuous reference to broader circumstances and related trends. Like all historical scholarship, our argument must be weighed on the twin balance of accuracy and relevance. Since the story is true to its sources and analogous to our experiences, we conclude that the 1980s were a consequential and important decade in the history of higher education and especially in the history of postsecondary writing instruction. We further assert that the 1980s, like our decade, were roiled by economic austerity and conflicts over political diversity, financial and cultural forces that still affect higher education, still shape writing pedagogy, still shadow over writing program administration. We finally contend that phronetic actors twisted imperfect achievements out of this knotty historical moment. Not the programs themselves, but the program administrators matter most. If our study of the writing program at the University of Texas at Austin from the mid-1970s through the mid-1990s can offer no best practices, it can at least promote suitable dispositions. This ethical argument must be weighed on the aesthetic scales of emotional impact and character identification.

With the narrative concluded, we return to the topic of scholarly method, discussed in our introduction and revived here so that we can contribute to an ongoing conversation among historians of rhetoric and composition. By highlighting the rhetorical properties of both our digital archive and our scholarly narrative, we encourage both archival and historiographic literacy, aiming toward the same effect that Jessica Enoch and Pamela VanHaitsma pursue in their undergraduate classes. Enoch and VanHaitsma want their students to see "how digital archives rhetorically constitute both group and individual identities."[5] Likewise, we want to give our readers "a deep sense" of what RhetCompUTX (https://rhetcomputx.dwrl.utexas.edu/) "does and what it asks users to do."[6] Additionally, we hope our readers will attain a similarly critical understanding of two other important elements in our historical research: the interviews with historical actors and the narrative told in these pages. Like Enoch and VanHaitsma, we believe that any archive, like every narrative, contributes to "*individual* constitutions and identity formations."[7] Since our digital archive and our scholarly narrative bear primarily on the writing program administrator's identity, we must circle back to the ethical concerns that underlie every historical project.

We began this project with an ethic of recovery in mind, wanting to remember people otherwise forgotten and record events already faded in the disciplinary imagination. This ethic of recovery is common among historians of rhetoric and composition, informing recent scholarly work and numerous pedagogical projects. Jacqueline Jones Royster's study of Black women essayists, for instance, reminds us that these women existed and exerted agency despite overwhelming obstacles. Royster aims to answer questions such as "Who are these writers?" and "What are the worlds of discourse they are entering?"[8] Her ethical commitment to recovery requires the skill that we mentioned in our introduction and you have exercised while reading this book's narrative chapters: "imagination . . . that is, the ability to see the possibility of certain experiences even if we cannot know the specificity of them."[9] The ethic of recovery and the exercise of critical imagination motivate numerous attempts to teach archival research and literacy in the undergraduate classroom.[10] However, when teaching these subjects, other scholars have found that the ethic of recovery does not suit their purposes. Jessica Enoch, for example, suggests that projects driven by an ethic of remembering or an ethic of gendering might offer historians of rhetoric potential not found in the predominant ethic of recovery.[11] Like Enoch, we began to look beyond the ethic of recovery and the exercise of critical imagination, wanting to supplement the recovery work that originally inspired our research. Like many other rhetoric and composition scholars, we began in the classroom.

As we were collecting materials and uploading them to the Omeka site that complements this book, one of us taught a graduate seminar on archival research in rhetoric and composition scholarship that used the Omeka site and its digitized artifacts as a case study and asked students to reflect on the site's potential as we read scholarship, visited repositories, and reviewed exhibits. This classroom experience inspired us to publicly display our research on an Omeka site, and it also revealed that, as historians, we are responsible to users of this digital archive and to many others. We borrow this notion of "archival responsibility" from J. J. Ghaddar and Michelle Caswell, who suggest that archivists and historians should practice "radical empathy" in our recognition of the many communities affected by our work. This practice of radical empathy requires reflection on four relationships: "the relationship between archivists and record creators, between archivists and record subjects, between archivists and record users, and between archivists and larger communities."[12] While working with a community of graduate students ("record users") in the early stages of our research, we began to reflect on our own responsibilities, and we adjusted our methods with these reflections in mind. What follows hereafter is an explanation of how we applied Ghaddar and Caswell's ethic of responsibility to the three primary components of our study: the collection, arrangement, and public display of our source material; the interviews with people who lived the events; and the narrative that we wrote based on these sources and interviews. Rather than the critical imagination that informs recovery work, we implemented what Gesa Kirsch and Jacqueline Jones Royster call "strategic contemplation . . . both speculation and the use of scholarly meditation as an enabling genre." Strategic contemplation allows the researcher to investigate their "passionate attachments and ethical commitments."[13] Better than critical imagination, strategic contemplation suits the ethic of responsibility guiding our efforts.

As mentioned earlier, we initially intended the Omeka site for private use, a "partner space" where we could collaboratively arrange our research materials across our geographic separation. To that end, we uploaded items with minimal metadata and arranged them chronologically on exhibit pages. We presented this to a group of graduate students, most of whom were interested in the field of rhetoric and composition. We simply wanted to "elucidate our own research endeavors."[14] Incorporating this site into a graduate seminar made us starkly aware that our site was not responsible to our users, for the graduate students themselves didn't understand how this material might relate to their interests. Toward the end of the semester, we began to discuss various ways to make the site more responsible to our users, which also prompted conversations about our responsibility to the record creators and those represented in the records, and that finally led to a publicly accessible digital archive that would be responsible to those who made the items exhibited by our digital archive, those represented in these items, and the users of the archive itself.

Matthew Kirschenbaum contends that technology has placed us "in a time of the forensic imagination" because digital "storage . . . is all about creating a systematized space where" we can "speak with the dead."[15] Kirschenbaum's enthusiasm captures the potential in digital archivism. But simply displaying historical materials is not enough, for bare exhibition may not serve the needs of those who seek communion and may violate the rights of those beyond the archival veil. In our efforts to be responsible, we focused on the metadata that accompanies each item and the digitized presentation of the items themselves. Queer theorists contributing to archival studies in rhetoric and composition have explained that the arrangement and presentation of items can shape the user's experience in purposeful ways and to political ends.[16] Awareness of this ability does not require that archivists absent themselves entirely. Rather, as Ghaddar and Caswell explain, strategic contemplation requires that we acknowledge and conscientiously assume "the archivist's ability to mediate" the user's "experience of the archives."[17]

Consider one of our efforts to be responsible to future researchers. Our graduate students expressed interest in tracing individuals through not just the items they produced but also the items in which they are represented, suggesting that responsibility to the record creator and those represented in the records requires that we allow the researcher to see a historical actor's full presence in the forensic traces of their actions. One such actor, Susan Rodi, exhibits such potential in metadata. Rodi created only three items in our digital archive, suggesting that she was a minor player. However, review of the items where her name is mentioned suggests a much larger impact. Like others contemplating archival potential in rhetoric and composition scholarship, we turned to the metadata, believing that the information about certain items can trace an actor's impact better than the presence of items created by a specific individual.[18] We decided, therefore, to include complete lists of all attendees in the metadata for minutes and other such administrative records. With this addition to the metadata, a search for "Rodi" reveals not three items but fifteen, demonstrating the full impact of her contribution. Since Rodi was a lecturer and lecturers are typically excluded from university governance or erased from university records, her vestige is faint when marked by the number of reports that she created. But when the metadata records her presence at important meetings, it reveals her deeper stamp on the writing program.

In addition to allowing us to be responsible to record creators, the metadata also allowed us to be responsible to our users. Our graduate students did not appreciate the spare metadata typically found in physical repositories, nor did they get much out of the typical categories featured in the Dublin Core metadata standard. Recent scholars have found that digital archives produced for a scholarly audience miss a chance to engage a wider public.[19] Our Omeka exhibit even failed to engage our scholarly users. The problem was a lack of context. Spare metadata prevented novice researchers and future administrators from understanding what the items were or why they mattered. We can't blame them for the confusion. University administration is byzantine, and its documentary traces are arcane. Those new to writing program administration or university life will necessarily be confused. Following our students' suggestion, we adapted the "description" metadata category to offer a brief prosaic explanation of each item and its content. We also used the "relations" category to explicitly mention and link to other items mentioned in a given agenda, a set of meeting minutes, or a departmental report. Robust descriptions and ample relations allow the user to more easily understand and better trace events through the documentary touchstones provided by the archive. The lines of administrative influence, the tiers of university bureaucracy, and the paths of managerial action all become easier to discern.

Pamela VanHaitsma believes that rhetoric and composition scholars share with archivists "a certain responsibility—the ability to respond to digital archives by stimulating participation." She furthermore contends that

Conclusion

"we possess particular pedagogical opportunities to do so."[20] In our effort to craft metadata that is responsive to novice requests and encourages their further exploration, we take advantage of the pedagogical opportunities that VanHaitsma indicates, both in the graduate classroom and in the digital exhibit. Our digital archive, if responsible to future users, is more likely to get appropriated in their research and pedagogy. Scholar/activist/teacher Whitney Douglas believes that strategic contemplation, which we have applied to our digital archive, invites "wonder, creativity, and inspiration."[21] Douglas's use of archival materials in her undergraduate classes and community theater certainly exemplifies this potential. We suggest that if users are going to do as Douglas intends—if they are going to "turn from viewing archives as passive repositories . . . to conceptualizing archives as active experiments in meaning-making"—then the archives must be responsible to the users' needs.[22]

While the metadata allowed us to be responsible to our users, the presentation of the items allows us to be responsible to their creators. Many of the people who wrote these reports or attended these meetings might want to be remembered, but some of the creators might not want their past scribblings preserved or publicized. We were led to this conclusion by archivists who follow the path of radical empathy, arriving at the belief that while many have a right to be remembered, many others have a right to be forgotten.[23] We were also led to this conclusion by the tense nature of our subject. In the items themselves, we can find evidence that, in retrospect, item creators regretted their actions and their words. Many of these subjects are still alive and likely still feel chagrin. Our desire to respect their right to be forgotten often conflicts with our responsibility to our users and the larger scholarly community. Our students expressed the greatest interest in the most salacious items, and the drama (as our narrative suggests) is an important part of the disciplinary history. In our efforts to balance the competing responsibilities to the creators who might want to be forgotten and the researchers who might want to remember, we decided to present all the items but redact some potentially embarrassing information from many. To future researchers, we could indicate that a documentary record exists without revealing its content. To the creators, we could offer some privacy. Sometimes the legal right to privacy allowed us to simply redact the contents of an entire item. Personal correspondence, for instance, is completely blacked out. The researcher can learn that John Ruszkiewicz and James Berlin exchanged letters about the Battle of Texas, but they cannot see the contents of those epistles. Sometimes, however, we have a legal right to display an item's content because the item was produced as part of an employee's work at a state-funded organization and therefore a matter of public record, but we have chosen to redact any material that a record creator might want removed. Handwritten comments on memos, for example, are typically redacted, though described in the metadata, as are some items of interoffice correspondence. We found that these handwritten notes were often impulsive and more extreme than the positions that principals actually advocated, and we don't wish for anyone to be judged on the basis of their initial reactionary thoughts. We have all had the experience of sitting in a meeting, feeling a strong internal reaction to a proposal, sleeping on it, and then composing a more reasoned, careful response than the one that initially flashed through our minds. Respecting the humanity of parties to the conflicts that we have described, even when we might personally disagree with them, has meant curating the archive, and our narrative, to reflect what people actually said and did publicly, rather than salaciously focusing on moments of emotion that are occasionally and inconsistently captured in the margins of the records that we inventoried.

As mentioned in our introduction, a fuller description of the digital archival exhibit and a more complete explanation of what it aims to achieve can be found in an article that we coauthored with the graduate students who participated in its construction.[24] In this section of our conclusion, we focus strictly on the ethic of responsibility and its impact on our decisions. We turn to the second phase of our process, the collection of interviews. Having assembled materials from personal papers, departmental records, university archives, and local print media, we knew enough about the events, but the people remained a mystery. Inspired by Kelly Ritter, who has similarly collected interviews in her research, we wanted to bring "forward voices to complement material artifacts" so that we could recover "lost histories of lesser-known instruction."[25] In short, we believed that interviews would allow us to be responsible to those people faintly represented in the archive despite their significant contribution in the classroom and to the writing program. We interviewed a number of senior male faculty and a few upper-level administrators, but we talked mostly with lecturers, undergraduates, untenured women, and graduate students. The written record is heavy with (mostly male) professors and administrators. The interviews are replete with the voices of people like James Skaggs (a lecturer), Susan Jarratt (a graduate instructor), Carol MacKay (a female junior professor), and Scott Henson (an undergraduate). Altogether, we found twenty-seven subjects willing to sit for lengthy recorded conversations. However, as we began interviewing subjects, we learned that their memories of particular events had faded significantly. Like many historians reliant on archival source material, we wanted to be responsible to the people who lived the events and who created the records. As Heidi McKee and James Porter note, "Those papers are people."[26] But when we talked with the people, we found that the papers promised a more accurate record of events. Our responsibility to future researchers conflicted with our responsibility to the record creators. We wanted an accurate history to serve scholars' interests, but we also wanted an inclusive record to honor participants' contributions.

McKee and Porter note that archival researchers are typically recursive, coming back to the same material with fresh eyes after exploring other sources. Based on their human subjects research, McKee and Porter notice that many archival researchers engage in not only informational recursion but also "ethical revisioning," rethinking their responsibility to their subjects at crucial moments in the research process.[27] Our initial interviews inspired such an ethical revisioning. We began to rethink the questions guiding our research, "questions of representation and interpretation."[28] Ann Cvetkovich helped us reimagine the interviews not as a complementary archive of information but rather as a necessary archive of affect. Cvetkovich herself collected interviews of AIDS activists, capturing "history's felt and even traumatic dimensions." Like Cvetkovich, in this ethically recursive moment of our research, we began to imagine our interviews as "an archive of emotions."[29] Just as she saw the activists' emotions as a "crucial part of the archive," so did we understand that the feelings expressed and experienced are an integral part of the story told in the preceding chapters.[30] By collecting these feelings in our interviews and displaying them kaleidoscopically in the historical narrative, we have tried to be responsible to both the record creators and the record users. We honor the creators by recording their sentiments; we honor researchers by including not only dates, names, and events but also emotions and motives.

Having arrived at this revision of our ethical responsibility, we changed the way that we conducted the interviews themselves. We still asked about dates and events, but we privileged questions about emotion, no longer inquiring, "What happened?" but instead, "How did you feel about or toward or during these events?" Since our archive was digitized and publicly available, we primed interview subjects by sharing specific documents with them, sometimes looking at these documents together during the interviews themselves, thus resuscitating past emotions attached to specific items. The new approach led to new interpretations. It is commonly believed, for example, that disciplinary hostility between literature and composition faculty contributed to many of the events chronicled in this book. In our interviews, we found little vestige of that hostility. Literature professors expressed more anxiety about the lecturers' plight than they did about the empire of rhetoric. The interviews also helped us sense something else about our subjects. Some subjects spoke garrulously, often professing that we could repeat anything that they said. Some spoke reluctantly, suggesting that they did not want to broadcast their sentiments. Some refused the interview altogether, saying they'd rather not dig up old skeletons. As historians, we have a responsibility to other scholars and the discipline, a duty to record as completely as we can. But we are also responsible to the subjects, and we are obliged to remember (or forget) them as they would prefer. We decided to keep the interviews private, not publishing them as we did the written records. And we furthermore decided to rely on all the interviews in our narrative but to foreground only the actors who spoke willingly and gave explicit permission to quote.

A few cases exemplify how our ethic of responsibility shaped the historical narrative's use of the interviews. James Skaggs spoke to us at length, repeatedly and explicitly telling us that we could publish anything that he said, as did David McMurrey and Rod Davis. So we featured their stories in chapter 2, making them main characters in the drama. Other lecturers and graduate students who played active roles in the Battle of Texas were much more reticent in their comments and explicitly asked us not to quote them on particular matters. We relied on the information that we gleaned from their interviews but did not feature these individuals in the narrative. We also looked for areas of common sentiment, so that we could cite multiple interviews at once, never directly attributing a feeling to one person and thus never accusing any individual of particular animus. A few interviewees were especially cautious, so we did not cite or quote them at all, allowing their contribution to inform our understanding and shape the narrative, but also respecting their right to be forgotten.

Following best practices in human subjects research, we provided all interview subjects with a transcript of the interview and invited them to edit or redact material. But three cases in particular stand out because they challenged our effort to balance our responsibility to future records users with our responsibility to past records creators. John Ruszkiewicz provided many of the papers that we rely on in this history. When we asked him to sit for an interview, he declined, saying: "In retirement, I write murder mysteries, not academic fiction, because they're less bloody." He added, "You can quote me on that."[31] Ruszkiewicz clearly did not want his sentiments to be a part of the story, and we have respected his wish, but Ruszkiewicz himself is an indelible part of the narrative. The story simply wouldn't make sense if we removed him completely. Two other cases offer a similar problem but with different solutions. James Duban and Alan Gribben both cordially declined to be interviewed despite several requests. Gribben offered to send us copies of his documents but later thought better of the offer. Duban directed us toward his previously cited *Daily Texan* article "A Modest Proposal: Teach Writing in Writing Courses," saying that it did and still does represent his full position. Again, we could not erase either constituent from the story, but we could refocus instead on those who did agree to an interview, such as Evan Carton, Scott Henson, and Geoff Henley.

One final example illustrates both the urgency and fragility of supplementing archival research with interviews. One of the most consistently phronetic actors in the events at UT Austin in the 1980s was Lester Faigley, whose opus *Fragments of Rationality* indicates that he grasped the changed political landscape within which both UT Austin and the discipline of rhetoric and composition operated well before his colleagues. Like Ruszkiewicz, Faigley contributed many documents in our archive and pointed us toward other established archives housed at UT Austin. We communicated informally with Lester frequently during the very early stages of this project, before the writing had even begun. More than willing to be interviewed despite his declining health, he was to be interviewed last, so he could fill in gaps exposed by the other interviewees. Lester Faigley passed before we were able to conduct his interview. Whatever modest contribution our narrative might make to rhetoric and composition and critical university studies, it is no doubt a poorer contribution for that loss, just as the field is richer for Lester's contributions.

Returning to the promise that Kelly Ritter saw in the combination of archival and human subjects research, we conclude that the informational and the affective content of historical research can be greatly enriched when archivists speak with records creators. We have also found that interviews allow archivists to fulfill their duties in service of record users and record creators. The historian can tell a rich story filled with details and emotions, events and sentiments, archives and affects. The historian can also gauge the level and quality of exposure to the record creators' interests in order to feature those who welcome the narrative limelight, while hiding others in the citational shadows. We end this strategic contemplation of our human subjects research with one final observation: Among our interviewees, the men spoke most freely, while the women often spoke reluctantly. We take this contrast as an affective indication of the precarity that women in academe still feel today. Some of our interviewees were lecturers or graduate students in the 1980s, so they had reason, at that time, to worry about public perception and professional retribution. But when they spoke with us, many of these same women were tenured professors at prestigious universities, and some were retired, yet they still professed a care and a concern that we rarely heard from the men. Trying to respect these sentiments, we favor male voices while relying on women's insights in our narrative. We conclude with this observation partly because we want to account for the masculine quality of this story but mostly because we want to emphasize the historian's responsibility to posterity and the explicit wishes of living subjects, real people. For posterity, we have recorded and reported the events and the outcomes as indicated in the archive. For people, we have respected the sentiments and the situations as gleaned in their interviews.

Having discussed the archive and the interviews, all that remains for strategic contemplation is the narrative. As mentioned several times already, we have privileged phronetic protagonists, but we don't intend to lionize these actors. They get pride of place in two chapters only because their disposition suits the circumstance. In another historical moment, a tragic or a romantic disposition might be more suitable. In fact, we agree with David Gold, who has argued that for historians of rhetoric and composition to get beyond the ethics of recovery, "we can . . . no longer afford narratives of heroes and villains."[32] Like Gold, we assumed from the start "a complex, multivocal past," using the characters as points of departure and telling each segment of the narrative from the perspective of one participant.[33] The result is a kaleidoscope of sympathetic figures (tragic, romantic, phronetic, or otherwise), each addressing a complicated and rapidly shifting historical moment with limited knowledge and admirable intentions. We hope that this narrative told from multiple viewpoints will "invite conversation" by presenting the reader with "mixtures of value." Wayne Booth assures us that all such "interesting cases" can invoke discussion and disagreement, offering the reader a rich experience and an opportunity for further conversation.[34] In crafting the narrative this way, we hope to fulfill our responsibility to the discipline of writing program administration.

A wealth of scholarly material aimed at training the would-be writing program administrator has been produced in the last decade. Among the more admirable and systematic efforts is *A Rhetoric for Writing Program Administrators*, which promises to offer "background on issues just about every WPA will, at some point in time or another, confront."[35] While we value such resources, we also suggest that historical scholarship can also serve the graduate program filled with students specializing in the discipline of rhetoric and composition. Pairing digital archivism and narrative historiography, historians can create a space for critical imagination and disciplinary debate. We are inspired in this effort by recent historians of composition studies who call for an expansive use of primary source evidence.[36] We are also inspired by historians and archivists who see the need for narrative interpretation.[37] Narratives naturally foreclose interpretation by offering a perspective and privileging a protagonist. We've narratively labored against such foreclosure, and we suggest that the archive itself further bends toward interpretive efflorescence. As Susan Wells has observed, an archive "refuses closure" because the copious evidence invites reinterpretation.[38] Wendy Hayden adds that, in the classroom, an archive's "lack of closure" encourages "re-reading."[39] In our effort to make sense of history without precluding interpretation, we blend the archive and the narrative, giving access to the evidence and featuring a range of actors.

We recommend that students and professors discuss and debate the issues presented in the preceding narrative, relying on the primary source evidence made available in the archive. Our pedagogical model for this exercise is not unfamiliar to rhetoric and composition specialists, as the first anthology of essays in this field was premised on debate. *Cross-Talk in Comp Theory*, now in its fourth edition, invites students and professors to debate by anthologizing canonical essays, conversing and often disagreeing with one another. We suggest that a similar disputational pedagogy can rely on studies like our own. A much older practice even better captures the pedagogical potential that we see in single-institution studies like this one. In ancient Rome, students were often asked to debate or expound imaginary cases and historical incidents. The *suasoria* exercise, recounted by Seneca the Elder in the first century CE, offers a model of how present-day instructors might use this book and its complementary archive in a graduate class.[40] Classicist D. A. Russell notes that the Roman exercise was distinct from the Greek in that Roman *suasoriae* drew from recent history, allowing students to make grounded and politically relevant arguments, while the Greek exercises relied on fantastic and literary cases, encouraging stylistic flourish but not contemporary reflection.[41]

One Roman case in particular would have been familiar to all of Seneca's students. After delivering fourteen vitriolic orations denouncing Marcus Antonius as a dictator and an enemy of the state, Marcus Tullius Cicero is told that he'll be spared execution if he burns his speeches and renounces their content. Seneca asked his students to compose orations addressed to

Cicero, suggesting one course of action or another. The students' speeches are rich in detail and advanced in technique, largely because every schoolboy knew the history of the Roman revolution, about the feud between Cicero and Antonius, and that Antonius proscribed Cicero, ultimately having him executed. But they also knew that Antonius was later defamed and then defeated by Octavian. More important, the subject of this ancient exercise, though roughly forty years removed from these students' living memory, pertained to their lives. During the early decades of the Roman Empire, Octavian (later "Caesar Augustus") was on the throne. By discoursing on Cicero and Antonius, students could deliberate matters relevant to their own political moments—such as demagoguery, dictatorship, speaking truth to power, and facing the consequences—without having to learn the complex and shifting political dynamics during the first imperial reign. The case was neatly contained yet wholly relevant, ripe for complicated deliberation without requiring elaborated expertise.

We suggest that something similar can be said about the writing program at UT Austin in the 1980s. It's a contained case study allowing students to debate actions that, though removed from our time, are relevant to present circumstances. We've crafted this narrative and constructed its complementary archive in the hope that graduate faculty will be able to present this case study for discussion in their seminars, just as Seneca asked his students to debate a historical scenario bearing some important similarity to their own political context. After reading chapter 2, review Susan Rodi's proposal for humane treatment of nontenure track faculty,[42] or John Ruszkiewicz's.[43] Compare these to the departmental subcommittee's initial recommendation.[44] Or, after reading the first half of chapter 4, look at the competing proposals for how to reorganize the writing program after the Saturday Night Massacre.[45] Or simply pick any of the issues discussed in the previous chapters: administrative autonomy for the writing program, abolition of the required writing course, critical literacy, writing across the curriculum. Every issue will yield multiple and competing items, thus allowing for further discussion and debate. And much contemporary scholarly literature on teaching with archival sources points to the creative possibility made available by presenting primary source information in the classroom not as resources for students' footnotes but as fodder for their conversation. Ryan Skinnell has argued that we need to get past the reverential "archival relationship." Instead of imagining archives as an altar of truth, we need to see them as "sites of *epistemic possibility*."[46] Echoing this sentiment while discoursing on her pedagogy, Katherine Tirabassi recommends approaching primary sources as "a resource for creative inspiration."[47] Finally, Laura Proszak and Ellen Cushman recommend bringing "storytelling methodologies" into students' archival research and inviting novice scholars "to think about the ideologies that undergird archives and artifacts."[48] In the spirit of epistemic delinking that animates Proszak and Cushman's advice, and in an attempt to approach RhetCompUTX as a site of possibility and a resource for creative inspiration, we now invite you, having read the narrative, to meander through the archive, placing yourself in the middle of tense meetings, joining the company of warring faculty, eavesdropping behind closed doors, marching among infuriated students, witnessing consequential decisions, and enduring their aftermath. Then tell your own version of the story. Most important, discuss your interpretation.

Notes

Introduction

1. M. Smith, *Abundant University*, 33.
2. M. Smith, *Abundant University*, 31.
3. Labaree, *Perfect Mess*, 194; M. Smith, *Abundant University*, 91.
4. Golden and Katz, *Race Between Education and Technology*, 249–60.
5. Golden and Katz, *Race Between Education and Technology*, 279; Kerr, *Uses of the University*, 186; Levine and Van Pelt, *Great Upheaval*, 99.
6. Guillory, *Professing Criticism*, 23–43.
7. Loss, *Between Citizens and the State*, 210–12.
8. Lee, *Unseen Unheard Minority*, 121.
9. For studies of student advocacy and its effect on diversity, see Johnson, *Undermining Racial Justice*, and Lee, *Unseen Unheard Minority*.
10. T. Miller, *Evolution of College English*, 67.
11. Loss, *Between Citizens and the State*, 2–3.
12. Loss, *Between Citizens and the State*, 72–76.
13. Loss, *Between Citizens and the State*, 112–17.
14. Loss, *Between Citizens and the State*, 158–61.
15. Loss, *Between Citizens and the State*, 202.
16. Loss, *Between Citizens and the State*, 168.
17. Kerr, *Uses of the University*, 198.
18. Kerr, *Uses of the University*, 165.
19. Slaughter and Leslie, *Academic Capitalism*, 7.
20. Bok, *Universities in the Marketplace*, 79–86.
21. C. Smith, *Market Values*, 19.
22. Labaree, *Perfect Mess*, 142.
23. Bok, *Universities in the Marketplace*, 96.
24. Donoghue, *Last Professors*, xxxiv–xxxv.
25. Bousquet, *How the University Works*, 12–13.
26. C. Smith, *Market Values*, 53.
27. Hartman, *War for the Soul of America*, 200.
28. Hartman, *War for the Soul of America*, 242.
29. Lauter, "'Political Correctness' and the Attack on American Colleges," 85.
30. Stabile, "Another Brick in the Wall," 116.
31. Levine and Van Pelt, *Great Upheaval*, 248–49.
32. Young and Friedman, "America's Censored Classrooms."
33. Barrow, *Universities and the Capitalist State*, 174.
34. Bauer and Vanhuisen, "Republicans Vote to Cut."
35. Carey, "Incredible Shrinking Future of College."
36. M. Smith, *Abundant University*, 103.
37. Levine and Van Pelt, *Great Upheaval*, 120–33.

38. Levine and Van Pelt, *Great Upheaval*, 215–30.
39. Stanton, "Culture War."
40. Domenech, "Thirty Years."
41. See Mastrangelo, *Writing a Progressive Past*; Mastrangelo and L'Eplattenier, "'Is It the Pleasure of This Conference?'"; and Suzanne Bordelon's "'Advance' Toward Democratic Administration."
42. In this collection, of particular interest are Ianetta, "'Stand Mum'"; Myers, "'Raise Your Right Arm'"; and Hays, "'Be Patient, but Don't Wait!'"
43. Gold and Hobbs, *Educating the New Southern Woman*.
44. For more on how racial diversity impacts writing instruction, see Baker-Bell, *Linguistic Justice*; and for more on how the assessment of student writing is tied up with diversity initiatives, see Inoue, *Antiracist Writing Ecologies*.
45. Schell and Stock, "Working Contingent Faculty in[to] Higher Education," 7.
46. Johnson, *Undermining Racial Justice*, 2.
47. Johnson, *Undermining Racial Justice*, 258.
48. Lee, *Unseen Unheard Minority*, 2–3.
49. Lee, *Unseen Unheard Minority*, 8.
50. McLeod, *Writing Program Administration*, 8, 22.
51. Powell et al., "Our Story Begins Here."
52. Martinez, *Counterstory*, 2, 21.
53. Hsu, *Constellating Home*, 4.
54. Martinez, *Counterstory*, 116.
55. Hsu, *Constellating Home*, 9.
56. Hsu, *Constellating Home*, 4, 146.
57. Gaillet, "Archival Survival," 36.
58. Hawhee, *Rhetoric in Tooth and Claw*, 13, 20.
59. Charlton et al., *GenAdmin*, 39.
60. Charlton et al., *GenAdmin*, 63.
61. W. Fisher, *Human Communication as Narration*, 17; Booth, *Company We Keep*, 201.
62. W. Fisher, *Human Communication as Narration*, 66.
63. White, *Metahistory*, 144–45.
64. White, *Metahistory*, 148–49.
65. Masters, *Practicing Writing*, 4.
66. Gold, *Rhetoric at the Margins*, 8.
67. Gold and Hobbs, *Educating the New Southern Woman*, 12.
68. Ritter, *To Know Her Own History*, 147.
69. White, *Metahistory*, 192–93.
70. Fleming, *From Form to Meaning*, 89, 148–52.
71. Fleming, *From Form to Meaning*, 200.
72. Skinnell, *Conceding Composition*, 137–38.
73. W. Fisher, *Human Communication as Narration*, 109.
74. Harris, *Teaching Subject*, 159.
75. Strickland, *Managerial Unconscious*, 121.
76. Gindlesparger, *Opening Ceremony*, 78–79.
77. Adler-Kassner, *Activist WPA*, 10.
78. Aristotle, *On Rhetoric*, 28.
79. Kerr, *Uses of the University*, 198.
80. Kerr, *Uses of the University*, 209.
81. White, *Metahistory*, 193–203.
82. Harris, *Teaching Subject*, 160.
83. L'Eplattenier, "Argument for Archival Research Methods," 71.
84. L'Eplattenier and Mastrangelo, "Why Administrative Histories?" xx.
85. Ferreira-Buckley, "Rescuing the Archives from Foucault," 577.
86. Purdy, "Three Gifts of Digital Archives," 40.
87. Longaker et al., "Archiving Our Own."
88. Purdy, "Three Gifts of Digital Archives," 37.
89. Ramsey-Tobienne, "Archives 2.0," 24.
90. Buehl, Chute, and Fields, "Training in the Archives," 278.
91. Morris, "Archival Turn in Rhetorical Studies," 115.
92. Wilde, Tetreault, and Franco, "Renegotiating the Public Memory of Writing Centers," 115. For another discussion of teaching archival research in the graduate classroom, see Jenna Morton-Aiken and Robert Schwegler, "Recursion and Responsiveness."
93. Wells, "Claiming the Archive," 60.
94. Purdy, "Three Gifts of Digital Archives," 35.
95. Jenny Rice, *Awful Archives*, 20.
96. Biesecker, "Of Historicity, Rhetoric."

97. Hayden, "And Gladly Teach," 148–49; Kirsch and Royster, "Feminist Rhetorical Practices," 648–56.
98. Kirsch and Royster, "Feminist Rhetorical Practices," 649–52.
99. Buehl, Chute, and Fields, "Training in the Archives," 297.

Chapter 1

1. Kerr, *Uses of the University*, 203.
2. Collini, *Speaking of Universities*, 23.
3. Whithaus and Thaiss, "Complex Ecology."
4. Beard and Park, "Forces Acting on a Departmental (Re-)Merger," 49.
5. Kerr, *Uses of the University*, 203.
6. Sledd, "Freshmen"; Megaw, "Spare that Freshman."
7. Nash, "Who's Minding Freshman English?," 126.
8. Nash, "Who's Minding Freshman English?," 128.
9. "Report of the Ad Hoc Committee on Composition," April 24, 1975, RhetCompUTX, https://rhetcomputx.dwrl.utexas.edu/s/DRW/item/3198.
10. Quoted in Nash, "Who's Minding Freshman English?," 127.
11. Regan, "Promises, Problems, and Politics," 87–90.
12. Wayne Rebhorn, telephone interview with Nate Kreuter, February 7, 2020.
13. Quoted in Nash, "Who's Minding Freshman English?," 126.
14. Reitter and Wellmon, *Permanent Crisis*, 68–70.
15. Kerr, *Uses of the University*, 14.
16. Labaree, *Perfect Mess*, 54.
17. Quoted in Nash, "Who's Minding Freshman English?," 127.
18. "Report of the Ad Hoc Committee on Composition," April 24, 1975, RhetCompUTX, https://rhetcomputx.dwrl.utexas.edu/s/DRW/item/3198.
19. "Minutes of the Department of English Meeting," April 24, 1975, RhetCompUTX, https://rhetcomputx.dwrl.utexas.edu/s/DRW/item/3196.
20. For documents testifying to the use of formal grammar as a proper measure of students' writing ability at UT Austin, see, for instance, "Freshman English Policy Committee Grade Inflation Memo," February 16, 1978, RhetCompUTX, https://rhetcomputx.dwrl.utexas.edu/s/DRW/item/253; "Freshman English Policy Committee Minutes," March 8, 1978, RhetCompUTX, https://rhetcomputx.dwrl.utexas.edu/s/DRW/item/352; and "Report of Freshman English Policy Committee Actions," October 13, 1978, RhetCompUTX, https://rhetcomputx.dwrl.utexas.edu/s/DRW/item/219.

21. Quoted in Nash, "Who's Minding Freshman English?," 127.
22. Gold, *Rhetoric at the Margins*, 14–62; B. Horner, "Traditions and Professionalization"; K. Fitzgerald, "Platteville Papers Revisited."
23. Pullman, "Stepping Yet Again," 17–23.
24. Wayne Rebhorn, "Letter to Lieb and King," February 9, 1979, RhetCompUTX, https://rhetcomputx.dwrl.utexas.edu/s/DRW/item/2179.
25. John Trimble, telephone interview with Nate Kreuter, June 16, 2020.
26. Rudolph, *American College and University*, 244.
27. Veysey, *Emergence of the American University*, 2.
28. Guillory, *Professing Criticism*, 160.
29. Rudolph, *American College and University*, 247–50.
30. Veysey, *Emergence of the American University*, 61.
31. Veysey, *Emergence of the American University*, 63.
32. Rudolph, *American College and University*, 294.
33. Berlin, *Writing Instruction*, 3–4.
34. Guillory, *Professing Criticism*, 131–32.
35. Brereton, *Origins of Composition Studies*, 34.
36. Brereton, *Origins of Composition Studies*, 11–12.
37. Ohmann and Douglas, *English in America*, 97–134; see also Fleming, *From Form to Meaning*, 29–31.
38. Guillory, *Professing Criticism*, 167.
39. North, *Making of Knowledge in Composition*, 36–45.
40. North, *Making of Knowledge in Composition*, 35.
41. Connors, "Rise and Fall of the Modes of Discourse," 454.
42. Applebee, *Tradition and Reform*, 80.

43. Applebee, *Tradition and Reform*, 97.
44. Applebee, *Tradition and Reform*, 107–19.
45. Mastrangelo, *Writing a Progressive Past*, 7–28.
46. Applebee, *Tradition and Reform*, 140.
47. Masters, *Practicing Writing*, 217.
48. Reitter and Wellmon, *Permanent Crisis*, 228.
49. Goggin, *Authoring a Discipline*, 59.
50. North, *Making of Knowledge in Composition*, 13; Applebee, *Tradition and Reform*, 198–204; Mason, "Project English."
51. Applebee, *Tradition and Reform*, 225–43.
52. John Trimble, "Synopsis of Past Proposals Affecting Freshman Composition," January 31, 1980, RhetCompUTX, https://rhetcomputx.dwrl.utexas.edu/s/DRW/item/1857.
53. Henze, Selzer, and Sharer, *1977*, 105–36.
54. Kinneavy, *Theory of Discourse*, 1.
55. Kinneavy, *Theory of Discourse*, 19–20.
56. "Slouching Through Theories of English for Fifty-Five Years," James Kinneavy Papers, Dolph Briscoe Center for American History, Box 4M800.
57. "Slouching Through Theories of English for Fifty-Five Years," James Kinneavy Papers, Dolph Briscoe Center for American History, Box 4M800.
58. For a more contemporary scholar reflecting on the interplay between critical theory and pedagogical practice, see Ede, *Situating Composition*, 31.
59. James Kinneavy, "E 306, 1976," August 1976, RhetCompUTX, https://rhetcomputx.dwrl.utexas.edu/s/DRW/item/662.
60. Sue Rodi, "E 306 Rodi Syllabus," 1978, RhetCompUTX, https://rhetcomputx.dwrl.utexas.edu/s/DRW/item/668.
61. James Kinneavy, Mary Trachsel, and John Ruszkiewicz, "E 306 Syllabus," August 1983, RhetCompUTX, https://rhetcomputx.dwrl.utexas.edu/s/DRW/item/652.
62. Wayne Rebhorn, telephone interview with Nate Kreuter, February 7, 2020; James Kinneavy Papers, Dolph Briscoe Center for American History, Box 4M800; Larry Carver, telephone interview with Nate Kreuter, January 7, 2020; Evan Carton, telephone interview with Nate Kreuter, February 20, 2020; Carol MacKay, telephone interview with Nate Kreuter, March 19, 2020.

63. Fred Kemp, telephone interview with Nate Kreuter, December 19, 2019.
64. Susan Jarratt, telephone interview with Nate Kreuter, October 22, 2019.
65. Susan Wells, telephone interview with Nate Kreuter, October 21, 2019.
66. James Skaggs, telephone interview with Nate Kreuter, November 7, 2019.
67. David Jolliffe, telephone interview with Nate Kreuter, October 15, 2019.
68. Susan Wells, telephone interview with Nate Kreuter, October 21, 2019.
69. Rod Davis, telephone interview with Nate Kreuter, December 11, 2019.
70. James Skaggs, telephone interview with Nate Kreuter, November 7, 2019.
71. Susan Wells, telephone interview with Nate Kreuter, October 21, 2019.
72. Flower and Hayes, "Cognitive Process Theory of Writing"; Emig, *Composing Processes of Twelfth Graders*.
73. Hairston, "Winds of Change," 1.
74. James Kinneavy, "E 306, 1976," August 1976, RhetCompUTX, https://rhetcomputx.dwrl.utexas.edu/s/DRW/item/662.
75. Sue Rodi, "E 306 Rodi Syllabus," 1978, RhetCompUTX, https://rhetcomputx.dwrl.utexas.edu/s/DRW/item/668; James Kinneavy, Mary Trachsel, and John Ruszkiewicz, "E 306 Syllabus," August 1983, RhetCompUTX, https://rhetcomputx.dwrl.utexas.edu/s/DRW/item/652.
76. James Kinneavy, "E 306, 1982," August 1982, RhetCompUTX, https://rhetcomputx.dwrl.utexas.edu/s/DRW/item/664.
77. James Kinneavy, Mary Trachsel, and John Ruszkiewicz, "E 306 Syllabus, 1984/5," August 1984–85 RhetCompUTX, https://rhetcomputx.dwrl.utexas.edu/s/DRW/item/656.
78. James Kinneavy and John Ruszkiewicz, "Syllabus for E 306, 1985," August 1985, RhetCompUTX, https://rhetcomputx.dwrl.utexas.edu/s/DRW/item/650.
79. Sledd, "And They Write Innumerable Books," 72.
80. John Meeker, "Formative Evaluation Research Associates Funding Application for Writing Program Study," January 13, 1978, RhetCompUTX, https://rhetcomputx.dwrl.utexas.edu/s/DRW/item/350.
81. Thomas Cameron, "Letter to John Meeker about Formative Evaluation Research Associates Study Procedure," March 20, 1978, RhetCompUTX, https://rhetcomputx.dwrl.utexas.edu/s/DRW/item

/344; see also "Freshman English Policy Committee Minutes," April 5, 1978, RhetCompUTX, https://rhetcomputx.dwrl.utexas.edu/s/DRW/item/338.

82. For samples of the reports that Faigley and Witte produced, see Stephen Witte et al., "The Goals of National Writing Programs as Perceived by a National Sample of Writing Program Directors and Teachers," January 1982, RhetCompUTX, https://rhetcomputx.dwrl.utexas.edu/s/DRW/item/3178; and Stephen Witte et al., "National Survey of College and University Writing Teachers, Technical Report No. 4," January 31, 1982, RhetCompUTX, https://rhetcomputx.dwrl.utexas.edu/s/DRW/item/3176. For an example of the collaborations between Faigley, Witte, and graduate students in the UT Austin rhetoric and composition PhD program, see Faigley and Miller, "What We Learn from Writing on the Job"; see also Faigley et al., *Assessing Writers' Knowledge and Processes of Composing*.

83. James Kinneavy, Stephen Witte, and Thomas Cameron, "Analytic and Synthetic Approaches to Composition: A Proposed Evaluation During the 1978–79 Academic Year of E 306 Options by the Freshman English Policy Committee," September 19, 1979, RhetCompUTX, https://rhetcomputx.dwrl.utexas.edu/s/DRW/item/233.

84. Stephen Witte, "Letter to John Weinstock," April 4, 1983, James Kinneavy Papers, Dolph Briscoe Center for American History, Box 4M811.

85. Goggin, *Authoring a Discipline*, 130–31.

86. Maxine Hairston, "Notes on Hairston's Visit with Ford Foundation," June 21, 1985, RhetCompUTX, https://rhetcomputx.dwrl.utexas.edu/s/DRW/item/1277.

87. Maxine Hairston, "Letter to Dean Robert King," June 14, 1985, RhetCompUTX, https://rhetcomputx.dwrl.utexas.edu/s/DRW/item/1281.

88. Thomas Miller, telephone interview with Nate Kreuter, October 9, 2019.

89. "Department of English Meeting Minutes," September 21, 1979, RhetCompUTX, https://rhetcomputx.dwrl.utexas.edu/s/DRW/item/2154.

90. Joseph Moldenhauer, "Memo on Faculty Recruitment," September 18, 1979, RhetCompUTX, https://rhetcomputx.dwrl.utexas.edu/s/DRW/item/2169.

91. James Kinneavy, "Proposal for a Rhetoric Concentration in the English Graduate Program," October 23, 1978, RhetCompUTX, https://rhetcomputx.dwrl.utexas.edu/s/DRW/item/223; see also "Freshman English Policy Committee Minutes," October 30, 1978, RhetCompUTX, https://rhetcomputx.dwrl.utexas.edu/s/DRW/item/241.

92. "Graduate Study in Rhetoric—Status Report," undated (1980), RhetCompUTX, https://rhetcomputx.dwrl.utexas.edu/s/DRW/item/63.

93. Fred Kemp, telephone interview with Nate Kreuter, December 19, 2019.

94. Joyce Locke Carter, telephone interview with Nate Kreuter, January 31, 2020.

95. John Trimble, "Welcome to All Assistant Instructors and Teaching Assistants," August 2, 1978, RhetCompUTX, https://rhetcomputx.dwrl.utexas.edu/s/DRW/item/58.

96. Mary Trachsel, telephone interview with Nate Kreuter, October 15, 2019.

97. For a review of this program, see Wittig, "Project C-BE English Drill and Practice." For discussion of Cameron's leadership in the Writing Lab project, see "Freshman English Policy Committee Minutes," January 24, 1979, RhetCompUTX, https://rhetcomputx.dwrl.utexas.edu/s/DRW/item/308; and Thomas Cameron, "Individualized Instruction Lab Course," RhetCompUTX, February 8, 1979, https://rhetcomputx.dwrl.utexas.edu/s/DRW/item/296.

98. Bill Francis, "Minutes of the University Council Meeting," May 16, 1977, RhetCompUTX, https://rhetcomputx.dwrl.utexas.edu/s/DRW/item/2658.

99. Lerner, *Idea of a Writing Laboratory*, 28–33.

100. "Freshman English Policy Committee Minutes," November 4, 1977, RhetCompUTX, https://rhetcomputx.dwrl.utexas.edu/s/DRW/item/382.

101. "University Catalog Listing E 106 and E 206 with Brief Descriptions," 1981, RhetCompUTX, https://rhetcomputx.dwrl.utexas.edu/s/DRW/item/518.

102. Valerie Balester, telephone interview with Nate Kreuter, October 11, 2019.

103. "Freshman English Policy Committee Meeting Minutes," January 30, 1985,

103. RhetCompUTX, https://rhetcomputx.dwrl.utexas.edu/s/DRW/item/572.

104. Fred Kemp, telephone interview with Nate Kreuter, December 19, 2019.

105. Fred Kemp, "Letter from 'Fred' About Computers," October 12, 1985, RhetCompUTX, https://rhetcomputx.dwrl.utexas.edu/s/DRW/item/2112.

106. Joyce Locke Carter, Letter to James Kinneavy, September 6, 1996, James Kinneavy Papers, Dolph Briscoe Center for American History, Box 4M800.

107. Bill Francis, "Minutes of the Second Regular Meeting of the General Faculty," May 3, 1977, RhetCompUTX, https://rhetcomputx.dwrl.utexas.edu/s/DRW/item/2708.

108. Susan Hereford and James Sledd, "Academic Success and Writing Ability: A Survey of Faculty and Student Opinion," February 1976, James Kinneavy Papers, Dolph Briscoe Center for American History, Box 4M802.

109. Maxine Hairston, "Report from the Ad Hoc Committee to Review the Change in the Plan I, B.A. Lower-Division English Requirement," 1976, RhetCompUTX, https://rhetcomputx.dwrl.utexas.edu/s/DRW/item/2656.

110. Newkirk, Cameron, and Selfe, "Why Johnny Can't Write," 68.

111. Susan Hereford and James Sledd, "Academic Success and Writing Ability: A Survey of Faculty and Student Opinion," February 1976, James Kinneavy Papers, Dolph Briscoe Center for American History, Box 4M802.

112. Joseph Moldenhauer, "Task Force on Composition Proposal Draft," April 30, 1980, RhetCompUTX, https://rhetcomputx.dwrl.utexas.edu/s/DRW/item/2001.

113. Joseph Moldenhauer, "Composition Proposal Vote Tally," June 3, 1980, RhetCompUTX, https://rhetcomputx.dwrl.utexas.edu/s/DRW/item/2006.

114. H. Paul Kelley, "Minutes of the University Council Meeting," April 20, 1981, RhetCompUTX, https://rhetcomputx.dwrl.utexas.edu/s/DRW/item/2666.

115. A program very similar to Kinneavy's plan was implemented at The Pennsylvania State University and remains in place as of this writing.

116. David Russell, *Writing in the Academic Disciplines*, 276–80.

117. Kinneavy, "Writing Across the Curriculum," 19.

118. Veysey, *Emergence of the American University*, 121–79.

119. Berlin, *Rhetoric and Reality*, 44–46; Goggin, *Authoring a Discipline*, 6, 66.

120. Brown, *Undoing the Demos*, 181.

121. "The Centrality of Rhetoric to the Liberal Arts Tradition," James Kinneavy Papers, Briscoe Center for American History, Box 4M796.

122. "Overall Summary of E 346K General Questionnaire," Kinneavy Papers, Dolph Briscoe Center for American History, Box 4M804.

123. K. Smith, "University Doesn't Care."

124. Grosky, "Remember Students."

125. Romano, "Keep Junior Course"; Head, "E 346K Teaches Key Skill"; Babcock, "Technical Majors Need E 346K Skills."

126. Skaggs, "English Lecturers Deserve Better Treatment."

127. Joseph Rice, "E 346K—The Write Stuff."

128. Fleming, *From Form to Meaning*, 205.

129. Porter et al., "Institutional Critique," 613.

130. Strickland, *Managerial Unconscious*, 121.

131. Adler-Kassner, *Activist WPA*, 174–75.

132. Charlton et al., *GenAdmin*, 108.

Chapter 2

1. Barrow, *Universities and the Capitalist State*, 257.

2. Sledd, "Disciplinarity and Exploitation," 34.

3. Bousquet, *How the University Works*, 173.

4. Connors, "Overwork/Underpay."

5. Bousquet, *How the University Works*, 174.

6. Bousquet, *How the University Works*, 159.

7. See the University of Texas at Austin Office of Institutional Studies, *Statistical Handbook, 1980–1981*, https://utexas.app.box.com/v/SHB80-81Complete, and *Statistical Handbook, 1990–91*," https://utexas.app.box.com/v/SHB90-91Complete.

8. "Coping with our 'Literacy Crisis.'"

9. "Skilled Writers."

10. Curtis, "Behind the Lines."

11. K. Kelly, "Aid with Composition."

12. See Thomas Cameron, "Cameron/Wainwright Proposal for Summer Provisional Section of E 306," April 25–26, 1978, RhetCompUTX, https://rhetcomputx.dwrl.utexas.edu/s/DRW/item/310.

13. Johnson, *Undermining Racial Justice*, 9–39.

14. Quoted in Williams, "Committee Probes English Program."

15. See Maxine Hairston, "Memo to James Kinneavy About Avoiding Scheduling Problems in E 306," September 15, 1977, RhetCompUTX, https://rhetcomputx.dwrl.utexas.edu/s/DRW/item/390; see also "Freshman English Policy Committee Minutes," September 30, 1977, RhetCompUTX, https://rhetcomputx.dwrl.utexas.edu/s/DRW/item/420.

16. "Freshman English Policy Committee Minutes," October 23, 1978, RhetCompUTX, https://rhetcomputx.dwrl.utexas.edu/s/DRW/item/227.

17. "Committee on Exemptions Report," March 6, 1980, RhetCompUTX, https://rhetcomputx.dwrl.utexas.edu/s/DRW/item/1859. In November 1982, the University Faculty Council considered removing E 306 from the provisional program; see "Recommended Curriculum for Provisional Admission Program Students," November 11, 1982, RhetCompUTX, https://rhetcomputx.dwrl.utexas.edu/s/DRW/item/1026. The council was still deliberating the matter in 1984; see "An Amendment to the Recommended Curriculum for Provisional Admission Program Students," 1984, RhetCompUTX, https://rhetcomputx.dwrl.utexas.edu/s/DRW/item/1024.

18. James Sledd, "Letter to English Department," March 28, 1980, RhetCompUTX, https://rhetcomputx.dwrl.utexas.edu/s/DRW/item/1072.

19. "Department of English Meeting Minutes," February 13, 1981, RhetCompUTX, https://rhetcomputx.dwrl.utexas.edu/s/DRW/item/2250.

20. "Projected Composition Offerings 1986–87," undated (likely 1985), RhetCompUTX, https://rhetcomputx.dwrl.utexas.edu/s/DRW/item/2082.

21. James Kinneavy Papers, Dolph Briscoe Center for American History, Box 4M799.

22. Newkirk, Cameron, and Selfe, "Why Johnny Can't Write," 68.

23. Susan Hereford and James Sledd, "Academic Success and Writing Ability: A Survey of Faculty and Student Opinion," February 1976, James Kinneavy Papers, Dolph Briscoe Center for American History, Box 4M802.

24. Henze, Selzer, and Sharer, *1977*, 23, 29–45, 56–57.

25. Maxine Hairston, "Report from the Ad Hoc Committee to Review the Change in the Plan I, B.A. Lower-Division English Requirement," 1976–77, RhetCompUTX, https://rhetcomputx.dwrl.utexas.edu/s/DRW/item/2656.

26. See James Vick, "Report of the University Council Committee on Basic Education Requirements," December 1980, RhetCompUTX, https://rhetcomputx.dwrl.utexas.edu/s/DRW/item/2660.

27. "Department of English Minutes," February 1, 1980, RhetCompUTX, https://rhetcomputx.dwrl.utexas.edu/s/DRW/item/2183.

28. "Department of English Minutes," February 29, 1980, RhetCompUTX, https://rhetcomputx.dwrl.utexas.edu/s/DRW/item/2190.

29. Rossinow, *Reagan Era*, 100.

30. "Department of English Meeting Minutes," January 25, 1980, RhetCompUTX, https://rhetcomputx.dwrl.utexas.edu/s/DRW/item/1086.

31. Joseph Moldenhauer, "Memo to Teaching Faculty," February 6, 1980, RhetCompUTX, https://rhetcomputx.dwrl.utexas.edu/s/DRW/item/2196.

32. "Department of English Minutes," January 25, 1980, RhetCompUTX, https://rhetcomputx.dwrl.utexas.edu/s/DRW/item/1086.

33. "Requirements Team Report," Undated (likely 1980), RhetCompUTX, https://rhetcomputx.dwrl.utexas.edu/s/DRW/item/1682.

34. Lester Faigley, "Format I Proposal," Undated (likely early 1980), RhetCompUTX, https://rhetcomputx.dwrl.utexas.edu/s/DRW/item/1659.

35. Quoted in Herring, "Report Reveals Students Weak in Composition."

36. James Kinneavy, "Proposal by the College of Liberal Arts for an Undergraduate Requirement in English," February 13, 1981, RhetCompUTX, https://rhetcomputx.dwrl.utexas.edu/s/DRW/item/2662.

37. Robberson, "New English Requirement Urged."

38. Locke, "Results of Graduation Requirement Study."

39. H. Paul Kelley, "Minutes of the University Council Meeting," February 16, 1981, RhetCompUTX, https://rhetcomputx.dwrl.utexas.edu/s/DRW/item/2664. See also Phyllis Richards, "Faculty Minutes Senate Meeting Notice and Agenda," October 5, 1981, RhetCompUTX, https://rhetcomputx.dwrl.utexas.edu/s/DRW/item/2768.

40. "College of Liberal Arts Faculty Meeting Minutes," October 6, 1980, RhetCompUTX, https://rhetcomputx.dwrl.utexas.edu/s/DRW/item/2210.

41. H. Paul Kelley, "Minutes of the University Council Meeting," April 20, 1981, RhetCompUTX, https://rhetcomputx.dwrl.utexas.edu/s/DRW/item/2666.

42. Mashberg, "General Faculty Approves New English Requirement."

43. H. Paul Kelley, "Minutes of the University Council Meeting," October 18, 1982, RhetCompUTX, https://rhetcomputx.dwrl.utexas.edu/s/DRW/item/2726.

44. For examples of the various proposals to amend the changes made to the core writing requirement, see "Proposed Changes to the College of Liberal Arts Part of the UT Austin Catalogue," January 20, 1983, RhetCompUTX, https://rhetcomputx.dwrl.utexas.edu/s/DRW/item/2732.

45. Joseph Moldenhauer, "Memo from Moldenhauer Establishing Subcommittees to Develop E 346K Syllabi," November 14, 1980, RhetCompUTX, https://rhetcomputx.dwrl.utexas.edu/s/DRW/item/825.

46. H. Paul Kelley, "Report on E 346K Approval," September 22, 1982, RhetCompUTX, https://rhetcomputx.dwrl.utexas.edu/s/DRW/item/2042.

47. H. Paul Kelley, "Minutes of the University Council Meeting," December 12, 1982, RhetCompUTX, https://rhetcomputx.dwrl.utexas.edu/s/DRW/item/2728.

48. H. Paul Kelley, "Minutes of the University Council Meeting," January 24, 1983, RhetCompUTX, https://rhetcomputx.dwrl.utexas.edu/s/DRW/item/2736.

49. Robert King, telephone interview with Nate Kreuter, November 18, 2019.

50. "Freshman English Policy Committee Minutes," March 21, 1979, RhetCompUTX, https://rhetcomputx.dwrl.utexas.edu/s/DRW/item/282.

51. Joseph Moldenhauer, "Memo on Faculty Recruitment," September 15, 1979, RhetCompUTX, https://rhetcomputx.dwrl.utexas.edu/s/DRW/item/2169. See also "Department of English Meeting Minutes," September 21, 1979, RhetCompUTX, https://rhetcomputx.dwrl.utexas.edu/s/DRW/item/2154.

52. Joseph Moldenhauer, "Memo on Faculty Workload," August 23, 1979, RhetCompUTX, https://rhetcomputx.dwrl.utexas.edu/s/DRW/item/2167.

53. Among other things, this committee recommended that faculty should receive 4.5 teaching credits for their writing classes. See Alan Friedman, Tony Hilfer, and Neill Megaw, "Teaching Load Credit Report to the English Department Faculty Senate," February 18, 1982, RhetCompUTX, https://rhetcomputx.dwrl.utexas.edu/s/DRW/item/1102.

54. "Minutes of the English Department Senate," February 19, 1982, RhetCompUTX, https://rhetcomputx.dwrl.utexas.edu/s/DRW/item/1112.

55. Robert King, telephone interview with Nate Kreuter, November 18, 2019.

56. Paul Meyer, telephone interview with Nate Kreuter, December 10, 2019.

57. Quoted in Hutcheson, "Sledd Faults 'Sorry' TA Program."

58. Bell, "House Subcommittee Urges Limits on TAs"; Ehrlich, "Bill Proposed to Limit TA Hiring Practices"; Reaves, "Workplace Compliance Hard, UT Prof Says"; "UT Faculty Airs Work Load Plan"; see also Philip Gough, Bonnie Rickelman, John Brockaw, James Daniel, and Neill Megaw, "Report from the Faculty Senate Committee on Ways and Means to Implement the General Faculty Resolutions Concerning Faculty Workloads and Teaching Assistants," March 2, 1978, RhetCompUTX, https://rhetcomputx.dwrl.utexas.edu/s/DRW/item/2755.

59. "Salty Sledd Strikes Again."

60. L. Kelly, "'Most Hated Man.'"

61. Bowen and Sosa, *Prospects for Faculty*, 99.

62. Quoted in L. Fisher, "English Lecturers Question Hiring."

63. Reitter and Wellmon, *Permanent Crisis*, 67.

64. "Association of Graduate Students of English Memo: Half-Time

Instructors," February 7, 1978, RhetCompUTX, https://rhetcomputx.dwrl.utexas.edu/s/DRW/item/376.

65. Regan, "Promises, Problems, and Politics," 20–25.

66. Berlin, *Rhetoric and Reality*, 90.

67. Robert King, telephone interview with Nate Kreuter, November 18, 2019.

68. Joseph Moldenhauer, "Memo on Faculty Recruitment, Additional Considerations," September 19, 1979, RhetCompUTX, https://rhetcomputx.dwrl.utexas.edu/s/DRW/item/2171.

69. "English Department Meeting Minutes," September 27, 1979, RhetCompUTX, https://rhetcomputx.dwrl.utexas.edu/s/DRW/item/2090.

70. "Minutes of the English Department Senate," February 19, 1982, RhetCompUTX, https://rhetcomputx.dwrl.utexas.edu/s/DRW/item/1112.

71. David McMurrey, telephone interview with Nate Kreuter, October 7, 2019.

72. James Skaggs, telephone interview with Nate Kreuter, November 7, 2019.

73. Rod Davis, telephone interview with Nate Kreuter, December 11, 2019.

74. "Freshman English Policy Committee Minutes," October 23, 1978, RhetCompUTX, https://rhetcomputx.dwrl.utexas.edu/s/DRW/item/227.

75. Childress, *Adjunct Underclass*, 60–61.

76. Joseph Moldenhauer, "Memo on Faculty Recruitment, Additional Considerations," September 19, 1979, RhetCompUTX, https://rhetcomputx.dwrl.utexas.edu/s/DRW/item/2171.

77. "English Department Meeting Minutes," April 25, 1980, RhetCompUTX, https://rhetcomputx.dwrl.utexas.edu/s/DRW/item/2244.

78. "Composition Proposals," June 3, 1980, RhetCompUTX, https://rhetcomputx.dwrl.utexas.edu/s/DRW/item/2006.

79. Joseph Moldenhauer, "Letter to King About Curriculum Revision Vote," July 15, 1980, RhetCompUTX, https://rhetcomputx.dwrl.utexas.edu/s/DRW/item/2116.

80. Childress, *Adjunct Underclass*, 75.

81. "Department of English Meeting Minutes," April 3, 1981, RhetCompUTX, https://rhetcomputx.dwrl.utexas.edu/s/DRW/item/2236.

82. Selby, "English Classes Added."

83. Joseph Moldenhauer, "Report on English Department Senate Actions," October 12, 1981, RhetCompUTX, https://rhetcomputx.dwrl.utexas.edu/s/DRW/item/1060.

84. "Proposed Resolution Concerning Lecturers," November 30, 1981, RhetCompUTX, https://rhetcomputx.dwrl.utexas.edu/s/DRW/item/1070.

85. Joseph Moldenhauer, "Report of the English Department Senate Actions," December 7, 1981, RhetCompUTX, https://rhetcomputx.dwrl.utexas.edu/s/DRW/item/1082.

86. Joseph Moldenhauer, "Memo on Minimum Teaching Requirements Policy," February 23, 1982, RhetCompUTX, https://rhetcomputx.dwrl.utexas.edu/s/DRW/item/1104.

87. Joseph Moldenhauer," National Recruitment of Lecturers Report," March 3, 1982, RhetCompUTX, https://rhetcomputx.dwrl.utexas.edu/s/DRW/item/1108.

88. "English Department Senate Minutes," March 5, 1982, RhetCompUTX, https://rhetcomputx.dwrl.utexas.edu/s/DRW/item/1114.

89. "English Department Senate Minutes," March 5, 1982, RhetCompUTX, https://rhetcomputx.dwrl.utexas.edu/s/DRW/item/1114.

90. Quoted in Pratt, "English Senate Votes to Limit."

91. Quoted in L. Fisher, "Lecturers Feel Jobs Are Too Dependent."

92. L. Fisher, "English Lecturers Question Hiring."

93. Quoted in L. Fisher, "English Lecturers Question Hiring."

94. Quoted in L. Fisher, "English Lecturers Question Teaching-Workload Ratio."

95. Quoted in L. Fisher, "Lecturers in English Department."

96. James Skaggs, telephone interview with Nate Kreuter, November 7, 2019.

97. "Department of English Meeting Minutes," April 3, 1981, RhetCompUTX, https://rhetcomputx.dwrl.utexas.edu/s/DRW/item/2236.

98. David Jolliffe, Wayne Lesser, James Skaggs, Sharon Wevill, and Thomas Whitbread, "Proposal from the Senate Subcommittee on Lecturers," February 1983, RhetCompUTX, https://rhetcomputx.dwrl.utexas.edu/s/DRW/item/689.

99. John Ruszkiewicz, "Proposal for Lecturers with Commentary #3," February 1983, RhetCompUTX, https://rhetcomputx.dwrl.utexas.edu/s/DRW/item/685.

100. Sledd, "Disciplinarity and Exploitation."

101. Bousquet, *How the University Works*, 184.

102. Sue Rodi, "Proposal for Lecturers," February 21, 1983, RhetCompUTX, https://rhetcomputx.dwrl.utexas.edu/s/DRW/item/679.

103. Schell, *Gypsy Academics and Mother-Teachers*, 55.

104. Bousquet, *How the University Works*, 175.

105. H. Paul Kelley, "Third Regular Meeting of the University Council for 1984–1985," November 19, 1984, RhetCompUTX, https://rhetcomputx.dwrl.utexas.edu/s/DRW/item/2715.

106. H. Paul Kelley, "Minutes of the University Council Meeting," of November 19, 1984, RhetCompUTX, https://rhetcomputx.dwrl.utexas.edu/s/DRW/item/2750.

107. Diane Shallert, Simon Bernau, William Duesterhoeft, Gaylord Jentz, Walter Reed, and Bonnie Rickelman, "Report of the Faculty Senate Committee on the Status and Role of the Lecturer," February 28, 1985, RhetCompUTX, https://rhetcomputx.dwrl.utexas.edu/s/DRW/item/2770.

108. Joseph Moldenhauer, "Task Force on Composition Proposal Draft," April 30, 1980, RhetCompUTX, https://rhetcomputx.dwrl.utexas.edu/s/DRW/item/2001.

109. Albert Goldbarth, Kurt Heinzelman, Joe Malof, Charles Rossman, Jim Shay, Gayatri Spivak, and Alan Friedman, "Governance Committee Memo to English Department," October 7, 1980, RhetCompUTX, https://rhetcomputx.dwrl.utexas.edu/s/DRW/item/2212.

110. See "Executive Committee Constitution," November 21, 1980, RhetCompUTX, https://rhetcomputx.dwrl.utexas.edu/s/DRW/item/2226, and Joe Malof, "Memo on Executive Committee Constitution," December 4, 1980, RhetCompUTX, https://rhetcomputx.dwrl.utexas.edu/s/DRW/item/2208.

111. "Minutes of the English Department Faculty Senate," January 29, 1982, RhetCompUTX, https://rhetcomputx.dwrl.utexas.edu/s/DRW/item/1096.

112. "English Department Meeting Minutes," April 18, 1980, RhetCompUTX, https://rhetcomputx.dwrl.utexas.edu/s/DRW/item/2240.

113. Maxine Hairston, "Letter to Bill Sutherland," March 24, 1984, RhetCompUTX, https://rhetcomputx.dwrl.utexas.edu/s/DRW/item/982.

114. Strickland, *Managerial Unconscious*, 121.

115. Greg Myers, "Letter to Bill Sutherland Regarding Hiring of Lecturers," March 27, 1984, RhetCompUTX, https://rhetcomputx.dwrl.utexas.edu/s/DRW/item/921.

116. James Kinneavy, "The Lecturers: Victims of Both Systems," March 24, 1984, RhetCompUTX, https://rhetcomputx.dwrl.utexas.edu/s/DRW/item/1554.

117. David Jollife, "Letter to the Faculty Senate," April 4, 1984, RhetCompUTX, https://rhetcomputx.dwrl.utexas.edu/s/DRW/item/984.

118. Susan Jarratt, telephone interview with Nate Kreuter, October 22, 2019.

119. Rod Davis, telephone interview with Nate Kreuter, December 11, 2019.

120. Ambrose Gordon, "English Department Senate Minutes," April 4, 1984, RhetCompUTX, https://rhetcomputx.dwrl.utexas.edu/s/DRW/item/1042.

121. William Sutherland, "Final Version of the Lecturer Document," April 6, 1984, RhetCompUTX, https://rhetcomputx.dwrl.utexas.edu/s/DRW/item/1176.

122. Neill Megaw, "Memo Opposing EC Action," April 5, 1984, RhetCompUTX, https://rhetcomputx.dwrl.utexas.edu/s/DRW/item/1552; see also James Kinneavy, "Lectures, the Issues," April 6, 1984, RhetCompUTX, https://rhetcomputx.dwrl.utexas.edu/s/DRW/item/1046.

123. Evan Carton, "Defense of Good Lecturer Policy," RhetCompUTX, https://rhetcomputx.dwrl.utexas.edu/s/DRW/item/1548.

124. Mark Burch, "English Department Senate Minutes," April 6, 1984, RhetCompUTX, https://rhetcomputx.dwrl.utexas.edu/s/DRW/item/1172.

125. Bowen and Sosa, *Prospects for Faculty*, 135–36.

126. Bousquet, *How the University Works*, 193, 200.

127. Donoghue, *Last Professors*, 34.

128. William Sutherland, "Memo Reconstituting the Agenda for the English

Faculty Senate Meeting," April 11, 1984, RhetCompUTX, https://rhetcomputx.dwrl.utexas.edu/s/DRW/item/1180.

129. Michael King, "Minutes of the English Faculty Senate," April 11, 1984, RhetCompUTX, https://rhetcomputx.dwrl.utexas.edu/s/DRW/item/1164.

130. Terence Odlin, "Minutes of the English Department Meeting," April 19, 1984, RhetCompUTX, https://rhetcomputx.dwrl.utexas.edu/s/DRW/item/1193.

131. Pratt, "New Rules Adopted for English Lecturers."

132. "Draft of English Department Letter to Dean Robert King Regarding Governance Issues," September 6, 1984, RhetCompUTX, https://rhetcomputx.dwrl.utexas.edu/s/DRW/item/1651.

133. Beebe, "Department Head Seeks Options."

134. Neill Megaw, "Letter to the University of Texas English Governance Committee," February 4, 1985, RhetCompUTX, https://rhetcomputx.dwrl.utexas.edu/s/DRW/item/1305.

135. Sledd, "Tale of 14 Stooges."

136. Simon Bernau, "Faculty Senate Meeting Minutes," April 29, 1985, RhetCompUTX, https://rhetcomputx.dwrl.utexas.edu/s/DRW/item/2230.

137. Robert King, "Memo to William Sutherland About English Governance Document," April 4, 1985, RhetCompUTX, https://rhetcomputx.dwrl.utexas.edu/s/DRW/item/626.

138. Quoted in Blessener, "English Department Members Approve." See also Blessener, "English Department Governance Unsettled."

139. Barrow, *Universities and the Capitalist State*, 75–90.

140. Strickland, *Managerial Unconscious*, 7, 9–12, 90–95.

141. Robert King, telephone interview with Nate Kreuter, November 18, 2019.

142. Barrow, *Universities and the Capitalist State*, 252.

143. Simpson, "Course May Be Dropped."

144. H. Paul Kelley, "Minutes of the University Council Meeting," March 18, 1985, RhetCompUTX, https://rhetcomputx.dwrl.utexas.edu/s/DRW/item/2752.

145. William Sutherland, "Memo to Faculty Re: E 346K," February 15, 1985, James Kinneavy Papers, Dolph Briscoe Center for American History, Box 4M804.

146. Beebe and Williams, "Deans Postpone E 346K Requirement."

147. Robert King, telephone interview with Nate Kreuter, November 18, 2019.

148. Steven Witte, "Review of 'Composition Problem,'" RhetCompUTX, https://rhetcomputx.dwrl.utexas.edu/s/DRW/item/2165.

149. Twombly, "UT Lecturers, a Survey."

150. Simon Bernau, "Minutes of the Faculty Senate," April 1, 1985, RhetCompUTX, https://rhetcomputx.dwrl.utexas.edu/s/DRW/item/2778.

151. Robert Wren, telephone interview with Nate Kreuter, October 21, 2019.

152. Alan Gribben, "Memo Regarding Bob Wren," October 16, 1985, RhetCompUTX, https://rhetcomputx.dwrl.utexas.edu/s/DRW/item/2334.

153. James Sledd, "Letter About Gribben," October 10, 1986, RhetCompUTX, https://rhetcomputx.dwrl.utexas.edu/s/DRW/item/2118.

154. Robert Wren, "Memo to English Department," undated, RhetCompUTX, https://rhetcomputx.dwrl.utexas.edu/s/DRW/item/925.

155. Alan Gribben, "Memo Regarding Bob Wren," October 16, 1985, RhetCompUTX, https://rhetcomputx.dwrl.utexas.edu/s/DRW/item/2334.

156. Megaw, "English Department Polarized over E 346K."

157. D. Woodruff, "Too Soon to Give Up on English 346K"; Kinneavy, "Course Suspension Weakens Troubled Writing Program"; Skaggs, "English Lecturers Deserve Better Treatment."

158. Watson, "Writing Essential Skill"; Grosky, "Remember Students"; Romano, "Keep Junior Course."

159. Quoted in Beebe, "Department Head Seeks Options."

160. Rebhorn, "English Course Fails"; Carver, "Literature, Composition Can Be."

161. Babcock, "Technical Majors Need E 346K Skills"; Rebec, "*Ad Hominem* Arguments Not Fair Play"; Welch, "Unite to Fight the Menace to E 346K."

162. Gribben, "Lecturers Selfish"; Skaggs, "English Lecturers Deserve Better Treatment."

163. T. McDonald, "UT Abounding in Bad Ideas"; T. Potts, "You Learned Me Well"; MacDonald, "Ode to Education."

164. Wren, "Danger of Public Promo"; Hadley, "Gribben's Attack Unfair."

165. E. Smith, "Letter on E 346K," March 1, 1985, RhetCompUTX, https://rhetcomputx.dwrl.utexas.edu/s/DRW/item/2274.

166. Megaw, "English Department Polarized over E 346K"; Wevill, "English Lecturers Highly Skilled"; Wadlington, "Stir Students' Interest"; Lesser, "Lower Division Classes Cannot Be Remedial." John Ruszkiewicz wrote a reply to Lesser's criticism of Kinneavy's curriculum, but the *Daily Texan* never published it; see John Ruszkiewicz, "Draft Letter to the Editor Explaining the Elimination of E 346K," March 7, 1985, RhetCompUTX, https://rhetcomputx.dwrl.utexas.edu/s/DRW/item/1253.

167. Simon Bernau, "Faculty Senate Meeting Minutes," March 4, 1985, RhetCompUTX, https://rhetcomputx.dwrl.utexas.edu/s/DRW/item/2254.

168. Harwood, "Discussion of English Composition Course."

169. "Departmental (A Poem)," March 15, 1985, RhetCompUTX, https://rhetcomputx.dwrl.utexas.edu/DRW/item/2248.

170. "Joe Boggs Goes to Slaughtergate," undated (likely 1985), RhetCompUTX, https://rhetcomputx.dwrl.utexas.edu/s/DRW/item/2222.

171. Heller, "50 Lecturers Lose Their Jobs."

172. Heller, "3 Tales of Life Off the Tenure Track."

173. Hairston, "We're Hiring Too Many Temporary Instructors."

174. Quoted in Heller, "50 Lecturers Lose Their Jobs," 24.

175. Quoted in Heller, "50 Lecturers Lose Their Jobs," 24.

176. Simon Bernau, "Faculty Senate Meeting Minutes," April 29, 1985, RhetCompUTX, https://rhetcomputx.dwrl.utexas.edu/s/DRW/item/2230.

177. Charles Rossman, "Letter to the *Austin Writer* About the E 346K Controversy," June 1985, RhetCompUTX, https://rhetcomputx.dwrl.utexas.edu/s/DRW/item/1955.

178. "Unsigned, Undated Memo to Departing Lecturers," undated (likely spring 1985), RhetCompUTX, https://rhetcomputx.dwrl.utexas.edu/s/DRW/item/1271.

179. Robert Twombly, "Apology," undated (likely 1985), RhetCompUTX, https://rhetcomputx.dwrl.utexas.edu/s/DRW/item/1265.

180. Joyce Locke Carter, telephone interview with Nate Kreuter, January 31, 2020.

181. Rod Davis, telephone interview with Nate Kreuter, December 11, 2019.

182. David McMurrey, "Resignation Letter," August 24, 1984, RhetCompUTX, https://rhetcomputx.dwrl.utexas.edu/s/DRW/item/1219.

183. Valerie Balester, telephone interview with Nate Kreuter, October 11, 2019.

184. Mary Trachsel, telephone interview with Nate Kreuter, October 15, 2019.

185. William Sutherland, "Memo Approving Special Assignment for Light German," January 27, 1986, RhetCompUTX, https://rhetcomputx.dwrl.utexas.edu/s/DRW/item/1311.

186. Balester, "Symposium on the 1991 Progress Report."

187. David McMurrey, "Proposal for Personal Computers in the Writing Lab," April 20, 1984, RhetCompUTX, https://rhetcomputx.dwrl.utexas.edu/s/DRW/item/1225.

188. David McMurrey, telephone interview with Nate Kreuter, October 7, 2019.

189. James Skaggs, telephone interview with Nate Kreuter, November 7, 2019.

190. Corbett, "From Literary Critic to Professional Rhetorician."

191. Quoted in McDonald and Schell, "Spirit and Influence of the Wyoming Resolution," 362.

192. McDonald and Schell, "Spirit and Influence of the Wyoming Resolution," 362–64.

193. Sledd, "See and Say," 138.

194. Wyche, "Reflections of an Anonymous Graduate Student," 8–10.

195. McDonald and Schell, "Spirit and Influence of the Wyoming Resolution," 370–71.

196. Schell and Stock, "Introduction," 18–21.

197. McClure, Goldstein, and Pemberton, "Introduction."

198. Harris, "Afterword," 285.

199. J. McDonald, "One of Many."

200. Gunner, "Elegy for a *Statement*," 63.

201. Donoghue, *Last Professors*, 59.

202. Murphy, "New Faculty for a New University," 25–26.
203. Lipson and Voorhies, "Material and the Cultural," 114–17.
204. Harris, "Meet the New Boss," 63.
205. Harris, "Meet the New Boss," 61.
206. Rogers, *Putting the Humanities PhD to Work*; Cassuto, *Graduate School Mess*.
207. Glenn, "Last Good Job," A12–A13.
208. Murphy, "New Faculty for a New University," 16.
209. Harris, "Meet the New Boss," 51.
210. James Sledd, "Memo to English Department," April 8, 1984, RhetCompUTX, https://rhetcomputx.dwrl.utexas.edu/s/DRW/item/1050.
211. Bousquet, *How the University Works*, 164–65.
212. Donoghue, *Last Professors*, 138.
213. Donoghue, *Last Professors*, 138.

Chapter 3

1. "Can't Teach This."
2. Ivins, "Austin Academics."
3. "Lower Division Policy Committee Minutes," October 5, 1988, RhetCompUTX, https://rhetcomputx.dwrl.utexas.edu/s/DRW/item/960. See also "Memo from Director of Writing Program to General Faculty About Various Issues," October 21, 1988, RhetCompUTX, https://rhetcomputx.dwrl.utexas.edu/s/DRW/item/954.
4. James Duban, "Memo from J. Duban Suggesting a Skills-Based Approach to Teaching Writing," September 13, 1990, RhetCompUTX, https://rhetcomputx.dwrl.utexas.edu/s/DRW/item/801.
5. Robert King, telephone interview with Nate Kreuter, November 18, 2019.
6. Hairston, "Winds of Change," 85.
7. Masters, *Practicing Writing*, 34.
8. Masters, *Practicing Writing*, 74.
9. James Duban, "Memo Suggesting a Skills-Based Approach to Teaching Writing," September 13, 1990, RhetCompUTX, https://rhetcomputx.dwrl.utexas.edu/s/DRW/item/801.
10. Sirc, *English Composition as a Happening*, 134.
11. Sirc, *English Composition as a Happening*, 155.
12. Crowley, "Around 1971," 205.
13. Hartman, *War for the Soul of America*, 216.
14. Faigley, *Fragments of Rationality*, 50.
15. Wan, *Producing Good Citizens*, 52.
16. Wan, *Producing Good Citizens*, 154.
17. Wan, *Producing Good Citizens*, 114.
18. Spellmeyer, *Common Ground*, 14–15.
19. James Kinneavy, "E 306 Syllabus, 1987," August 1987, RhetCompUTX, https://rhetcomputx.dwrl.utexas.edu/s/DRW/item/644.
20. Bruffee, *Collaborative Learning*, 20.
21. Bruffee, *Collaborative Learning*, 41.
22. Cooper and Holzman, *Writing as Social Action*, 204–5.
23. Cooper and Holzman, *Writing as Social Action*, 206–12.
24. Bizzell, *Academic Discourse and Critical Consciousness*, 139.
25. Loss, *Between Citizens and the State*, 215.
26. Harris, *Teaching Subject*, 140.
27. Harris, *Teaching Subject*, 142.
28. Harris, *Teaching Subject*, 149.
29. Kent, "Introduction," 5.
30. Linda Brodkey, "Letter to Kinneavy," August 4, 1983, James Kinneavy Papers, Dolph Briscoe Center for American History, Box 4M806.
31. James Kinneavy, "Letter to William Sutherland," February 24, 1988, James Kinneavy Papers, Dolph Briscoe Center for American History, Box 4M797.
32. Brandt, *Literacy as Involvement*, 103.
33. Brandt, *Literacy in American Lives*, 3.
34. Loss, *Between Citizens and the State*, 168.
35. Brodkey, "Writing Permitted in Designated Spaces Only," 234.
36. Brodkey, "Writing Permitted in Designated Spaces Only," 221.
37. Brodkey, "Writing Permitted in Designated Spaces Only," 224.
38. Spellmeyer, *Common Ground*, 59.
39. Spellmeyer, *Common Ground*, 32.
40. Spellmeyer, *Common Ground*, 59.
41. Linda Brodkey, "Packet for New E 306 Syllabus," August 1990, RhetCompUTX, https://rhetcomputx.dwrl.utexas.edu/s/DRW/item/2380.
42. C. Anderson, "Faculty Supports New E 306 Theme."
43. Branson, "When Writing Goes Public," 49.

44. Peckham, *Going North, Thinking West*, 65.
45. Rodgers, *Age of Fracture*, 5.
46. Giroux and Aronowitz, *Education Under Siege*, 3–5.
47. Loss, *Between Citizens and the State*, 229–30.
48. Kenneth Kirk, "Report and Recommendations from the Faculty Senate Curriculum Committee," April 18, 1990, RhetCompUTX, https://rhetcomputx.dwrl.utexas.edu/s/DRW/item/3058.
49. Linda Brodkey, "Memo to Lower Division English Policy Committee," March 20, 1990, RhetCompUTX, https://rhetcomputx.dwrl.utexas.edu/s/DRW/item/1038.
50. Standish Meacham, "Memoir," 2003, Standish Meacham Papers, Dolph Briscoe Center for American History, Box 2.325/C113d.
51. Ackerman, "UT Comp Class Fuels Controversy."
52. Johnson, *Undermining Racial Justice*, 78.
53. Kinneavy, *Theory of Discourse*, 96–105.
54. "Lower Division English Policy Committee Minutes," April 3, 1990, RhetCompUTX, https://rhetcomputx.dwrl.utexas.edu/s/DRW/item/913.
55. James Duban, John Ruszkiewicz, and Linda Brodkey, "Lower Division English Policy Committee Meeting Agenda," April 4, 1990, RhetCompUTX, https://rhetcomputx.dwrl.utexas.edu/s/DRW/item/911.
56. "Lower Division English Policy Committee Meeting Minutes," April 10, 1990, RhetCompUTX, https://rhetcomputx.dwrl.utexas.edu/s/DRW/item/905.
57. Frost, "'University Perspective.'"
58. H. Eldon Sutton, "Report and Recommendations from the Faculty Senate Curriculum Committee," April 18, 1990, RhetCompUTX, https://rhetcomputx.dwrl.utexas.edu/s/DRW/item/3058.
59. Susan Wells, interview with Nate Kreuter, October 21, 2019.
60. Linda Brodkey and John Ruszkiewicz, "Memo to Lower Division English Policy Committee," April 15, 1990, RhetCompUTX, https://rhetcomputx.dwrl.utexas.edu/s/DRW/item/915.
61. John Ruszkiewicz, "Motions to Alter the E 306 Syllabus and Implementation," April 6, 1990, RhetCompUTX, https://rhetcomputx.dwrl.utexas.edu/s/DRW/item/174.
62. "Lower Division English Policy Committee Meeting Minutes," April 17, 1990, RhetCompUTX, https://rhetcomputx.dwrl.utexas.edu/s/DRW/item/903.
63. Maxine Hairston, "Letter to Dean Standish Meacham," August 27, 1990, RhetCompUTX, https://rhetcomputx.dwrl.utexas.edu/s/DRW/item/721.
64. Draft of Hartzog's "Through the Looking Glass," RhetCompUTX, https://rhetcomputx.dwrl.utexas.edu/s/DRW/item/727. See also Cunningham, *The Texas Way*, 164.
65. Jan Bruell, Joseph Horn, and Lee Willerman, "Memo to Donald Foss, Chair of Psychology, Expressing Concern About Racism and Sexism Anthology in E 306," May 1, 1990, RhetCompUTX, https://rhetcomputx.dwrl.utexas.edu/s/DRW/item/168.
66. "English Department Minutes," May 8, 1990, RhetCompUTX, https://rhetcomputx.dwrl.utexas.edu/s/DRW/item/873.
67. "University Co-Operative Society (UT Austin Bookstore) Textbook Invoices for Paula Rothenberg's *Racism and Sexism*," May 10, 1990, and June 25, 1990, RhetCompUTX, https://rhetcomputx.dwrl.utexas.edu/s/DRW/item/709.
68. Standish Meacham, "Memo from Dean Standish Meacham Announcing That the New E 306 Syllabus Would Not Be Implemented," July 23, 1990, RhetCompUTX, https://rhetcomputx.dwrl.utexas.edu/s/DRW/item/166.
69. The details in this paragraph and other notes of this chapter draw from Carol Hartzog's excellent article "Through the Looking Glass: The Controversy over E 306 at the University of Texas at Austin," undated (1992), RhetCompUTX, https://rhetcomputx.dwrl.utexas.edu/s/DRW/item/727.
70. Loy, "English 306 Controversy Called 'Sobering.'"
71. John Ruszkiewicz, "Letter to Joe Kruppa," February 10, 1991, RhetCompUTX, https://rhetcomputx.dwrl.utexas.edu/s/DRW/item/923.
72. James Kinneavy, "Memo Attached to E 306 Ad Hoc Committee Report," April 30, 1990, RhetCompUTX, https://rhetcomputx.dwrl.utexas.edu/s/DRW/item/2106.
73. Allen, "Debate Continues."

74. Quoted in Bosco, "New E 306 Able to Unite."
75. Connally, "State Involved in E 306 Debate."
76. Cunningham, *Texas Way*, 166.
77. Huppé, "Academic Concerns vs. Media Perceptions."
78. Robinson and Brodkey, "Not Just a Matter of Course," 23.
79. Schudson, *Good Citizen*, 92.
80. James Kinneavy, "The Centrality of Rhetoric to the Liberal Arts Tradition," March 1984, James Kinneavy Papers, Dolph Briscoe Center for American History, Box 4M796.
81. Schudson, *Good Citizen*, 92.
82. Mortenson, "Going Public"; V. Anderson, "Property Rights"; Skinnell, "Problem of Publics."
83. Driver, "Gribben Asks Faculty Senate to Screen E 306."
84. Driver, "Gribben Suggests Control."
85. John Ruszkiewicz, "Letter to Lynne Munson," August 5, 1991, RhetCompUTX, https://rhetcomputx.dwrl.utexas.edu/s/DRW/item/1331.
86. Lynne Cheney, "Political Correctness and Beyond," September 25, 1991, RhetCompUTX, https://rhetcomputx.dwrl.utexas.edu/s/DRW/item/741. See also Lynn Cheney, *Telling the Truth: A Report on the State of the Humanities in Higher Education*, September 1992, RhetCompUTX, https://rhetcomputx.dwrl.utexas.edu/s/DRW/item/751.
87. John Ruszkiewicz, "Letter to Ted Koppel," May 23, 1986, RhetCompUTX, https://rhetcomputx.dwrl.utexas.edu/s/DRW/item/2142.
88. Moss, "UT English Classes Changed"; "UT's Including Ethnic Study Is a Good Step."
89. Utter, "E 306 to Add Readings on Racism"; Hays, "E 306 Changes Bring Something New."
90. "Civil Rights Theme."
91. Duban, "Teach Writing in Writing Courses."
92. Duban, "Stick to Writing in E 306 at UT."
93. Duban, "Teach Writing in Writing Courses."
94. Ruszkiewicz, "Altered E 306 Format Compromised."

95. "Memo from Tom Cable (?) to John Ruszkiewicz About His *Daily Texan* Article," July 29, 1990, RhetCompUTX, https://rhetcomputx.dwrl.utexas.edu/s/DRW/item/12.
96. Mary Blockley, "Memo to John Ruszkiewicz from Mary Blockley," July 24, 1990, RhetCompUTX, https://rhetcomputx.dwrl.utexas.edu/s/DRW/item/8.
97. Duban, "Teach Writing in Writing Courses."
98. Brodkey and Slatin, "E 306 Reforms Would Protect Students."
99. Brodkey and Slatin, "New E 306 Keeps Commitment to Writing."
100. Brodkey and Slatin, "New E 306 Keep Commitment to Writing."
101. Hairston, "Committee Does Good."
102. Hairston, "Required Writing Courses."
103. Hairston, "Diversity, Ideology, and Teaching Writing."
104. Maxine Hairston and Mali, "Letter Exchange Between Hairston and 'Mali' at Northern Arizona U," March 1991, RhetCompUTX, https://rhetcomputx.dwrl.utexas.edu/s/DRW/item/813.
105. Skinnell, "Problem of Publics," 159.
106. V. Anderson, "Property Rights."
107. Branson, "When Writing Goes Public," 49.
108. D'Souza, *Illiberal Education*, 17.
109. Carton, "Self Besieged."
110. D'Souza, *Illiberal Education*, 13.
111. Quoted in Barton, "Protesters Demand Participation."
112. Joseph Kruppa and Linda Brodkey, "Memo from Joseph Kruppa Calling an English Department Meeting and Attached Memo from Linda Brodkey About the New Curriculum," May 1, 1990, RhetCompUTX, https://rhetcomputx.dwrl.utexas.edu/s/DRW/item/176.
113. Carton, "Self Besieged."
114. Cole, *Cult of True Victimhood*, 27–28.
115. Scott Henson, telephone interview with Nate Kreuter, May 20, 2020.
116. Rene Williams, "Letter to John Ruszkiewicz," November 11, 1990, RhetCompUTX, https://rhetcomputx.dwrl.utexas.edu/s/DRW/item/996.
117. H. Paul Kelley, "Minutes of the University Council Meeting," September 17, 1990,

RhetCompUTX, https://rhetcomputx.dwrl.utexas.edu/s/DRW/item/3053.
118. Henson and Philpott, "E 306: Chronicle of a Smear Campaign."
119. Will, "Radical English."
120. Innis and Yioutas, "New E 306 Disregards Western Culture."
121. Scott Henson, telephone interview with Nate Kreuter, May 20, 2020.
122. Henson and Philpott, "E 306: Chronicle of a Smear Campaign."
123. Henson and Philpott, "'Tejas.'"
124. Henson and Philpott, "Extracurricular Activity."
125. McHargue, "English Department's Delay."
126. Garcia, "Fix E 306 and Stop Bitching."
127. Henry and Mitchell, "Gribben, Colleagues."
128. M. Taylor, "English 306 Not for Politics."
129. Tom McLaughlin, "Letter to Alan Gribben," August 31, 1990, RhetCompUTX, https://rhetcomputx.dwrl.utexas.edu/s/DRW/item/1058.
130. Heinzelman and Saldívar, "Rhetoric and Composition."
131. "Statement of Academic Concern," October 15, 1990.
132. Tom McLaughlin, "Letter to Alan Gribben," August 31, 1990, RhetCompUTX, https://rhetcomputx.dwrl.utexas.edu/s/DRW/item/1058.
133. Budziszewski, "English or Indoctrination?"
134. "Dean Delays Changes in a Disputed Course."
135. Willats, "Readin', Writin', and Racism."
136. Mays, "English as a Second Language."
137. Gribben, "E 306: Oppressing English Composition."
138. Connally, "Happy Trails."
139. Murchison, "UT Prof Goes Out a Winner?"
140. Marvel, "Education of Alan Gribben."
141. Brooks, "Professor Leaves."
142. Bernstein, *Dictatorship of Virtue*, 311.
143. Bernstein, *Dictatorship of Virtue*, 297.
144. D'Souza, *Illiberal Education*, 6.
145. Murchison, "Eyes of Texas."
146. Brooks, "UT English Professor."
147. Connally, "Power Play."
148. Galinsky, "Duban a Victim of Politics."
149. Walker, "'Undoing Progress,'" 62–80.
150. Geoff Henley, telephone interview with Nate Kreuter, April 24, 2020.
151. Huang and Loy, "Speech to Parents Avoids Controversy."
152. Henley, "Class Warfare."
153. "Statement of Academic Concern," October 15, 1990.
154. Quoted in Bernstein, *Dictatorship of Virtue*, 329.
155. Henley, "Brodkey's 'Diversity' Only One-Sided."
156. Vivian, *Campus Misinformation*, 28–30.
157. Yioutas, "KLRU Panel on Campus Issues Unbalanced."
158. Roberts-Miller, *Rhetoric and Demagoguery*, 35.
159. "Public Letter to *Austin American-Statesman*," July 14, 1990, RhetCompUTX, https://rhetcomputx.dwrl.utexas.edu/s/DRW/item/2098.
160. "Statement of Academic Concern," July 18, 1990.
161. Bizzell and Trimbur, "Letter," 37.
162. Collier, "Incorrect English."
163. Curtis, "Behind the Lines."
164. Murchison, "Radical Left Has Won."
165. Gribben, "New E 306 Format Flawed."
166. "UT Co-operative Society (UT Bookstore) Textbook Invoices for Paula Rothenberg's *Racism and Sexism*," May 19, 1990, and June 25, 1990, RhetCompUTX, https://rhetcomputx.dwrl.utexas.edu/s/DRW/item/709.
167. "Civil Rights Theme."
168. Murchison, "English Faculty Should Stick to English."
169. Stanford, "No Thanks"; see also McHargue, "Recomposition."
170. Gribben, "'Texan' Goes Too Far."
171. Will, "Radical English."
172. Leo, "Academy's New Ayatollahs."
173. Yardley, "On Dasher! On Dancer! To Albania!"
174. Diamond, "Readin', Writin', and Repressin'."

175. Brodkey and Fowler, "Political Suspects."

176. Newberry, "UT Official Sees Introduction."

177. Baudrillard, *Gulf War Did Not Take Place*, 31.

178. Baudrillard, *Gulf War Did Not Take Place*, 58 and 62.

179. Gogan, *Jean Baudrillard*, 65.

180. Maxine Hairston, "Note to Ruszkiewicz with Attached Letter to Woodward," July 10, 1992, RhetCompUTX, https://rhetcomputx.dwrl.utexas.edu/s/DRW/item/753.

181. Standish Meacham, "Handwritten Notes on Community," no date, Standish Meacham Papers, Dolph Briscoe Center for American History, Box 2.325/C113d.

182. Linda Brodkey, "Memo to James Kinneavy," August 1, 1990, Kinneavy Papers, Dolph Briscoe Center for American History, Box 4M797.

183. John Slatin, "Reply to Query on Texas Writing Course," July 27, 1990, https://rhetcomputx.dwrl.utexas.edu/s/DRW/item/1991.

184. Roberts-Miller, *Rhetoric and Demagoguery*, 185.

185. Geoff Henley, telephone interview with Nate Kreuter, April 24, 2020; Scott Henson, telephone interview with Nate Kreuter, May 20, 2020.

186. James Berlin, "Reply to Ruszkiewicz," August 21, 1991, RhetCompUTX, https://rhetcomputx.dwrl.utexas.edu/s/DRW/item/707.

187. John Ruszkiewicz, "Letter to James Berlin Re: Maxine Hairston's Presentation at CCCC," August 31, 1991, RhetCompUTX, https://rhetcomputx.dwrl.utexas.edu/s/DRW/item/705.

188. John Ruszkiewicz, "1992 Legal Pad," June–October 1992, RhetCompUTX, https://rhetcomputx.dwrl.utexas.edu/s/DRW/item/3192.

189. Bleich, "Comment on Property Rights," 370.

190. Rodgers, *Age of Fracture*, 260.

191. Baker-Bell, *Linguistic Justice*, 30.

192. E. Smith, *Critique of Anti-Racism*, 9.

193. Bouie, "What the Republican Push."

194. Cunningham, *Texas Way*, 166.

195. Faigley, *Fragments of Rationality*, 50.

Chapter 4

1. Two representative volumes about the marketization of higher education include David Labaree's *A Perfect Mess* and Arthur Levine and Scott Van Pelt's *The Great Upheaval*. Two representative books recently published about the rights revolution in American higher education include Matthew Johnson's *Undermining Racial Justice* and Sharon Lee's *An Unseen Unheard Minority*.

2. Bloom, *Closing of the American Mind*, 339.

3. Bloom, *Closing of the American Mind*, 346.

4. Sledd, "Reply to Bizzell and Trimbur's 'Letter,'" 50.

5. Jameson, *Postmodernism*, 417.

6. O'Connell, "What Goes On."

7. Connors, "Abolition Debate."

8. Ruszkiewicz, "Documents of Dissent," 180.

9. Simon Bernau, "Faculty Senate Meeting Minutes," April 29, 1985, RhetCompUTX, https://rhetcomputx.dwrl.utexas.edu/s/DRW/item/2230.

10. Wayne Rebhorn, telephone interview with Nate Kreuter, February 7, 2020; Lance Bertelson, telephone interview with Nate Kreuter, February 26, 2020.

11. Larry Carver, telephone interview with Nate Kreuter, January 7, 2020.

12. Carol MacKay, telephone interview with Nate Kreuter, March 19, 2020.

13. James Sledd, "Letter to the English Department," March 28, 1980, RhetCompUTX, https://rhetcomputx.dwrl.utexas.edu/s/DRW/item/1072.

14. James Vick, "Report of the University Council Committee on Basic Education Requirements," December 1980, RhetCompUTX, https://rhetcomputx.dwrl.utexas.edu/s/DRW/item/2660.

15. Goggin and Miller, "What is *New* About the 'New Abolitionists,'" 91–92.

16. Lesser, "Lower Division Classes Cannot Be Remedial."

17. Carver, "Literature, Composition Can Be Taught."

18. James Kinneavy and Phyllis Richards, "Minutes of the Faculty Senate and Proposal by the College of Liberal Arts for an Undergraduate University Requirement in English," February 2, 1981, RhetCompUTX,

https://rhetcomputx.dwrl.utexas.edu/s/DRW/item/2766.

19. H. Paul Kelley, "Minutes of the University Council," March 23, 1981, RhetCompUTX, https://rhetcomputx.dwrl.utexas.edu/s/DRW/item/2710.

20. H. Paul Kelley, "Minutes of the University Council Meeting," January 24, 1983, RhetCompUTX, https://rhetcomputx.dwrl.utexas.edu/s/DRW/item/2736.

21. John Trimble, "Summary of Remarks by Robert King About E 346K and E 306," April 1, 1985, RhetCompUTX, https://rhetcomputx.dwrl.utexas.edu/s/DRW/item/1299.

22. Larry Carver, telephone interview with Nate Kreuter, January 7, 2020.

23. Evan Carton, telephone interview with Nate Kreuter, February 20, 2020.

24. Joseph Kruppa, "Memo Establishing E 346K Evaluation," May 28, 1985, RhetCompUTX, https://rhetcomputx.dwrl.utexas.edu/s/DRW/item/2138.

25. Joseph Kruppa, "Memo Recapping 10 June 1985 Meeting of E 346K Evaluation Committee," June 10, 1985, RhetCompUTX, https://rhetcomputx.dwrl.utexas.edu/s/DRW/item/1283.

26. Joseph Kruppa, "Letter About E 346K Evaluation," July 12, 1985, RhetCompUTX, https://rhetcomputx.dwrl.utexas.edu/s/DRW/item/2136.

27. Quoted in Williams, "Committee Probes English Program."

28. Quoted in Williams, "Committee Reviews E 346K Proposal."

29. Joseph Kruppa, Jerome Bump, Lester Faigley, Alan Gribben, Charles Rossman, and William Sutherland, "E 346K Report," August 30, 1985, RhetCompUTX, https://rhetcomputx.dwrl.utexas.edu/s/DRW/item/2124.

30. Quoted in Matejowski, "English 306 Proposal Passes in a Landslide Victory."

31. Ewing, "New Elective Composition Course."

32. Ewing, "Some Professors Oppose Dropping E 306."

33. Quoted in Shaw, "English 346K Abolished."

34. Quoted in Ewing, "New Elective Composition Course."

35. "E 346K Committee Report," March 6, 1986, RhetCompUTX, https://rhetcomputx.dwrl.utexas.edu/s/DRW/item/2312.

36. H. Paul Kelley, "University Council Minutes," February 17, 1986, RhetCompUTX, https://rhetcomputx.dwrl.utexas.edu/s/DRW/item/2298.

37. Quoted in Borden, "Cunningham Defends Student Government."

38. John Ruszkiewicz, "Letter to Joe Kruppa in Support of E 306," RhetCompUTX, https://rhetcomputx.dwrl.utexas.edu/s/DRW/item/1285.

39. Maxine Hairston, "Letter to Joe Kruppa," June 14, 1985, RhetCompUTX, https://rhetcomputx.dwrl.utexas.edu/s/DRW/item/1279.

40. R. Renwick, "English Department Meeting Minutes," September 11, 1985, RhetCompUTX, https://rhetcomputx.dwrl.utexas.edu/s/DRW/item/2128.

41. Quoted in Ewing, "Some Professors Oppose Dropping E 306."

42. James Kinneavy, "Request for Faculty Action Concerning the English Composition Program," March 12, 1986, RhetCompUTX, https://rhetcomputx.dwrl.utexas.edu/s/DRW/item/2781.

43. John Ruszkiewicz, "Letter to Cunningham," January 23, 1986, RhetCompUTX, https://rhetcomputx.dwrl.utexas.edu/s/DRW/item/2302.

44. H. Paul Kelley, "University Council Minutes," February 17, 1986, RhetCompUTX, https://rhetcomputx.dwrl.utexas.edu/s/DRW/item/2298.

45. Joseph Kruppa, Jerome Bump, Lester Faigley, Alan Gribben, Charles Rossman, and William Sutherland, "Response of the E 346K Evaluation Committee to James Kinneavy's Message to the University Council," March 17, 1986, RhetCompUTX, https://rhetcomputx.dwrl.utexas.edu/s/DRW/item/2788.

46. W. Horner, "Historical Introduction," 1–5.

47. "Modern Language Association Commission on Writing and Literature Surveys," 1984, James Kinneavy Papers, Dolph Briscoe Center for American History, Box 4M805.

48. Quoted in Williams, "Committee Probes English Program."

49. Charles Rossman, "Memo to Format 1 Committee," RhetCompUTX, https://rhetcomputx.dwrl.utexas.edu/s/DRW/item/2018.

50. D. G. Kehl and John Ruszkiewicz, "Survey of Writing Programs," October 21,

2005, RhetCompUTX, https://rhetcomputx.dwrl.utexas.edu/s/DRW/item/114. For a comparable sentiment expressed in more recent scholarly literature, see Lindemann, "Freshman Composition, No Place for Literature."

51. Kinneavy, "Course Suspension Weakens Troubled Writing Program."

52. James Kinneavy, "The Decomposition of English," 1985, RhetCompUTX, https://rhetcomputx.dwrl.utexas.edu/s/DRW/item/2286.

53. Hairston, "Breaking Our Bonds and Reaffirming Our Connections," 275–77.

54. John Ruszkiewicz, "Three Tips on Writing," 1984/1985, RhetCompUTX, https://rhetcomputx.dwrl.utexas.edu/s/DRW/item/1.

55. Edward Corbett, "How Did Rhetoric Acquire the Reputation of Being the Art of Flim Flam?," August 23, 1985, RhetCompUTX, https://rhetcomputx.dwrl.utexas.edu/s/DRW/item/112.

56. Edward Corbett, "Letter from Edward Corbett to John Ruszkiewicz," August 25, 1985, RhetCompUTX, https://rhetcomputx.dwrl.utexas.edu/s/DRW/item/102.

57. See Muller, "Alternate Writing Plan"; Muller, "Faculty Debates Changing"; and Muller, "Freshman Course May Be Dropped."

58. S. Taylor, "Proposed E 306 Changes."

59. S. Taylor, "Department Plans Structure."

60. Nather, "If You're Going to Require It."

61. Rubio, "English Proposal Overlooks Students."

62. Goodwin, "Politics Jeopardize Writing Skills."

63. Kelley, "Confusion of the First Class."

64. Quoted in S. Taylor, "Proposed E 306 Changes."

65. Maxine Hairston, James Kinneavy, John Ruszkiewicz, and John Trimble, "Rhetoric Faculty Problems with Recommendations for E 346K," September 10, 1985, RhetCompUTX, https://rhetcomputx.dwrl.utexas.edu/s/DRW/item/2140.

66. James Kinneavy, "Request for Faculty Action Concerning the English Composition Program," March 12, 1986, RhetCompUTX, https://rhetcomputx.dwrl.utexas.edu/s/DRW/item/2781.

67. Elkind, "UT Versus A&M."

68. H. Paul Kelley, "Ninth Regular Meeting of the University Council," May 7, 1986, RhetCompUTX, https://rhetcomputx.dwrl.utexas.edu/s/DRW/item/2792.

69. H. Paul Kelley, "University Council Minutes," February 17, 1986, RhetCompUTX, https://rhetcomputx.dwrl.utexas.edu/s/DRW/item/2298.

70. "Unattributed Draft of Letter to Fonken," February 25, 1986, RhetCompUTX, https://rhetcomputx.dwrl.utexas.edu/s/DRW/item/2330; H. Paul Kelley, "University Council Minutes," February 17, 1986, RhetCompUTX, https://rhetcomputx.dwrl.utexas.edu/s/DRW/item/2298.

71. H. Paul Kelley, "Ninth Regular Meeting of the University Council," May 12, 1986, RhetCompUTX, https://rhetcomputx.dwrl.utexas.edu/s/DRW/item/2792.

72. William Sutherland, "Letter to Ruszkiewicz Regarding E 306," March 10, 1986, RhetCompUTX, https://rhetcomputx.dwrl.utexas.edu/s/DRW/item/2288.

73. Lance Bertelson, telephone interview with Nate Kreuter, February 26, 2020.

74. "Lower Division Policy Committee Description," 1988–89, RhetCompUTX, https://rhetcomputx.dwrl.utexas.edu/s/DRW/item/1014.

75. Neil Nehring, "Letter from Neil Nehring to John Ruszkiewicz," August 18, 1988, RhetCompUTX, https://rhetcomputx.dwrl.utexas.edu/s/DRW/item/3.

76. John Ruszkiewicz, "Reason Is But Choosing: Ideology in Freshman English," 1991, RhetCompUTX, https://rhetcomputx.dwrl.utexas.edu/s/DRW/item/713.

77. Brodkey, "Writing Permitted in Designated Spaces Only," 225–27.

78. "Freshman English Policy Committee Minutes," October 30, 1978, RhetCompUTX, https://rhetcomputx.dwrl.utexas.edu/s/DRW/item/241.

79. Ewing, "Some Professors Oppose Dropping E 306."

80. Bradley, "UT Students Writing Without Tools."

81. Elizabeth McGonigal, Frank Pool, Joan Hall, Daniel Munger, Marcia Hilsabeck, Martha Hastedt, J. Patrick Schmidt, R. N. Wightman, and Sara Gaetjins, "Letter from Texas High School Teachers to Gerard Fonken," April 17, 1991, RhetCompUTX, https://rhetcomputx.dwrl.utexas.edu/s/DRW/item/1054.

82. Longaker et al., "Growing Despite Austerity," 187. For enrollment data, see the University of Texas 2014–2015 *Statistical Handbook*, https://utexas.app.box.com/v/SHB14–15Complete.
83. Ritter, *Before Shaughnessy*.
84. R. Renwick, "English Department Meeting Minutes," September 11, 1985, RhetCompUTX, https://rhetcomputx.dwrl.utexas.edu/s/DRW/item/2128.
85. Muller, "Faculty Debates Changing."
86. Joseph Kruppa, Jerome Bump, Lester Faigley, Alan Gribben, Charles Rossman, and William Sutherland, "Response of the E 346K Evaluation Committee to James Kinneavy's Message to the University Council," March 17, 1986, RhetCompUTX, https://rhetcomputx.dwrl.utexas.edu/s/DRW/item/2788.
87. Robert Wren, "Letter Regarding E 346K," undated (1985), RhetCompUTX, https://rhetcomputx.dwrl.utexas.edu/s/DRW/item/2126.
88. Robert Wren, telephone interview with Nate Kreuter, October 21, 2019.
89. Mary Robertson, "Letter to Bob Wren," undated (1985), RhetCompUTX, https://rhetcomputx.dwrl.utexas.edu/s/DRW/item/2336.
90. John Ruszkiewicz, "Memo to Charles Rossman," 1985, RhetCompUTX, https://rhetcomputx.dwrl.utexas.edu/s/DRW/item/1275.
91. Charles Rossman, "Letter to John Ruszkiewicz," June 28, 1985, RhetCompUTX, https://rhetcomputx.dwrl.utexas.edu/s/DRW/item/1287.
92. H. Paul Kelley, "Minutes of the University Council Meeting," March 17, 1986, RhetCompUTX, https://rhetcomputx.dwrl.utexas.edu/s/DRW/item/1287.
93. H. Paul Kelley, "Minutes of the University Council," March 23, 1981, RhetCompUTX, https://rhetcomputx.dwrl.utexas.edu/s/DRW/item/2710.
94. James Sledd, "Note from James Sledd," February 22, 1985, RhetCompUTX, https://rhetcomputx.dwrl.utexas.edu/s/DRW/item/2266; see also "Note Referring to Sledd's Proposal," February 23, 1985, RhetCompUTX, https://rhetcomputx.dwrl.utexas.edu/s/DRW/item/2264.
95. John Slatin, "Open Letter on Composition Draft," 1985(?), RhetCompUTX, https://rhetcomputx.dwrl.utexas.edu/s/DRW/item/2177.
96. James Sledd, "Note from James Sledd," February 22, 1985, RhetCompUTX, https://rhetcomputx.dwrl.utexas.edu/s/DRW/item/2266.
97. John Slatin, "Open Letter on Composition Draft," 1985(?), RhetCompUTX, https://rhetcomputx.dwrl.utexas.edu/s/DRW/item/2177.
98. Joseph Kruppa, Jerome Bump, Lester Faigley, Alan Gribben, Charles Rossman, and William Sutherland, "E 346K Report," August 30, 1985, RhetCompUTX, https://rhetcomputx.dwrl.utexas.edu/s/DRW/item/2124.
99. "Minutes of the Faculty Senate Meeting," April 3, 1989, RhetCompUTX, https://rhetcomputx.dwrl.utexas.edu/s/DRW/item/3056; see also Joseph Legowski and H. Paul Kelley, "University Council Education Policy Committee Recommendations Based on the 'Fowler' Report on Substantial Writing Courses, 1988–1989," April 11, 1989, RhetCompUTX, https://rhetcomputx.dwrl.utexas.edu/s/DRW/item/87.
100. Joseph Legowski, "Revised Recommendations Concerning Substantial Writing Courses," May 3, 1989, RhetCompUTX, https://rhetcomputx.dwrl.utexas.edu/s/DRW/item/3063.
101. H. Eldon Sutton and Kenneth Kirk, "Report and Recommendations from the Faculty Senate Curriculum Committee," April 18, 1990, RhetCompUTX, https://rhetcomputx.dwrl.utexas.edu/s/DRW/item/3058.
102. "Lower Division English Policy Committee English Packet Guide," Fall 1989, RhetCompUTX, https://rhetcomputx.dwrl.utexas.edu/s/DRW/item/194.
103. Connors, "Abolition Debate in Composition," 61.
104. Goggin and Miller, "What Is New About the 'New Abolitionists,'" 93.
105. S. Miller, *Textual Carnivals*, 6–7.
106. S. Miller, *Textual Carnivals*, 39–42.
107. Crowley, "Personal Essay on Freshman English," 162.
108. Crowley, "Personal Essay on Freshman English," 170.
109. Faigley, *Fragments of Rationality*, 16.
110. Faigley, *Fragments of Rationality*, 162.

111. Stephen Witte, "Review of Composition Problem," undated (1985), RhetCompUTX, https://rhetcomputx.dwrl.utexas.edu/s/DRW/item/2165.

112. John Ruszkiewicz, "Memo to Charles Rossman," 1985, RhetCompUTX, https://rhetcomputx.dwrl.utexas.edu/s/DRW/item/1275.

113. H. Paul Kelley, "Minutes of the University Council Meeting," March 17, 1986, RhetCompUTX, https://rhetcomputx.dwrl.utexas.edu/s/DRW/item/2786.

114. Stephen Witte, "Review of Composition Problem," undated (1985), RhetCompUTX, https://rhetcomputx.dwrl.utexas.edu/s/DRW/item/2165; see also Simon Bernau, "Minutes of the Faculty Senate," April 1, 1985, RhetCompUTX, https://rhetcomputx.dwrl.utexas.edu/s/DRW/item/2778.

115. John Trimble, "Memo to Rhetoric Interest Group," April 1, 1985, RhetCompUTX, https://rhetcomputx.dwrl.utexas.edu/s/DRW/item/1297.

116. John Trimble, "Summary of Remarks by Robert King about E 306 and E 346K," April 2, 1985, RhetCompUTX, https://rhetcomputx.dwrl.utexas.edu/s/DRW/item/1299.

117. Maxine Hairston, James Kinneavy, John Ruszkiewicz, and John Trimble, "Rhetoric Faculty Letter to Robert King," May 16, 1985, RhetCompUTX, https://rhetcomputx.dwrl.utexas.edu/s/DRW/item/2080.

118. Williams, "At the Crossroads."

119. R. Renwick, "English Department Meeting Minutes," September 11, 1985, RhetCompUTX, https://rhetcomputx.dwrl.utexas.edu/s/DRW/item/2128.

120. H. Paul Kelley, "Minutes of the University Council Meeting," March 17, 1986, RhetCompUTX, https://rhetcomputx.dwrl.utexas.edu/s/DRW/item/2786.

121. Quoted in Muller, "Alternate Writing Plan."

122. See Bizzell, "Cognition, Convention, and Certainty."

123. John Ruszkiewicz and Elizabeth Cullingford, "Exchange Between Cullingford and Ruszkiewicz Regarding Department Climate," November 11, 1991, RhetCompUTX, https://rhetcomputx.dwrl.utexas.edu/s/DRW/item/819.

124. John Ruszkiewicz and Elizabeth Cullingford, "Communication Between Liz Cullingford and John Ruszkiewicz," November 20, 1991, RhetCompUTX, https://rhetcomputx.dwrl.utexas.edu/s/DRW/item/2114.

125. Loy, "King to Return to Position."

126. Henley, "English Rule."

127. Henley, "Rough Draft."

128. Connally and Bezanson, "Changing Course."

129. Henson, "Illiberal Arts." See also Henson, "Kingmaker."

130. Feistel, "Motivations Questioned."

131. Bosco, "English Department to Vote."

132. Frank Bean, "Enriching the Undergraduate Experience at the University of Texas at Austin," November 1991, RhetCompUTX, https://rhetcomputx.dwrl.utexas.edu/s/DRW/item/703.

133. H. Paul Kelley, "Minutes of the University Council Meeting," January 27, 1992, RhetCompUTX, https://rhetcomputx.dwrl.utexas.edu/s/DRW/item/3084.

134. "Cunningham Announces Decisions."

135. Quoted in Williamson, "English Department Could Be Redesigned."

136. Henley, "Rough Draft."

137. Ratliff, "Changes Necessary for English Program."

138. John Ruszkiewicz, "Memo to King About Division of Rhetoric and Composition Budget," April 3, 1992, RhetCompUTX, https://rhetcomputx.dwrl.utexas.edu/s/DRW/item/160.

139. Robert King, interview with Nate Kreuter, November 18, 2019.

140. Cunningham, *Texas Way*, 167.

141. Quoted in Franke, "Writing Shifts to New Division."

142. Joseph Kruppa and William Cunningham, "Kruppa and Cunningham Memos Announcing the Formation of Division of Rhetoric and Composition," September 1, 1992, and August 28, 1992, RhetCompUTX, https://rhetcomputx.dwrl.utexas.edu/s/DRW/item/143.

143. Quoted in T. Woodruff, "Professors Claim New Department."

144. Evan Carton, "Memo Announcing English Department Meeting on Rhetoric and Composition Proposal," September 9, 1992, RhetCompUTX, https://rhetcomputx.dwrl.utexas.edu/s/DRW/item/137.

145. John Ruszkiewicz, "1992 Legal Pad," June–October 1992, RhetCompUTX,

https://rhetcomputx.dwrl.utexas.edu/s/DRW/item/3192.

146. Brooks, "UT Council to Hear."
147. Causey, "Committee Created."
148. John Durbin, "Memo from Durbin with Questions About Division of Rhetoric and Composition Proposal," September 15, 1992, RhetCompUTX, https://rhetcomputx.dwrl.utexas.edu/s/DRW/item/135.
149. H. Paul Kelley, "Minutes of the University Council Meeting," September 21, 1992, RhetCompUTX, https://rhetcomputx.dwrl.utexas.edu/s/DRW/item/3090.
150. H. Paul Kelley, "Minutes of the University Council Meeting," October 19, 1992, RhetCompUTX, https://rhetcomputx.dwrl.utexas.edu/s/DRW/item/3094.
151. Carton, "New Division."
152. Gainer, "Committee Still Unformed."
153. See, for instance, Hindman, "Learning as We G(r)o(w)"; see also Maid, "Creating Two Departments of Writing."
154. See Agnew and Dallas; "Internal Friction"; Anson, "Who Wants Composition?"; Matzen, "Great Recession"; Yood, "Revising the Dream"; Zimmerman, "'And So Two Shall Become One.'"
155. Joseph Kruppa and William Cunningham, "Kruppa and Cunningham Memos Announcing the Formation of Division of Rhetoric and Composition," September 1, 1992, and August 28, 1992, RhetCompUTX, https://rhetcomputx.dwrl.utexas.edu/s/DRW/item/143.
156. Quoted in Neff, "New Education Initiative."
157. Joseph Kruppa and William Cunningham, "Kruppa and Cunningham Memos Announcing the Formation of Division of Rhetoric and Composition," September 1, 1992, and August 28, 1992, RhetCompUTX, https://rhetcomputx.dwrl.utexas.edu/s/DRW/item/143.
158. John Ruszkiewicz, "Ruszkiewicz's Notes Preparing for Sept 1992 Meeting about DRC formation," September 18, 1992, RhetCompUTX, https://rhetcomputx.dwrl.utexas.edu/s/DRW/item/3187.
159. Ruch, *Higher Ed, Inc.*, 14.
160. Ruch, *Higher Ed, Inc.*, 83–84.
161. Joseph Kruppa and William Cunningham, "Kruppa and Cunningham Memos Announcing the Formation of Division of Rhetoric and Composition," September 1, 1992, and August 28, 1992, RhetCompUTX, https://rhetcomputx.dwrl.utexas.edu/s/DRW/item/143.
162. Swearingen, "Prim Irony."
163. Collini, *Speaking of Universities*, 34.
164. Barrow, *Entrepreneurial Intellectual*, 9.
165. Alaniz, "Rhetoric Division Faces Scrutiny." See also J. Parker Lamb, "Minutes of the Faculty Senate," October 5, 1992, RhetCompUTX, https://rhetcomputx.dwrl.utexas.edu/s/DRW/item/3077.
166. H. Paul Kelley, "Minutes of the University Council Meeting," November 16, 1992, RhetCompUTX, https://rhetcomputx.dwrl.utexas.edu/s/DRW/item/3096.
167. Robert Berdahl, "Memo Creating the University Committee to Examine the Undergraduate Writing Program," February 10, 1993, RhetCompUTX, https://rhetcomputx.dwrl.utexas.edu/s/DRW/item/761.
168. Robert King, "Letter Appointing Faigley as Director and John Ruszkiewicz as Associate Director of the New Division of Rhetoric and Composition," January 21, 1993, RhetCompUTX, https://rhetcomputx.dwrl.utexas.edu/s/DRW/item/17.
169. Neff, "New Education Initiative."
170. Lester Faigley, "Memo from Faigley to King Ahead of Meeting About Division of Rhetoric and Composition," September 29, 1992, RhetCompUTX, https://rhetcomputx.dwrl.utexas.edu/s/DRW/item/791.
171. John Ruszkiewicz, "1992 Legal Pad," June–October 1992, RhetCompUTX, https://rhetcomputx.dwrl.utexas.edu/s/DRW/item/3192.
172. John Ruszkiewicz, "Notes from Meeting of Rhetoric Faculty Regarding Division of Rhetoric and Composition," October 5, 1992, RhetCompUTX, https://rhetcomputx.dwrl.utexas.edu/s/DRW/item/783.
173. John Ruszkiewicz, "Notes on the Division of Rhetoric and Composition," October 12, 1992, RhetCompUTX, https://rhetcomputx.dwrl.utexas.edu/s/DRW/item/775.
174. Robert King, "Memo from King About Advisory Committee for the Division of Rhetoric and Composition," October 15, 1992, RhetCompUTX, https://rhetcomputx.dwrl.utexas.edu/s/DRW/item/779.

175. James Kinneavy, Lester Faigley, John Ruszkiewicz, Linda Ferreira-Buckley, John Slatin, Evan Carton, and Terry Kelley, "Memo and Report on Division of Rhetoric and Composition," December 2, 1992, RhetCompUTX, https://rhetcomputx.dwrl.utexas.edu/s/DRW/item/759.

176. John Ruszkiewicz, "Things I Want in/from a Rhetoric Division," 1992–93(?), RhetCompUTX, https://rhetcomputx.dwrl.utexas.edu/s/DRW/item/149.

177. Linda Ferreira-Buckley, "Working Notes," 1992–93(?), RhetCompUTX, https://rhetcomputx.dwrl.utexas.edu/s/DRW/item/151; "Points of Difference," 1992–93(?), RhetCompUTX, https://rhetcomputx.dwrl.utexas.edu/s/DRW/item/147.

178. "Memo Re: Final Version of the Division of Composition Committee," January 28, 1993, RhetCompUTX, https://rhetcomputx.dwrl.utexas.edu/s/DRW/item/771.

179. John Ruszkiewicz, "Division of Rhetoric and Composition Course Proposals," July 14, 1993, RhetCompUTX, https://rhetcomputx.dwrl.utexas.edu/s/DRW/item/145.

180. Vinokur, "University Adds Writing Courses."

181. Barton, "Devising a Division."

182. Maxine Hairston, "Unattributed Letter to Robert King," May 6, 1994, RhetCompUTX, https://rhetcomputx.dwrl.utexas.edu/s/DRW/item/749.

183. Sledd, "Division Just Rhetoric."

184. Schendel, "Locating Writing Programs," 189–93.

185. Hindman, "Learning as We G(r)o(w)," 109.

186. Kearns and Turner, "Outsider's Perspective," 54.

187. Sorapure and Adler-Kassner, "Context, Strategy, Identity," 116.

Conclusion

1. Labaree, *Perfect Mess*, 149.
2. Labaree, *Perfect Mess*, 153.
3. Faigley, *Fragments of Rationality*, 16.
4. Harris, *Teaching Subject*, 159.
5. Enoch and VanHaitsma, "Archival Literacy," 230.
6. Enoch and VanHaitsma, "Archival Literacy," 219.
7. Enoch and VanHaitsma, "Archival Literacy," 230.
8. Royster, *Traces of a Stream*, 78.
9. Royster, *Traces of a Stream*, 83.
10. See, for instance, Hayden, "And Gladly Teach"; Kennedy and Walker, "Pedagogy"; and Shaver, "Cultivating a Feminist Consciousness."
11. Enoch, "Releasing Hold."
12. Ghaddar and Caswell, "'To Go Beyond.'"
13. Kirsch and Royster, "Feminist Rhetorical Practices," 658–59.
14. Ramsey-Tobienne, "Archives 2.0," 24.
15. Kirschenbaum, *Mechanisms*, 250–51.
16. K. J. Rawson emphasizes the potential for "political activism" in archival construction; see Rawson, "Rhetorical Power of Archival Description," 348. According to Jean Bessette, archival organization presents the user with opportunities to notice a pattern, which "generates new ideas and identifications." Bessette, *Retroactivism in the Lesbian Archives*, 83.
17. Ghaddar and Caswell, "'To Go Beyond,'" 38.
18. Graban, "From Location(s) to Locatability."
19. L. Potts, "Archive Experiences."
20. VanHaitsma, "Digital LGBTQ Archives," 259.
21. Douglas, "Looking Outward," 33.
22. Douglas, "Looking Outward," 38.
23. Culbertson and Lanthorne, "Praxis, Not Practice."
24. Longaker et al., "Archiving Our Own."
25. Ritter, *To Know Her Own History*, 87. For a similar use of interviews as a complement to material primary source research, see chapter 1 in David Gold's *Rhetoric at the Margins*.
26. McKee and Porter, "Ethics of Archival Research," 60.
27. McKee and Porter, "Ethics of Archival Research," 63.
28. McKee and Porter, "Ethics of Archival Research," 75.
29. Cvetkovich, *Archive of Feelings*, 167.
30. Cvetkovich, *Archive of Feelings*, 204.
31. John Ruszkiewicz, personal correspondence, May 20, 2020.
32. Gold, "Remapping Revisionist Historiography," 24.

33. Gold, "Remapping Revisionist Historiography," 17.
34. Booth, *Company We Keep*, 207.
35. Malenczyk, "Introduction with Some Rhetorical Terms," 4.
36. From Cheryl Glenn and Jessica Enoch, who assert that we should "search for new kinds of evidence," to Lori Ostergaard and Henrietta Rix Wood, who contend that we should explore "composition and rhetoric in the educational institutions," compositionist-archivists creatively compile primary source evidence. See Glenn and Enoch, "Invigorating Historiographic Practices," 16; Ostergaard and Wood, "Adding New Stories," 2. Gretchen Flesher Moon promotes "a complex layering of institutional, teacher, and student documents," a methodological stratification of archival sources that weighs the crushing mass of historical circumstance and thus provides the context wherein any assertion of agency seems a victory. Moon, "Locating Composition History," 10.
37. Instead of seeing primary source evidence as a sure route to historical truth, we follow the advice of the historian Carol Steedman, who approaches the "Archive" as "something that, through the cultural activity of History, can become Memory's potential space, one of the few realms of the modern imagination where a hard-won and carefully constructed place, can return to boundless, limitless space." Steedman, *Dust*, 83. The archivist Michelle Caswell elaborates when saying that "archives are multilayered, dynamic, and in constant motion," leading her to conclude that "narrative creation is integral to the archives." Caswell, *Archiving the Unspeakable*, 133.
38. Wells, "Claiming the Archive," 58.
39. Hayden, "And Gladly Teach," 145–46.
40. Seneca, *Declamations, Volume II*, 561–93.
41. D. Russell, *Greek Declamation*, 106.
42. "Proposal for Lecturers," February 21, 1983, RhetCompUTX, https://rhetcomputx.dwrl.utexas.edu/s/DRW/item/679.
43. "A Proposal on the Lecturer Situation," 1984, RhetCompUTX, https://rhetcomputx.dwrl.utexas.edu/s/DRW/item/1034.
44. "Proposal from the Senate Subcommittee on Lecturers," February 1983, RhetCompUTX, https://rhetcomputx.dwrl.utexas.edu/s/DRW/item/689.
45. Stephen Witte, "Review of the 'Composition Problem,'" 1985, RhetCompUTX, https://rhetcomputx.dwrl.utexas.edu/s/DRW/item/2165; "E 346K Committee Report," August 30, 1985, RhetCompUTX, https://rhetcomputx.dwrl.utexas.edu/s/DRW/item/2124; "Rhetoric Faculty Letter to Robert King," May 16, 1985, RhetCompUTX, https://rhetcomputx.dwrl.utexas.edu/s/DRW/item/2080.
46. Skinnell, "Archives of Epistemic Possibility," xiii.
47. Tirabassi, "Creative Storytelling," 76.
48. Proszak and Cushman, "Delinking Student Perceptions," 205.

Bibliography

Ackerman, Todd. "UT Comp Class Fuels Controversy." *Houston Chronicle*, June 27, 1990.

Adler-Kassner, Linda. *The Activist WPA: Changing Stories About Writing and Writers*. Logan: Utah State University Press 2008.

Agnew, Eleanor, and Phyllis Surrency Dallas. "Internal Friction in a New Independent Department of Writing and What the External Conflict Resolution Consultants Recommended." In *A Field of Dreams: Independent Writing Programs and the Future of Composition Studies*, edited by Peggy O'Neill, Angela Crow, and Larry W. Burton, 38–49. Logan: Utah State University Press, 2002.

Alaniz, José. "Rhetoric Division Faces Scrutiny by New Committee." *Daily Texan*, November 17, 1992.

Allen, Diane. "Debate Continues: What Focus for Freshman Writing." *Council Grams*, March/April 1991.

Anderson, Christopher. "Faculty Supports New E 306 Theme." *Daily Texan*, September 17, 1990.

Anderson, Virginia. "Property Rights: Exclusion as Moral Action in 'The Battle of Texas.'" *College English* 62, no. 4 (March 2000): 445–72.

Anson, Chris. "Who Wants Composition? Reflections on the Rise and Fall of an Independent Writing Program." In *A Field of Dreams: Independent Writing Programs and the Future of Composition Studies*, edited by Peggy O'Neill, Angela Crow, and Larry W. Burton, 152–69. Logan: Utah State University Press, 2002.

Applebee, Arthur. *Tradition and Reform in the Teaching of English: A History*. Urbana, IL: National Council of Teachers of English, 1974.

Aristotle. *On Rhetoric: A Theory of Civic Discourse*. Introduced, edited, and translated by George Kennedy. New York: Oxford University Press, 1991.

Arola, Kristin L. and Victor Villanueva, eds. *Cross-Talk in Comp Theory: A Reader*. 4th ed. Urbana, IL: National Council of Teachers of English, 2024.

Babcock, John. "Technical Majors Need E 346K Skills." *Daily Texan*, February 25, 1985.

Baker-Bell, April. *Linguistic Justice: Black Language, Literacy, Identity and Pedagogy*. New York: Routledge, 2020.

Balester, Valerie. "Symposium on the 1991 Progress Report from the CCCC Committee on Professional Standards: Revising the 'Statement': On the Work of Writing Centers." *College Composition and Communication* 43, no. 2 (1992): 167–71.

Barrow, Clyde. *The Entrepreneurial Intellectual in the Corporate University*. London: Palgrave, 2018.

———. *Universities and the Capitalist State: Corporate Liberalism and the*

Reconstruction of American Higher Education, 1894–1928. Madison: University of Wisconsin Press, 1990.

Barton, Chris. "Devising a Division." *The Alcalde*, January/February 1994.

———. "Protesters Demand Participation in Decision on Diversity." *Daily Texan*, July 30, 1990.

Baudrillard, Jean. *The Gulf War Did Not Take Place*. Translated and introduced by Paul Patton. Sydney: Power Publications, 1995.

Bauer, Scott, and Harm Vanhuisen. "Republicans Vote to Cut University of Wisconsin System's Budget by $32 Million in Diversity Program Spat." *Associated Press*, June 22, 2023. https://apnews.com/article/university-wisconsin-budget-legislature/-cut-tuition-c654d9cb21317c7d0a86860 2019c2dcf.

Beard, David, and Chongwong Park. "Forces Acting on a Departmental (Re-) Merger: Budgets, Spaces, Disciplines, Identities." In *Weathering the Storm: Independent Writing Programs in the Age of Fiscal Austerity*, edited by Richard Matzen and Matthew Abraham, 38–50. Logan: Utah State University Press, 2019.

Beebe, Andrea. "Department Head Seeks Options to Fill E 346K Component." *Daily Texan*, February 20, 1985.

Beebe, Andrea, and Ellen Williams. "Deans Postpone E 346K Requirement." *Daily Texan*, February 18, 1985.

Bell, Brenda. "House Subcommittee Urges Limits on TAs." *Austin American-Statesman*, September 21, 1976.

Berlin, James. *Rhetoric and Reality: Writing Instruction in American Colleges, 1900–1985*. Carbondale: Southern Illinois University Press, 1987.

———. *Writing Instruction in Nineteenth-Century American Colleges*. Carbondale: Southern Illinois University Press, 1984.

Bernstein, Richard. *Dictatorship of Virtue: Multiculturalism and the Battle for America's Future*. New York: Alfred A. Knopf, 1994.

Bérubé, Michael, and Cary Nelson, eds. *Higher Education Under Fire: Politics, Economics, and the Crisis of the Humanities*. New York: Routledge, 1995.

Bessette, Jean. *Retroactivism in the Lesbian Archives: Composing Pasts and Futures*. Carbondale: Southern Illinois University Press, 2018.

Biesecker, Barbara. "Of Historicity, Rhetoric: The Archive as Scene of Invention." *Rhetoric and Public Affairs* 9, no. 1 (2006): 124–31.

Bizzell, Patricia. *Academic Discourse and Critical Consciousness*. Pittsburgh: Pittsburgh University Press, 1992.

———. "Cognition, Convention, and Certainty: What We Need to Know About Writing." *PRE/TEXT* 2 (1982): 213–43.

Bizzell, Patricia, and John Trimbur. "Letter on Linda Brodkey Case." *Radical Teacher* 39 (1990): 37.

Bleich, David. "A Comment on Property Rights: Exclusion as Moral Action in 'the Battle of Texas.'" *College English* 63, no. 3 (January 2001): 370.

Blessener, Paula. "English Department Governance Unsettled." *Daily Texan*, February 8, 1985.

———. "English Department Members Approve Revised Governance Plan." *Daily Texan*, February 18, 1985.

Bloom, Allan. *The Closing of the American Mind*. New York: Simon and Schuster, 1987.

Bok, Derek. *Universities in the Marketplace: The Commercialization of Higher Education*. Princeton, NJ: Princeton University Press, 2003.

Booth, Wayne. *The Company We Keep: An Ethics of Fiction*. Berkeley: University of California Press, 1988.

Bordelon, Suzanne. "The 'Advance' Toward Democratic Administration: Laura Johnson Wylie and Gertrude Buck of Vassar College." In *Historical Studies of Writing Program Administration*, edited by Barbara L'Eplattenier and Lisa Mastrangelo, 91–115. West Lafayette, IN: Parlor Press, 2004.

Borden, Keefe. "Cunningham Defends Student Government." *Daily Texan*, January 22, 1986.

Bosco, Francine. "English Department to Vote on New Governing Body." *Daily Texan*, December 4, 1991.

———. "New E 306 Able to Unite Divided English Department." *Daily Texan*, June 4, 1991.

Bouie, Jamelle. "What the Republican Push for 'Parents' Rights' Is Really About." *New York Times*, March 28, 2023.

Bousquet, Marc. *How the University Works: Higher Education and the Low-Wage Nation*. New York: New York University Press, 2008.

Bowen, William, and Julie Ann Sosa. *Prospects for Faculty in the Arts and Sciences: A Study of Factors Affecting Demand and Supply, 1987 to 2012*. Princeton, NJ: Princeton University Press, 1989.

Bradley, Jennifer. "UT Students Writing Without Tools Needed for Employment." *Daily Texan*, December 5, 1988.

Brandt, Deborah. *Literacy as Involvement: The Acts of Writers, Readers, and Texts*. Carbondale: Southern Illinois University Press, 1990.

———. *Literacy in American Lives*. Cambridge: Cambridge University Press, 2001.

Branson, Tyler. "When Writing Goes Public: Agitation, Intervention, and Disruption in Public Arguments About Writing." PhD diss., Texas Christian University, 2015.

Brereton, John, ed. *The Origins of Composition Studies in the American College, 1875–1925*. Pittsburgh: University of Pittsburgh Press, 1995.

Brodkey, Linda. "Writing Permitted in Designated Spaces Only." In *Higher Education Under Fire: Politics, Economics, and the Crisis of the Humanities*, edited by Michael Bérubé and Cary Nelson, 214–37. New York: Routledge, 1995.

Brodkey, Linda, and Sherri Fowler. "Political Suspects." *Voice*, April 23, 1991.

Brodkey, Linda, and John Slatin. "E 306 Reforms Would Protect Students from Indoctrination." *Daily Texan*, September 5, 1990.

———. "New E 306 Keeps Commitment to Writing." *Daily Texan*, September 4, 1990.

Brooks, Phillips A. "Professor Leaves in the Wake of Course Debate." *Austin American-Statesman*, May 30, 1990.

———. "UT Council to Hear English Department Plan for Division." *Austin American-Statesman*, September 21, 1992.

———. "UT English Professor Heading to Denton." *Austin-American Statesman*, May 16, 1992.

Brown, Wendy. *Undoing the Demos: Neoliberalism's Stealth Revolution*. New York: Zone Books, 2015.

Bruffee, Kenneth. *Collaborative Learning: Higher Education, Interdependence, and the Authority of Knowledge*. Baltimore, MD: Johns Hopkins University Press, 1993.

Budziszewski, Jay. "English or Indoctrination." *Daily Texan*, July 27, 1990.

Buehl, Jonathan, Tamar Chute, and Anne Fields. "Training in the Archives: Archival Research and Professional Development." *College Composition and Communication* 64, no. 2 (December 2012): 274–305.

"Can't Teach This." *University Review* (Austin, Texas), November/December 1990.

Carey, Kevin. "The Incredible Shrinking Future of College." *Vox*, November 21, 2022. https://www.vox.com/the-highlight/23428166/college-enrollment-population-education-crash.

Carter, Shannon, and Kelly Dent. "East Texas Activism (1966–68): Locating the Literary Scene Through the Digital Humanities." *College English* 76, no. 2 (2013): 152–70.

Carton, Evan. "New Division Has Nothing to Do with Writing Education." *Daily Texan*, November 4, 1992.

———. "The Self Besieged: American Identity on Campus and in the Gulf." *Tikkun*, July/August 1991.

Carver, Larry. "Literature, Composition Can Be Taught in the Same Class." *Daily Texan*, February 25, 1985.

Cassuto, Leonard. *The Graduate School Mess: What Caused It and How to Fix It*. Cambridge, MA: Harvard University Press, 2015.

Caswell, Michelle. *Archiving the Unspeakable: Silence, Memory, and the Photographic Record in Cambodia*. Madison: University of Wisconsin Press, 2014.

Causey, Gigi. "Committee Created to Clarify Rhetoric Division." *Daily Texan*, September 21, 1992.

Charlton, Colin, Jonikka Charlton, Tarez Samra Graban, Kathleen J. Ryan, and Amy Ferdinandt Stolley. *GenAdmin: Theorizing WPA Identities in the Twenty-First Century*. Anderson, SC: Parlor Press, 2011.

Charney, Davida. "Lone Geniuses in Popular Science: The Devaluation of Scientific Consensus." *Written Communication* 20, no. 3 (2003): 215–41.

Childress, Herb. *The Adjunct Underclass: How America's Colleges Betrayed Their Faculty, Their Students, and Their Mission*. Chicago: University of Chicago Press, 2019.

"A Civil Rights Theme for a Writing Course." *New York Times*, June 24, 1990.

Cole, Alyson. *The Cult of True Victimhood: From the War on Welfare to the War on Terror*. Stanford, CA: Stanford University Press, 2006.

Collier, Peter. "Incorrect English." *Heterodoxy*, May 1992.

Collini, Stefan. *Speaking of Universities*. New York: Verso, 2017.

Connally, Matthew. "Happy Trails: Gribben Leaves Fight with Honor." *Daily Texan*, June 3, 1991.

———. "Power Play: English Faculty Dispute Gets Bolder." *Daily Texan*, September 25, 1991.

———. "State Involved in E 306 Debate: Bill Filed for UT Class." *Daily Texan*, February 19, 1991.

Connally, Matthew, and David Bezanson. "Changing Course: Budget Council Would Benefit Department of English." *Daily Texan*, August 28, 1991.

Connors, Robert. "The Abolition Debate in Composition: A Short History." In *Composition in the Twenty-First Century: Crisis and Change*, edited by Lynn Bloom, Donald Daiker, and Edward White, 47–63. Carbondale: Southern Illinois University Press, 1996.

———. "Overwork/Underpay: Labor and Status of Composition Teachers Since 1880." *Rhetoric Review* 9, no. 1 (1990): 108–26.

———. "The Rise and Fall of the Modes of Discourse." *College Composition and Communication* 32, no. 4 (1981): 444–55.

Cooper, Marylin, and Michael Holzman. *Writing as Social Action*. Portsmouth, NH: Boynton/Cook, 1989.

"Coping with Our 'Literacy Crisis.'" *Daily Texan*, June 21, 1977.

Corbett, Edward. "From Literary Critic to Professional Rhetorician: A Professional Journey." Paper Presented at the Annual Meeting of the Conference on College Composition and Communication, Cincinnati, Ohio, March 19–21, 1992. https://files.eric.ed.gov/fulltext/ED358482.pdf.

Crowley, Sharon. "Around 1971: The Emergence of Process Pedagogy." In *Composition in the University: Historical and Polemical Essays*, 187–214. Pittsburgh: University of Pittsburgh Press, 1998.

———. "A Personal Essay on Freshman English." *PRE/TEXT* 12, nos. 3–4 (1991): 155–76.

Culbertson, Anna, and Amanda Lanthorne. "Praxis, Not Practice: The Ethics of Consent and Privacy in 21st-Century Archival Stewardship." *Across the Disciplines* 18, no. 1/2 (November 2021). https://wac.colostate.edu/docs/atd/volume18/Culbertson,Lanthorne.pdf.

Cunningham, William, with Monty Jones. *The Texas Way: Money, Power, Politics, and Ambition at the University*. Austin, TX: Tower Books, 2013.

"Cunningham Announces Decisions on Recommendations Proposed by Committee on the Undergraduate Experience." *OnCampus*, May 11, 1992.

Curtis, Gregory. "Behind the Lines." *Texas Monthly*, July 1983.

———. "Behind the Lines: The Bring-Something-Texan-That-You-Want-to-Burn Party." *Texas Monthly*, May 1990.

Cvetkovich, Ann. *An Archive of Feelings: Trauma, Sexuality, and Lesbian Public Cultures*. Durham, NC: Duke University Press, 2003.

Davis, Rod. "The English Wars." *Texas Observer*, September 28, 1984.

"Dean Delays Changes in a Disputed Course." *New York Times*, July 29, 1990.

Diamond, Sara. "Readin', Writin', and Repressin'." *Z Magazine*, February 1991.

Domenech, Ben. "Pat Buchanan and Thirty Years of Culture Wars." *Spectator World*, October 22, 2022. https://thespectator.com/topic/pat-buchanan-and-thirty-years-of-culture-wars/.

Donoghue, Frank. *The Last Professors: The Corporate University and the Fate of the Humanities*. New York: Fordham University Press, 2018.

Douglas, Whitney. "Looking Outward: Archival Research as Community Engagement." *Community Literacy Journal* 11, no. 2 (2017): 30–42.

Driver, Candice. "Gribben Asks Faculty Senate to Screen E 306." *Daily Texan*, July 20, 1990.

———. "Gribben Suggests Control of E 306 Go to Arbitrator." *Daily Texan*, August 6, 1990.

D'Souza, Dinesh. *Illiberal Education: The Politics of Race and Sex on Campus*. New York: Free Press, 1991.

Duban, James. "A Modest Proposal: Stick to Writing in E 306 at UT." *Austin American-Statesman*, August 26, 1990.

———. "A Modest Proposal: Teach Writing in Writing Courses." *Daily Texan*, August 9, 1990.

Ede, Lisa. *Situating Composition: Composition Studies and the Politics of Location*. Carbondale: Southern Illinois University Press, 2004.

Ehrlich, Dana. "Bill Proposed to Limit TA Hiring Practices." *Daily Texan*, February 8, 1977.

Elkind, Peter. "UT Versus A&M." *Texas Monthly*, May 1986.

Emig, Janet. *The Composing Processes of Twelfth Graders*. Urbana, IL: National Council of Teachers of English, 1971.

Enoch, Jessica. "Releasing Hold: Feminist Historiography Without the Tradition." In *Theorizing Histories of Rhetoric*, edited by Michelle Ballif, 58–73. Carbondale: Southern Illinois University Press, 2013.

Enoch, Jessica, and David Gold. "Seizing the Methodological Moment: The Digital Humanities and Historiography in Rhetoric and Composition." *College English* 76, no. 2 (2013): 105–14.

Enoch, Jessica, and Pamela VanHaitsma. "Archival Literacy: Reading the Rhetoric of Digital Archives in the Undergraduate Classroom." *College Composition and Communication* 67, no. 2 (December 2015): 216–42.

Everett, Justin, and Cristina Hanganu-Bresch, eds. *Minefield of Dreams: Triumphs and Travails of Independent Writing Programs*. Boulder: University Press of Colorado, 2017.

Ewing, Darryl. "New Elective Composition Course to Become Requirement in '88." *Daily Texan*, February 21, 1985.

———. "Some Professors Oppose Dropping E 306." *Daily Texan*, February 24, 1986.

Faigley, Lester. *Fragments of Rationality: Postmodernity and the Subject of Composition*. Pittsburgh: University of Pittsburgh Press, 1992.

Faigley, Lester, Roger Cherry, David Jolliffe, and Anna Skinner. *Assessing Writers' Knowledge and Processes of Composing*. Norwood, NJ: Ablex, 1985.

Faigley, Lester, and Thomas Miller. "What We Learn from Writing on the Job." *College English* 44, no. 6 (1982): 557–69.

Feistel, Eric. "Motivations Questioned in Re-Formation of AAUP." *Daily Texan*, October 29, 1991.

Ferreira-Buckley, Linda. "Rescuing the Archives from Foucault." *College English* 61, no. 5 (May 1999): 577–83.

Fisher, Laura. "English Lecturers Question Hiring on Short Notice." *Daily Texan*, October 10, 1982.

———. "English Lecturers Question Teaching-Workload Ratio." *Daily Texan*, October 20, 1982.

———. "Lecturers Feel Jobs Are Too Dependent on Student Evaluations." *Daily Texan*, October 7, 1982.

———. "Lecturers in English Department Note Hiring Workload Issues." *Daily Texan*, November 19, 1982.

Fisher, Walter. *Human Communication as Narration: Toward a Philosophy of*

Reason, Value, and Action. Columbia: University of South Carolina Press, 1987.

Fitzgerald, Kathryn. "The Platteville Papers Revisited: Gender and Genre in a Normal School Writing Assignment." In *Local Histories: Reading the Archives of Composition*, edited by Patricia Donohue and Gretchen Flesher Moon, 115–33. Pittsburgh: University of Pittsburgh Press, 2007.

Fitzgerald, Margot. "Students, AIs Deserve Changes in E 306." *Daily Texan*, August 8, 1990.

Fleming, David. *From Form to Meaning: Freshman Composition and the Long Sixties, 1957–1974*. Pittsburgh: University of Pittsburgh Press, 2011.

Flower, Linda, and John Hayes. "A Cognitive Process Theory of Writing." *College Composition and Communication* 32, no. 4 (1981): 365–87.

Foss, K. A., and S. K. Foss. "Personal Experience as Evidence in Feminist Scholarship." *Western Journal of Communication* 58, no. 1 (1994): 39–43.

Franke, Johanna. "Writing Shifts to New Division." *Daily Texan*, September 2, 1992.

Frost, Kate. "'A University Perspective': An Award-Winning Teacher Indicts the UT Education Factor." *Daily Texan*, April 13, 1990.

Gaillet, Lynée Lewis. "Archival Survival." In *Working in the Archives: Practical Research Methods for Rhetoric and Composition*, edited by Alexis E. Ramsey, Wendy B. Sharer, Barbara L'Eplattenier, and Lisa S. Mastrangelo, 28–39. Carbondale: Southern Illinois University Press, 2010.

Gainer, Anne. "Committee Still Unformed." *Daily Texan*, October 30, 1992.

Galinsky, Karl. "Duban a Victim of Politics." *Daily Texan*, September 26, 1991.

Garcia, Ernest. "Fix E 306 and Stop Bitching." *Daily Texan*, July 27, 1990.

Ghaddar, J. J., and Michelle Caswell. "'To Go Beyond': Towards a Decolonial Archival Praxis." *Archival Science* 19 (May 2019): 71–85. https://doi.org/10.1007/s10502-019-09311-1.

Gindlesparger, Kathryn. *Opening Ceremony: Inviting Inclusion into University Governance*. Minneapolis: University of Minnesota Press, 2023.

Giroux, Henry, and Stanley Aronowitz. *Education Still Under Siege*. 2nd ed. Westport, CT: Bergin and Garvey, 1993.

Glenn, Cheryl. "The Last Good Job in America." *College Composition and Communication* 52, no. 1 (2000): A12–A13.

Glenn, Cheryl, and Jessica Enoch. "Invigorating Historiographic Practices in Rhetoric and Composition Studies." In *Working in the Archives: Practice Research Methods for Rhetoric and Composition*, edited by Alexis E. Ramsey, Wendy B. Sharer, Barbara L'Eplattenier, and Lisa S. Mastrangelo, 11–27. Carbondale: Southern Illinois University Press, 2010.

Gogan, Brian. *Jean Baudrillard: The Rhetoric of Symbolic Exchange*. Carbondale: Southern Illinois University Press, 2017.

Goggin, Maureen Daly. *Authoring a Discipline: Scholarly Journals and the Post–World War II Emergence of Rhetoric and Composition*. New York: Routledge, 2000.

Goggin, Maureen Daly, and Susan Kay Miller. "What Is *New* About the 'New Abolitionists': Continuities and Discontinuities in the Great Debate." *Composition Studies* 28, no. 2 (2000): 85–112.

Gold, David. "Remapping Revisionist Historiography." *College Composition and Communication* 64, no. 1 (September 2012): 15–34.

———. *Rhetoric at the Margins: Revising the History of Writing Instruction in American Colleges, 1873–1947*. Carbondale: Southern Illinois University Press, 2008.

Gold, David, and Catherine Hobbs. *Educating the New Southern Woman: Speech, Writing, and Race at the Public Women's Colleges, 1884–1945*. Carbondale: Southern Illinois University Press, 2014.

Golden, Claudia, and Lawrence Katz. *The Race Between Education and Technology*. Cambridge, MA: Harvard University Press, 2008.

Goodwin, Scott. "Politics Jeopardize Writing Skills." *Daily Texan*, April 2, 1986.

Graban, Tamra Sarez. "From Location(s) to Locatability: Mapping Feminist Recovery and Archival Activity Through Metadata." *College English* 76, no. 2 (November 2013): 171–93.

Gribben, Alan. "E 306: Oppressing English Composition." *University Review*, October 1990.

———. "Lecturers Selfish." *Daily Texan*, February 22, 1985.

———. "New E 306 Format Flawed." *Daily Texan*, June 18, 1990.

———. "'Texan' Goes Too Far in Debating E 306." *Daily Texan*, July 23, 1990.

Grosky, Jay. "Remember Students." *Daily Texan*, February 20, 1985.

Guillory, John. *Professing Criticism: Essays on the Origin of Literary Study*. Chicago: University of Chicago Press, 2022.

Gunner, Jeanne. "Elegy for a *Statement*." In *Labored: The State(ment) and Future of Work in Composition*, edited by Randall McClure, Dayna V. Goldstein, and Michael A. Pemberton, 52–68. Anderson, SC: Parlor Press, 2017.

Hadley, David. "Gribben's Attack Unfair." *Daily Texan*, March 1, 1985.

Hairston, Maxine. "Breaking Our Bonds and Reaffirming Our Connections." *College Composition and Communication* 36, no. 3 (1985): 272–82.

———. "Committee Does Good." *Daily Texan*, September 19, 1991.

———. "Diversity, Ideology, and Teaching Writing." *College Composition and Communication* 43, no. 2 (May 1992): 179–93.

———. "Required Writing Courses Should Not Focus on Politically Charged Social Issues." *Chronicle of Higher Education*, January 23, 1991.

———. "We're Hiring Too Many Temporary Instructors." *Chronicle of Higher Education*, April 17, 1985.

———. "The Winds of Change: Thomas Kuhn and the Revolution in the Teaching of Writing." *College Composition and Communication* 33, no. 1 (1982): 76–88.

Harris, Joseph. "Afterword." In *Labored: The State(ment) and Future of Work in Composition*, edited by Randall McClure, Dayna V. Goldstein, and Michael A. Pemberton, 285–88. Anderson, SC: Parlor Press, 2017.

———. "Meet the New Boss, Same as the Old Boss: Class Consciousness in Composition." *College Composition and Communication* 52, no. 1 (2000): 43–68.

———. *A Teaching Subject: Composition Since 1966*. 2nd ed. Logan: Utah State University Press, 2012.

Hartman, Andrew. *A War for the Soul of America: A History of the Culture Wars*. 2nd ed. Chicago: University of Chicago Press, 2019.

Harwood, Quittner. "Discussion of English Composition Course Becomes Faculty Feud." *Daily Texan*, March 5, 1985.

Hawhee, Debra. *Rhetoric in Tooth and Claw: Animals, Language, and Sensation*. Chicago: University of Chicago Press, 2017.

Hayden, Wendy. "And Gladly Teach: The Archive's Pedagogical Turn." *College English* 80, no. 2 (November 2017): 133–58.

Hayes, Susan. "E 306 Changes Bring Something New—Critical Thought." *Daily Texan*, June 11, 1990.

Hays, Elaine. "'Be Patient, but Don't Wait!': The Activist Ethos of Student Journalism at the Colored State Normal School, Elizabeth City, North Carolina, 1892–1937." In *In The Archives of Composition: Writing and Rhetoric in High Schools and Normal Schools*, edited by Lori Ostergaard and Henrietta Rix Wood, 149–66. Pittsburgh: University of Pittsburgh Press, 2015.

Head, Hayley. "E 346K Teaches Key Skill." *Daily Texan*, February 28, 1985.

Heinzelman, Kurt, and Ramon Saldívar. "Rhetoric and Composition: Provost Meddles in E 306 Decision." *Daily Texan*, July 31, 1990.

Heller, Scott. "3 Tales of Life off the Tenure Track." *Chronicle of Higher Education*, April 17, 1985.

———. "50 Lecturers Lose Their Jobs in a Dispute over How—and If—Writing Can Be Taught." *Chronicle of Higher Education*, April 17, 1985.

Henley, Geoff. "Brodkey's 'Diversity' Only One-Sided." *Daily Texan*, October 10, 1990.

———. "Class Warfare." *Images*, April 18, 1991.

———. "English Rule: Budget Council Would Aid Department." *Daily Texan*, June 30, 1991.

———. "Rough Draft: Kruppa Wrong for Predetermining Department's Position." *Daily Texan*, August 2, 1991.

Henry, Liz, and Kathy Mitchell. "Gribben, Colleagues Make English Department a Battlefield." *Daily Texan*, August 13, 1990.

Henson, Scott. "Illiberal Arts." *Texas Observer*, September 6, 1991.

———. "Kingmaker." *Texas Observer*, September 20, 1991.

Henson, Scott, and Thomas Philpott. "E 306: Chronicle of a Smear Campaign." *The Polemicist*, September 1990.

———. "Extracurricular Activity." *Images*, October 18, 1990.

———. "'Tejas': The Attack on Diverse Press." *The Polemicist*, September 1990.

Henze, Brent, Jack Selzer, and Wendy Sharer. *1977: A Cultural Moment in Composition*. West Lafayette, IN: Parlor Press, 2007.

Herring, Klaus. "Report Reveals Students Weak in Composition." *Daily Texan*, February 21, 1981.

Hindman, Jane. "Learning as We G(r)o(w): Strategizing the Lessons of a Fledgling Rhetoric and Writing Department." In *A Field of Dreams: Independent Writing Programs and the Future of Composition Studies*, edited by Peggy O'Neill, Angela Crow, and Larry W. Burton, 107–29. Logan: Utah State University Press, 2002.

Horner, Bruce. "Traditions and Professionalization: Reconceiving Work in Composition." *College Composition and Communication* 51, no. 3 (2000): 366–98.

Horner, Winifred Bryan. "Historical Introduction." In *Composition and Literature: Bridging the Gap*, edited by Winifred Bryan Horner, 1–13. Chicago: University of Chicago Press, 1983.

Hsu, V. Jo. *Constellating Home: Trans and Queer Asian American Rhetorics*. Columbus: Ohio State University Press, 2022.

Huang, Jenny, and David Loy. "Speech to Parents Avoids Controversy." *Daily Texan*, October 29, 1990.

Huppé, Alex. "Academic Concerns vs. Media Perceptions." *Council Chronicle*, September 1991.

Hutcheson, Ron. "Sledd Faults 'Sorry' TA Program." *Daily Texan*, August 30, 1976.

Ianetta, Melissa. "'Stand Mum': Women's Silence at the Lexington Academy, 1839–1841." In *In the Archives of Composition: Writing and Rhetoric in High Schools and Normal Schools*, edited by Lori Ostergaard and Henrietta Rix Wood, 97–114. Pittsburgh: University of Pittsburgh Press, 2015.

Innis, Amanda, and Paul Yioutas. "New E 306 Disregards Western Culture." *Daily Texan*, September 18, 1990.

Inoue, Asao. *Antiracist Writing Ecologies: Teaching and Assessing Writing for a Socially Just Future*. Anderson, SC: Parlor Press, 2015.

Ivins, Molly. "Austin Academics Are People with NOT ENOUGH TO DO." *Dallas Times Herald*, August 14, 1990.

Jameson, Fredric. *Postmodernism; or, the Cultural Logic of Late Capitalism*. Durham, NC: Duke University Press, 1991.

Johnson, Matthew. *Undermining Racial Justice: How One University Embraced Inclusion and Inequality*. Ithaca, NY: Cornell University Press, 2020.

Kearns, Judith, and Brian Turner. "An Outsider's Perspective: Curriculum Design and Strategies for Sustainability in a Canadian IWP." *Minefield of Dreams: Triumphs and Travails of Independent Writing Programs*, edited by Justin Everett and Cristina Hanganu-Bresch, 43–62. Boulder: University Press of Colorado, 2017.

Kelley, Mike. "Confusion of the First Class." *Austin American-Statesman*, September 13, 1985.

Kelly, Kathryn. "Aid with Composition." *Daily Texan*, September 28, 1984.

Kelly, Lee. "'Most Hated Man' UT Professor Has Made Enemies for Speaking Out." *Austin American-Statesman*, June 11, 1978.

Kennedy, Tammy, and Angelika Walker. "A Pedagogy for the Ethics of Remembering: Producing Public Memory for the *Women's Archive Project*." In *Pedagogies of Public Memory: Teaching Writing and Rhetoric in Museums, Memorials, and Archives*, edited by Jane Greer and Laurie Grobman, 91–104. New York: Routledge, 2015.

Kent, Thomas. "Introduction." In *Post-Process Theory: Beyond the Writing Process Paradigm*, edited by Thomas Kent, 1–6. Carbondale: Southern Illinois University Press, 1999.

Kerr, Clark. *The Uses of the University*. 5th ed. Cambridge, MA: Harvard University Press, 2001.

Kinneavy, James. "Course Suspension Weakens Troubled Writing Program." *Daily Texan*, February 20, 1985.

———. *A Theory of Discourse*. New York: W. W. Norton, 1971.

———. "Writing Across the Curriculum." *ADE Bulletin* 76 (Winter 1983): 14–21.

Kirsch, Gesa, and Jacqueline Jones Royster. "Feminist Rhetorical Practices: In Search of Excellence." *College Composition and Communication* 61, no. 4 (June 2010): 640–72.

Kirschenbaum, Matthew. *Mechanisms: New Media and the Forensic Imagination*. Cambridge, MA: MIT Press, 2008.

Labaree, David. *A Perfect Mess: The Unlikely Ascendancy of American Higher Education*. Chicago: University of Chicago Press, 2017.

Lauter, Paul. "'Political Correctness' and the Attack on American Colleges." In *Higher Education Under Fire: Politics, Economics, and the Crisis of the Humanities*, edited by Michael Bérubé and Cary Nelson, 73–90. New York: Routledge, 1995.

Lee, Sharon. *An Unseen Unheard Minority: Asian American Students at the University of Illinois*. New Brunswick, NJ: Rutgers University Press, 2022.

Leo, John. "The Academy's New Ayatollahs." *US News and World Report*, December 10, 1990.

L'Eplattenier, Barbara. "An Argument for Archival Research Methods: Thinking Beyond Methodology." *College English* 72, no. 1 (September 2009): 67–79.

L'Eplattenier, Barbara, and Lisa Mastrangelo. "Why Administrative Histories?" In *Historical Studies of Writing Program Administration*, edited by Barbara L'Eplattenier and Lisa Mastrangelo, xvii–xxvi. West Lafayette, IN: Parlor Press, 2004.

Lerner, Neal. *The Idea of a Writing Laboratory*. Carbondale: Southern Illinois University Press, 2009.

Lesser, Wayne. "Lower Division Classes Cannot Be Remedial." *Daily Texan*, March 7, 1985.

Levine, Arthur, and Scott Van Pelt. *The Great Upheaval: Higher Education's Past, Present, and Uncertain Future*. Baltimore, MD: Johns Hopkins University Press, 2021.

Lindemann, Erika. "Freshman Composition: No Place for Literature." *College English* 55, no. 3 (March 1993): 311–16.

Lipson, Carol, and Molly Voorhies. "The Material and the Cultural as Interconnected Texts: Revising Material Conditions for Part-Time Faculty at Syracuse University." In *Moving a Mountain: Transforming the Role of Contingent Faculty in Composition Studies and Higher Education*, edited by Eileen E. Schell and Patricia Lambert Stock, 107–31. Urbana, IL: National Council of Teachers of English, 2001.

Locke, Michelle. "Results of Graduation Requirement Study Draw Mixed Responses." *Daily Texan*, February 12, 1981.

Longaker, Mark Garrett, Davida Charney, Diane Davis, and Alice Batt. "Growing Despite Austerity." *College Composition and Communication* 68, no. 1 (2016): 185–91.

Longaker, Mark Garrett, Nathan Kreuter, Stephen Kwame Dadugblor, Hannah Foltz, Tristin Brynn Hooker, Martha Sue Karnes, Bethany Caye Radcliffe, K. J. Schaeffner, and Kiara Walker. "Archiving Our Own: The Digital

Archive of Rhetoric and Composition at the University of Texas at Austin, 1975–1995." *College Composition and Communication* 73, no. 4 (2022): 774–805.

Loss, Christopher. *Between Citizens and the State: The Politics of Higher Education in the Twentieth Century*. Princeton, NJ: Princeton University Press, 2012.

Loy, David. "E 306 Controversy Called 'Sobering.'" *Daily Texan*, February 7, 1991.

———. "King to Return to Position as Liberal Arts Dean." *Daily Texan*, April 8, 1991.

MacDonald, David. "Ode to Education." *Daily Texan*, March 18, 1985.

Maid, Barry. "Creating Two Departments of Writing: One Past and One Future." In *A Field of Dreams: Independent Writing Programs and the Future of Composition Studies*, edited by Peggy O'Neill, Angela Crow, and Larry W. Burton, 130–52. Logan: Utah State University Press, 2002.

Malenczyk, Rita. "Introduction with Some Rhetorical Terms." In *A Rhetoric for Writing Program Administrators*, edited by Rita Malenczyk, 3–8. Anderson, SC: Parlor Press, 2012.

———, ed. *A Rhetoric for Writing Program Administrators*. Anderson, SC: Parlor Press, 2012.

Martinez, Aja. *Counterstory: The Rhetoric and Writing of Critical Race Theory*. Urbana, IL: National Council of Teachers of English, 2020.

Marvel, Bill. "The Education of Alan Gribben." *Dallas Morning News*, June 17, 1991.

Mashberg, Amy. "General Faculty Approves New English Requirement." *Daily Texan*, June 2, 1981.

Mason, Curtis. "Project English: Cold War Paradigms and the Teaching of Composition." In *In the Archives of Composition: Writing and Rhetoric in High Schools and Normal Schools*, edited by Lori Ostergaard and Henrietta Rix Wood, 206–22. Pittsburgh: University of Pittsburgh Press, 2015.

Masters, Thomas. *Practicing Writing: The Postwar Discourse of Freshman English*. Pittsburgh: University of Pittsburgh Press, 2004.

Mastrangelo, Lisa. *Writing a Progressive Past: Women Teaching and Writing in the Progressive Era*. Anderson, SC: Parlor Press, 2012.

Mastrangelo, Lisa, and Barbara L'Eplattenier. "'Is It the Pleasure of This Conference to Have Another?': Women's Colleges Meeting and Talking About Writing in the Progressive Era." In *Historical Studies of Writing Program Administration*, edited by Barbara L'Eplattenier and Lisa Mastrangelo, 117–43. West Lafayette, IN: Parlor Press, 2004.

Matejowski, Matthew. "English 306 Proposal Passes in a Landslide Victory." *Daily Texan*, September 19, 1985.

Matzen, Richard. "The Great Recession: Helping and Hurting Writing Faculty in an Independent Writing Program." In *Weathering the Storm: Independent Writing Programs in the Age of Fiscal Austerity*, edited by Richard Matzen and Matthew Abraham, 68–80. Logan: Utah State University Press, 2019.

Matzen, Richard, and Matthew Abraham, eds. *Weathering the Storm: Independent Writing Programs in the Age of Fiscal Austerity*. Logan: Utah State University Press, 2019.

Mays, Steven. "English as a Second Language." *University Review*, September 1990.

McClure, Randall, Dayna V. Goldstein, and Michael. A. Pemberton. "Introduction: Labor Practices, the *Statement*, and the Future of Work in Composition." In *Labored: The State(ment) and Future of Work in Composition*, edited by Randall McClure, Dayna V. Goldstein, and Michael A. Pemberton, ix–xix. Anderson, SC: Parlor Press, 2017.

McDonald, James. "One of Many: The *Statement* in the Context of Other Position Statements on Academic Labor." In *Labored: The State(ment) and Future of Work in Composition*, edited by Randall McClure, Dayna V. Goldstein, and Michael A. Pemberton, 69–92. Anderson, SC: Parlor Press, 2017.

McDonald, James, and Eileen Schell. "The Spirit and Influence of the Wyoming Resolution: Looking Back to Look Forward." *College English* 73, no. 4 (2011): 360–78.

McDonald, Terry. "UT Abounding in Bad Ideas." *Daily Texan*, February 25, 1985.

McHargue, Kevin. "English Department's Delay Does Not End Debate of E 306." *Daily Texan*, July 24, 1990.

———. "Recomposition: Confusion Reigns in the World of Alan Gribben." *Daily Texan*, July 20, 1990.

McKee, Heidi, and James Porter. "The Ethics of Archival Research." *College Composition and Communication* 64, no. 1 (September 2012): 59–81.

McLeod, Susan. *Writing Program Administration*. West Lafayette, IN: Parlor Press, 2007.

Megaw, Neill. "English Department Polarized over E 346K." *Daily Texan*, March 7, 1985.

———. "Teacher, Spare that Freshman." *The Alcalde*, April 1970.

Miller, Susan. *Textual Carnivals: The Politics of Composition*. Carbondale: Southern Illinois University Press, 1991.

Miller, Thomas. *The Evolution of College English: Literacy Studies from the Puritans to the Postmoderns*. Pittsburgh: University of Pittsburgh Press, 2011.

Moon, Gretchen Flesher. "Locating Composition History." In *Local Histories: Reading the Archives of Composition*, edited by Patricia Donahue and Gretchen Flesher Moon, 1–13. Pittsburgh: University of Pittsburgh Press, 2007.

Morris, Charles III. "The Archival Turn in Rhetorical Studies; or, the Archive's Rhetorical (Re)Turn." *Rhetoric and Public Affairs* 9, no. 1 (Spring 2006): 113–15.

Mortenson, Peter. "Going Public." *College Composition and Communication* 50, no. 2 (1998): 182–205.

Morton-Aiken, Jenna, and Robert Schwegler. "Recursion and Responsiveness: Archival Pedagogy and Archival Infrastructures in the Same Conversation." In *Teaching Through the Archives: Text, Collaboration, and Activism*, edited by Tarez Samra Graban and Wendy Hayden, 136–57. Carbondale: Southern Illinois University Press, 2022.

Moss, Kirby. "UT English Classes Changed to Study Civil Rights Cases." *Austin American-Statesman*, May 31, 1990.

Muller, Debra. "Alternate Writing Plan Yet to Be Evaluated." *Daily Texan*, September 13, 1985.

———. "Faculty Debates Changing E 306 Requirements." *Daily Texan*, September 12, 1985.

———. "Freshman Course May Be Dropped." *Daily Texan*, September 3, 1985.

Murchison, William. "English Faculty Should Stick to English." *Dallas Morning News*, July 7, 1990.

———. "Eyes of Texas Now Function as Big Brother." *Dallas Morning News*, October 2, 1991.

———. "Radical Left Has Won the Battle for Lecterns." *Dallas Morning News*, May 19, 1990.

———. "UT Prof Goes Out a Winner?" *Dallas Morning News*, May 1, 1991.

Murphy, Michael. "New Faculty for a New University: Toward a Full-Time Teaching-Intensive Faculty Track in Composition." *College Composition and Communication* 52, no. 1 (2000): 14–42.

Myers, Whitney. "'Raise Your Right Arm / And Pull on Your Tongue!': Reading Silence(s) at the Albuquerque Indian School." In *In The Archives of Composition: Writing and Rhetoric in High Schools and Normal Schools*, edited by Lori Ostergaard and Henrietta Rix Wood, 42–60. Pittsburgh: University of Pittsburgh Press, 2015.

Nash, George. "Who's Minding Freshman English at UT Austin?" *College English* 38, no. 2 (1976): 125–31.

Nather, David. "If You're Going to Require It, You Ought to Teach It." *Daily Texan*, September 4, 1985.

Neff, Nancy. "New Education Initiative Provides One-on-One Assistance to University Students Seeking Improved Writing Skills." *OnCampus*, October 25, 1993.

———. "University Establishes New Division for Teaching Writing, Composition." *OnCampus*, September 8, 1992.

Newberry, Robert. "UT Official Sees Introduction of Diversity Course." *Houston Post*, September 5, 1990.

Newkirk, Thomas, Thomas Cameron, and Cynthia Selfe. "Why Johnny Can't Write: A University View of Freshman Writing Ability." *English Journal* 66, no. 8 (1977): 65–69.

North, Stephen. *The Making of Knowledge in Composition: Portrait of an Emerging Field*. Portsmouth, NH: Boynton/Cook, 1987.

O'Connell, Chris. "What Goes On." *The Alcalde*, August 26, 2016. https://medium.com/the-alcalde/what-goes-on-524982f49915.

Ohmann, Richard, and Wallace Douglas. *English in America: A Radical View of the Profession*. New York: Oxford University Press, 1976.

O'Neill, Peggy, Angela Crow, and Larry W. Burton, eds. *A Field of Dreams: Independent Writing Programs and the Future of Composition Studies*. Logan: Utah State University Press, 2002.

Ostergaard, Lori, and Henrietta Rix Wood. "Adding New Stories to the History of Composition and Rhetoric." In *the Archives of Composition: Writing and Rhetoric in High Schools and Normal Schools*, edited by Lori Ostergaard and Henrietta Rix Wood, 1–24. Pittsburgh: University of Pittsburgh Press, 2015.

Peckham, Irvin. *Going North, Thinking West: The Intersections of Social Class, Critical Thinking, and Politicized Writing Instruction*. Logan: Utah State University Press, 2010.

Piore, Michael, and Charles Sabel. *The Second Industrial Divide: Possibilities for Prosperity*. New York: Basic Books, 1984.

Porter, James, Patricia Sullivan, Stuart Blythe, Jeffrey Grabill, and Libby Miles. "Institutional Critique: A Rhetorical Methodology for Change." *College Composition and Communication* 51, no. 4 (June 2000): 610–42.

Potts, Liza. "Archive Experiences: A Vision for the User-Centered Design in the Digital Humanities." In *Rhetoric and the Digital Humanities*, edited by Jim Rudolpho and William Hart-Davidson, 255–63. Chicago: University of Chicago Press, 2015.

Potts, Terri. "You Learned Me Well." *Daily Texan*, February 22, 1985.

Powell, Malea, Daisy Levy, Andrea Riley-Mukavetz, Marilee Brooks-Gillies, Maria Novotny, and Jennifer Fisch-Ferguson. "Our Story Begins Here: Constellating Cultural Rhetorics." *enculturation*, October 25, 2014, https://enculturation.net/our-story-begins-here.

Pratt, Todd. "English Senate Votes to Limit Lecturers' Teaching Time." *Daily Texan*, April 9, 1982.

———. "New Rules Adopted for English Lecturers." *Daily Texan*, April 20, 1984.

Proszak, Laura, and Ellen Cushman. "Delinking Student Perceptions of Place with/in the University Archive." In *Teaching Through the Archives: Text, Collaboration, and Activism*, edited by Tarez Samra Graban and Wendy Hayden, 197–211. Carbondale: Southern Illinois University Press, 2022.

Pullman, George. "Stepping Yet Again into the Same Current." In *Post-Process Theory: Beyond the Writing-Process Paradigm*, edited by Thomas Kent, 16–29. Carbondale: Southern Illinois University Press, 1999.

Purdy, James. "Three Gifts of Digital Archives." *Journal of Literacy and Technology* 12, no. 3 (November 2011): 24–44.

Ramsey-Tobienne, Alexis. "Archives 2.0: Digital Archives and the Formation of New Research Methods." *Peitho Journal* 15, no. 1 (Fall/Winter 2012): 4–28. https://cfshrc.org/article/archives-2-0-digital-archives-and-the-formation-of-new-research-methods.

Ratliff, George. "Changes Necessary for English Program." *Daily Texan*, June 30, 1992.

Rawson, K. J. "The Rhetorical Power of Archival Description: Classifying Images of Gender Transgression." *Rhetoric Society Quarterly* 48, no. 4 (2018): 327–51.

Reaves, Gail. "Workplace Compliance Hard, UT Prof Says." *Austin American-Statesman*, September 12, 1978.

Rebec, Thomas. "*Ad Hominem* Arguments Not Fair Play." *Daily Texan*, February 25, 1985.

Rebhorn, Wayne. "English Course Fails to Be Discipline Specific." *Daily Texan*, February 25, 1985.

Regan, Alison Elizabeth. "Promises, Problems, and Politics: The History of Rhetoric, English Studies, and Writing Instruction at the University of Texas at Austin, 1883–1994." PhD diss., University of Texas at Austin, 1996.

Reitter, Paul, and Chad Wellmon. *Permanent Crisis: The Humanities in a Discontented Age*. Chicago: University of Chicago Press, 2021.

Rice, Jenny. *Awful Archives: Conspiracy Theory, Rhetoric, and Acts of Evidence*. Columbus: Ohio State University Press, 2020.

Rice, Joseph. "E 346K—The Write Stuff." *Houston Post*, May 6, 1985.

Ritter, Kelly. *Before Shaughnessy: Basic Writing at Yale and Harvard, 1920–1960*. Carbondale: Southern Illinois University Press, 2009.

———. *To Know Her Own History: Writing at the Woman's College, 1943–1963*. Pittsburgh: University of Pittsburgh Press, 2012.

Robberson, Michelle. "New English Requirement Urged." *Daily Texan*, February 3, 1981.

Roberts-Miller, Patricia. *Rhetoric and Demagoguery*. Carbondale: Southern Illinois University Press, 2019.

Robinson, Lillian, and Linda Brodkey. "Not Just a Matter of Course: Lillian Robinson Talks with Linda Brodkey." *Women's Review of Books* 9, no. 5 (February 1992): 23–24.

Rodgers, Daniel. *Age of Fracture*. Cambridge, MA: Belknap Press of Harvard University Press, 2011.

Rogers, Katina. *Putting the Humanities PhD to Work: Thriving in and Beyond the Classroom*. Durham, NC: Duke University Press, 2020.

Romano, Debbie. "Keep Junior Course." *Daily Texan*, February 20, 1985.

Rossinow, Doug. *The Reagan Era: A History of the 1980s*. New York: Columbia University Press, 2015.

Royster, Jacqueline Jones. *Traces of a Stream: Literacy and Social Change Among African American Women*. Pittsburgh: University of Pittsburgh Press, 2000.

Rubio, Joe. "English Proposal Overlooks Students." *Daily Texan*, September 30, 1985.

Ruch, Richard. *Higher Ed, Inc.: The Rise of the For-Profit University*. Baltimore, MD: Johns Hopkins University Press, 2001.

Rudolph, Frederick. *The American College and University: A History*. New York: Alfred A. Knopf, 1962.

Russell, D. A. *Greek Declamation*. Cambridge: Cambridge University Press, 1983.

Russell, David. *Writing in the Academic Disciplines: A Curricular History*. 2nd ed. Carbondale: Southern Illinois University Press, 2001.

Ruszkiewicz, John. "Altered E 306 Format Compromised by Ideological Freight." *Daily Texan*, July 24, 1990.

———. "Documents of Dissent: Hairston's 'Breaking Our Bonds' in Context." *College Composition and Communication* 68, no. 1 (2017): 179–85.

"Salty Sledd Strikes Again." *Daily Texan*, April 18, 1978.

Schell, Eileen. *Gypsy Academics and Mother-Teachers: Gender, Contingent Labor, and Writing Instruction*. Portsmouth, NH: Boynton/Cook, 1998.

Schell, Eileen, and Patricia Lambert Stock. "Introduction: Working Contingent Faculty in[to] Higher Education." In *Moving a Mountain: Transforming the Role of Contingent Faculty in Composition Studies and Higher Education*, edited by Eileen E. Schell and Patricia Lambert Stock, 1–44. Urbana, IL: National Council of Teachers of English, 2001.

Schendel, Ellen. "Locating Writing Programs in Research Universities." In *A Field of Dreams: Independent Writing Programs and the Future of Composition Studies*, edited by Peggy O'Neill, Angela Crow, and Larry W. Burton, 186–212. Logan: Utah State University Press, 2002.

Schudson, Michael. *The Good Citizen: A History of American Civic Life*. Cambridge, MA: Harvard University Press, 1998.

Schultz, Lucille. *The Young Composers: Composition's Beginnings in Nineteenth-Century Schools*. Carbondale: Southern Illinois University Press, 1999.

Selby, Gardner. "English Classes Added." *Daily Texan*, September 1, 1981.

Seneca the Elder. *Declamations, Volume II*. Translated by Michael Winterbottom. Cambridge, MA: Harvard University Press, 1974.

Shaver, Lisa. "Cultivating a Feminist Consciousness in the University Archive." In *Teaching Through the Archives: Text, Collaboration, and Activism*, edited by Tarez Samra Graban and Wendy Hayden, 46–59. Carbondale: Southern Illinois University Press, 2022.

Shaw, Mark. "English 346K Abolished as Deans Plan New Requirements." *Daily Texan*, February 18, 1986.

Simpson, Brian. "Course May Be Dropped Due to Inadequate Staffing." *Daily Texan*, February 13, 1985.

Sirc, Geoffrey. *English Composition as a Happening*. Logan: Utah State University Press, 2002.

Skaggs, James. "E 346K Helps Excellence." *Daily Texan*, February 26, 1985.

———. "English Lecturers Deserve Better Treatment." *Daily Texan*, February 20, 1985.

"Skilled Writers: A Vanishing Breed?" *The Alcalde*, May/June 1979.

Skinnell, Ryan. "The Archives of Epistemic Possibility." In *Teaching Through the Archives: Text, Collaboration, and Activism*, edited by Tarez Samra Graban and Wendy Hayden, xi–xvi. Carbondale: Southern Illinois University Press, 2022.

———. *Conceding Composition: A Crooked History of Composition's Institutional Fortunes*. Logan: Utah State University Press, 2015.

———. "A Problem of Publics and the Curious Case of Texas." *JAC* 30, nos. 1–2 (2010): 143–73.

Slaughter, Sheila, and Larry Leslie. *Academic Capitalism: Politics, Policies, and the Entrepreneurial University*. Baltimore, MD: Johns Hopkins University Press, 1997.

Sledd, James. "And They Write Innumerable Books." *Writing Instructor* 2, no. 2 (1983): 69–78.

———. "Disciplinarity and Exploitation: Compositionists as Good Professionals." *Workplace: A Journal for Academic Labor* 7 (2001): 31–39.

———. "Division Just Rhetoric." *Daily Texan*, January 15, 1993.

———. "Freshmen: Victims of Tainted Teaching." *The Alcalde*, January 1970.

———. "Reply to Bizzell and Trimbur's 'Letter on Linda Brodkey Case.'" *Radical Teacher* 40 (1991): 50.

———. "See and Say." In *Eloquent Dissent: The Writings of James Sledd*, edited by Richard Freed, 135–47. Portsmouth, NH: Boynton/Cook, 1996.

———. "Tale of 14 Stooges." *Daily Texan*, February 18, 1985.

———. "TAs Shoulder 60 Percent of Workload." *Daily Texan*, January 27, 1975.

Smith, Charles. *Market Values in American Higher Education: The Pitfalls and Promises*. Lanham, MD: Rowman and Littlefield, 2000.

Smith, Erec. *A Critique of Anti-Racism in Rhetoric and Composition: The Semblance of Empowerment*. Lanham, MD: Lexington Books, 2020.

Smith, Kurt. "University Doesn't Care." *Daily Texan*, March 25,1985.

Smith, Michael. *The Abundant University: Remaking Higher Education for a Digital World*. Cambridge, MA: MIT Press, 2023.

Sorapure, Madeleine, and Linda Adler-Kassner. "Context, Strategy, Identity: A History of Change in the UC Santa Barbara Writing Program." *Weathering the Storm: Independent Writing Programs in the Age of Fiscal Austerity*, edited by Richard N. Matzen and Matthew Abraham, 110–17. Logan: Utah State University Press, 2019.

Spellmeyer, Kurt. *Common Ground: Dialogue, Understanding, and the Teaching of Composition*. Englewood Cliffs, NJ: Prentice Hall, 1993.

Stabile, Carol. "Another Brick in the Wall: (Re)contextualizing the Crisis." In *Higher Education Under Fire: Politics, Economics, and the Crisis of the Humanities*, edited by Michael Bérubé and Cary Nelson, 108–25. New York: Routledge, 1995.

Stanford, Scott. "No Thanks: Administration's Poor Planning Sinks E 306 Proposal." *Daily Texan*, July 4, 1990.

Stanton, Zach. "How the 'Culture War' Could Break Democracy." *Politico*, May 20, 2021. https://www.politico.com/news/magazine/2021/05/20/culture-war-politics-2021-democracy-analysis-489900.

"A Statement of Academic Concern." *Daily Texan*, July 18, 1990.

"A Statement of Academic Concern." *Daily Texan*, October 15, 1990.

Steedman, Carolyn. *Dust*. Manchester: Manchester University Press, 2001.

Strickland, Donna. *The Managerial Unconscious in the History of Composition Studies*. Carbondale: Southern Illinois University Press, 2011.

Strickland, Donna, and Jeanne Gunner, eds. *The Writing Program Interrupted: Making Space for Critical Discourse*. Portsmouth, NH: Heinemann, 2009.

Swearingen, Jan. "Prim Irony: Suzuki Method Composition in the Twenty-First Century." In *Composition in the Twenty-First Century: Crisis and Change*, edited by Lynn Bloom, Donald Daiker, and Edward White, 75–80. Carbondale: Southern Illinois University Press, 1996.

Taylor, Mark. "English 306 Not for Politics." *Daily Texan*, July 27, 1990.

Taylor, Suzanne. "Department Plans Structure of New English Requirement." *Daily Texan*, April 9, 1986.

———. "Proposed E 306 Changes Could Cost Students More." *Daily Texan*, September 6, 1985.

Tirabassi, Katherine E. "Creative Storytelling: Archives as Sites for Nonfiction Research and Writing." In *Teaching Through the Archives: Text, Collaboration, and Activism*, edited by Tarez Samra Graban and Wendy Hayden, 76–90. Carbondale: Southern Illinois University Press, 2022.

Trimble, John. *Writing with Style*. New York: Prentice Hall, 1975.

Twombly, Robert. "UT Lecturers, a Survey." *Santa Rita Express*, February 1985.

University of Texas at Austin Office of Institutional Studies. *Statistical Handbook, 1980–1981*. https://utexas.app.box.com/v/SHB80-81Complete.

University of Texas at Austin Office of Institutional Studies. *Statistical Handbook, 1990–91*. https://utexas.app.box.com/v/SHB90-91Complete.

"UT Faculty Airs Work Load Plan." *Austin American-Statesman*, January 18, 1977.

"UT's Including Ethnic Study Course Is a Good Step." *Austin American-Statesman*, June 4, 1990.

Utter, Shane. "E 306 to Add Readings on Racism." *Daily Texan*, June 4, 1990.

VanHaitsma, Pamela. "Digital LGBTQ Archives as Sites of Public Memory and Pedagogy." *Rhetoric and Public Affairs* 22, no. 2 (2019): 253–80.

Veysey, Laurence. *The Emergence of the American University*. Chicago: University of Chicago Press, 1965.

Vinokur, Marina. "University Adds Writing Courses for Undergrads." *Daily Texan*, June 25, 1994.

Vivian, Bradford. *Campus Misinformation: The Real Threat to Free Speech in American Higher Education*. New York: Oxford University Press, 2022.

Wadlington, Warwick. "Stir Students' Interest." *Daily Texan*, March 7, 1985.

Walker, Kiara. "'Undoing Progress': Reactionary Rhetoric and Appeals to Rhetorical Liberalism." PhD diss., University of Texas at Austin, 2023.

Wan, Amy. *Producing Good Citizens: Literacy Training in Anxious Times*. Pittsburgh: University of Pittsburgh Press, 2014.

Watson, Andrea. "Writing Essential Skill." *Daily Texan*, February 20, 1985.

Welch, Cheryl. "Unite to Fight the Menace to E 346K." *Daily Texan*, February 25, 1985.

Wells, Susan. "Claiming the Archive for Rhetoric and Composition." In *Rhetoric and Composition as Intellectual Work*, edited by Gary Olson, 55–64. Carbondale: Southern Illinois University Press, 2002.

Wevill, David. "English Lecturers Highly Skilled, Hard Working." *Daily Texan*, March 7, 1985.

White, Hayden. *Metahistory: The Historical Imagination in Nineteenth-Century Europe*. Baltimore, MD: Johns Hopkins University Press, 1973.

Whithaus, Carl, and Chris Thaiss. "A Complex Ecology: The Growth of an Independent Writing Program in the Aftermath of the Great Recession." In *Weathering the Storm: Independent Writing Programs in the Age of Fiscal Austerity*, edited by Richard Matzen and Matthew Abraham, 128–40. Logan: Utah State University Press, 2019.

Wilde, Patty, Molly Tetreault, and Sarah B. Franco. "Renegotiating the Public Memory of Writing Centers." In *Pedagogies of Public Memory: Teaching Writing and Rhetoric in Museums, Memorials, and Archives*, edited by Jane Greer and Laurie Grobman, 105–16. New York: Routledge, 2015.

Will, George. "Radical English." *Washington Post*, September 16, 1990.

Willats, Brian. "Readin', Writin', and Racism: The Rise and Fall of E 306." *University Review*, September 1990.

Williams, Ellen. "At the Crossroads." *Daily Texan*, September 10, 1985.

———. "Committee Probes English Program." *Daily Texan*, July 15, 1985.

———. "Committee Reviews E 346K Proposal." *Daily Texan*, August 2, 1985.

Williamson, Kevin. "English Department Could Be Redesigned." *Daily Texan*, June 10, 1992.

Wittig, Susan. "Project C-BE English Drill and Practice: A Package by Susan Wittig, University of Texas at Austin." *Pipeline* (Fall 1978): 20–22.

Woodruff, David. "Too Soon to Give Up on English 346K." *Daily Texan*, February 20, 1985.

Woodruff, Thea. "Professors Claim New Department Is Authority Breach." *Daily Texan*, September 3, 1992.

Wren, Robert. "Danger of Public Promo." *Daily Texan*, February 28, 1985.

Wyche, Susan. "Reflections of an Anonymous Graduate Student on the Wyoming Conference Resolution." In *Labored: The State(ment) and Future of Work in Composition*, edited by Randall McClure, Dayna V. Goldstein, and Michael A. Pemberton, 3–13. Anderson, SC: Parlor Press, 2017.

Yardley, Jonathan. "On Dasher! On Dancer! To Albania!" *Washington Post*, December 24, 1990.

Yioutas, Paul. "KLRU Panel on Campus Issues Unbalanced." *Daily Texan*, September 4, 1990.

Yood, Jessica. "Revising the Dream: Graduate Students, Independent Writing Programs, and the Future of English Studies." In *A Field of Dreams: Independent Writing Programs and the Future of Composition Studies*, edited by Peggy O'Neill, Angela Crow, and Larry W. Burton, 170–85. Logan: Utah State University Press, 2002.

Young, Jeremy, and Jonathan Friedman. "America's Censored Classrooms." Pen America, August 17, 2022, https://pen.org/report/americas-censored-classrooms/.

Zebroski, James. *Thinking Through Theory: Vygotskian Perspectives on the Teaching of Writing*. Portsmouth, NH: Heinemann, 1994.

Zimmerman, Traci. "'And So Two Shall Become One': Being (and Becoming) the School of Writing, Rhetoric, and Technical Communication." In *Weathering the Storm: Independent Writing Programs in the Age of Fiscal Austerity*, edited by Richard Matzen and Matthew Abraham, 60–67. Logan: Utah State University Press, 2019.

Index

AAUP, 10, 61, 74, 91
abolition of first-Year writing, 114–17, 124–28
academic precarity
    Activism, 62
    adjuncts, 7–8, 49, 57–56, 71–72, 141
    CCCC "Statement of Standards and Principles," 73
    Wyoming Resolution, 72–73
antivictimism, 96–97, 100–101

Berlin, James, 107–8
Bertelson, Lance, 122–23
Brodkey, Linda, 82–83
Bump, Jerome, 42

Cactus Café, 68
Carter, Joyce Locke, 41–42, 70–71
Carton, Evan, 95–96, 116–17
Carver, Larry, 114
Cheney, Lynne, 91–92
civic education, 5–6, 8, 43–44, 80–81, 96, 124
Computer Writing and Research Lab / Digital Writing and Research Lab, 41–42, 58
Corbett, Edward, 72, 120
Cullingford, Elizabeth, 131–32

Daedalus Networked Writing Environment, 42
Davis, Rod, 58, 61
diversity, 1–4, 6, 85
digital archivism
    archival responsibility, 147–48
    ethic of recovery, 146–47
    RhetCompUTX, 20–22, 146–51
Duban, James, 78, 101

D'Souza, Dinesh, 95–96

enrollments, 32–34, 50–51

faculty governance
    Executive Committee, English Department, 63, 132
    Faculty Senate, English Department, 63
    managerialism, 7, 10, 48, 66–67, 109–10, 237
    market values, 65, 73–75, 109–10, 137
Faigley, Lester, 39–40, 124–25, 138
Fereirra-Buckley, Linda, 138
first-year writing
    classical rhetoric, 35, 80–81
    E 306, 24, 81
    E 309K, 124–27
    Kinneavy syllabus, 36, 38
    critical literacy, 80–82
    current traditional rhetoric, 28–29, 32–34, 78–79
    process pedagogy, 37–38, 78–80
    Writing About Difference, 83–84, 86, 106
fox, foxes, 19, 145
Friedman, Alan, 52, 62

Gribben, Alan, 68–69, 99–101, 105–6

Hairston, Maxine, 32–38, 88
Henley, Geoff, 102
Henson, Scott, 97–98
historiography
    ethics, 15–19
    narrative, 13–19, 24–25, 47, 155–56

independent writing programs, 131, 140
    Division of Rhetoric and Composition, 132–35
interviews
    ethics, 151–52
    methodology, 152–55

Kemp, Fred, 41
King, Robert, 55, 67
Kinneavy, James, 35–37, 80

lecturers. *See* academic precarity
Liberal Arts Foundation Council, 91
literacy. *See* first-year writing

MacKay, Carol, 114–15
McCarthyism, 106, 107
McMurrey, David, x, 58, 64, 71–72, 153
Meacham, Standish, 85, 98
Megaw, Neill, 26–29
Michigan Mandate, 85
Michigan State, 14
Miller, Thomas, 5
Modern Language Association (MLA), 91, 119
Morrill Land-Grant Acts, 31
Morrison, Sterling, 114
multiculturalism. *See* diversity
Myers, Greg, 35

National Association of Scholars (NAS), 91, 98, 104, 106, 107
National Defense Act, 34
National Defense Education Act, 5, 34, 39
National Endowment for the Humanities (NEH), 91
neo-abolitionism. *See* abolition of first-year writing
Nightline, 92
Northern Arizona University, 94

Oswego State University, 74

pandemic, 1, 8, 9
Parlin Hall, 36, 86, 117
Persian Gulf War, 106
Philpott, Thomas, 97–98
Polemicist, The, 97, 98–99
Postrhetorical curriculum, 32
Practitioners, 32–33, 44–45, 129
Progressive era, 33–34, 91
proportional representation, 4, 13

racism, 9, 77, 90, 95–96
    and fraternities, 86
Racism and Sexism, 86, 88, 89, 102, 105, 106

radical empathy, 147, 150
Radical Teacher, 105
Reagan, Ronald, 45, 52, 95, 113
    Reaganite, 65
Rebhorn, Wayne, 27–30
Rhetoric Interest Group, 68
rights revolution, 5–8, 77, 82, 91, 96, 112, 133, 141
Rodi, Susan, 36
Rogers, Lorene, 56
Rothenberg, Paula. See *Racism and Sexism*
Ruszkiewicz, John, 36, 41

San Diego State University, 136, 141
Skaggs, James, 58–61
Slatin, John, 93–95
Sledd, James, 25–29
    labor rights, 51, 54–56, 62, 75
    Wyoming Resolution, 72–74
social justice, 10, 99
Spivak, Gayatri, 58
Stanford University, 85
state funding, 112, 141
"Statement of Academic Concern," 99, 104
Students Advocating Valid Education (SAVE), 102
suasoria, suasoriae, 156–57
Supreme Court, 5, 112
    Cases in Brodkey Syllabus, 84, 86–88, 98
Sutherland, William, 66
Syracuse University, 74

Task Force on Composition, 52–53, 59
teaching load, 55–63
Teaching-Load Credit Committee, 55
tenure
    for lecturers, 49–50
    threats to, 10
Texas A&M, 122, 137
Texas Association of Scholars (TAS), 98, 104
Texas State Legislature, 9, 56, 77, 109
Todos Unidos, 96
Trachsel, Mary, 36
Trimble, John, 29–35
Trudy's Texas Star, 131
tuition
    efforts to expand access, 4
    G.I. Bill of Rights, 5
    efforts to increase, 6
    as percentage of institution funding, 7
    raises in, 112, 113

University of California, Santa Barbara, 141
Undergraduate Writing Center, 41, 138, 139, 146

University Faculty Council, 42, 43, 51
University of Illinois, 9, 13
University of Michigan, 13, 39, 51
University Review, 100
USSR, 113

Velvet Underground, 114
Victimist, 97, 101, 103
Vick, James, 51
Vick Report, 52–54, 126
Vygotsky, Lev, 34, 43

Washington Post, 98, 105, 106

Western State College, 35, 36
Witte, Steven, 35–40
writing program administration (WPA), 16–23, 45–47, 75, 146–49, 155
writing across the curriculum, 24, 38, 42–45, E 325, 29–30, 118, 130, 139
E 346K, 43–46, 53–54, 67–70, 80, 116, 118–20, 124–26, 128, 130
Writing Lab, 41–42, 48, 71–72
Wyoming Resolution, 72–74
Written Communication, 39–40

Z Magazine, 106

www.ingramcontent.com/pod-product-compliance
Ingram Content Group UK Ltd.
Pitfield, Milton Keynes, MK11 3LW, UK
UKHW031442060125
3971UKWH00039B/476